Basic AutoCAD® for Interior Designers Using AutoCAD® 2002

Basic AutoCAD® for Interior Designers Using AutoCAD® 2002

Jin Feng

Purdue University

Upper Saddle River, New Jersey
Columbus, Ohio

Editor in Chief: Stephen Helba
Executive Editor: Debbie Yarnell
Media Development Editor: Michelle Churma
Production Editor: Louise N. Sette
Production Supervision: Lisa Garboski, bookworks
Design Coordinator: Diane Ernsberger
Text Designer: STELLARViSIONs
Cover Designer: Jeff Vanik
Production Manager: Brian Fox
Marketing Manager: Jimmy Stephens

Screen representations used with permission from and under the copyright of
Autodesk, Inc.

This book was set in Adobe Garamond by STELLARViSIONs and was printed and bound by
Courier Kendallville, Inc. The cover was printed by Phoenix Color Corp.

Pearson Education Ltd., *London*
Pearson Education Australia Pty. Limited, *Sydney*
Pearson Education Singapore Pte. Ltd.
Pearson Education North Asia Ltd., *Hong Kong*
Pearson Education Canada, Ltd., *Toronto*
Pearson Educación de Mexico, S.A. de C.V.
Pearson Education—Japan, *Tokyo*
Pearson Education Malaysia Pte. Ltd.
Pearson Education, *Upper Saddle River, New Jersey*

Prentice
Hall

10 9 8 7 6 5 4 3
ISBN: 0-13-097720-9

For Jiang

Preface

AutoCAD and Learning AutoCAD

Since its introduction into the world of design in 1982 by Autodesk, AutoCAD has become the most widely used PC design software for many disciplines, including interior design and architecture. In today's building industry, AutoCAD is a standard tool of design, drafting, and management. Without competent AutoCAD skills, a college graduate may find it difficult to find an entry-level job; a veteran designer may feel at a disadvantage. The importance of adequate AutoCAD training can never be overemphasized. AutoCAD is a comprehensive, complex computer-aided design system used in many different fields among which interior design is only a small area of application. This makes learning AutoCAD a difficult task for interior designers and interior design students because very few AutoCAD books are written specifically for interior designers. Most AutoCAD books are overloaded with information that is irrelevant to interior design. Those inexperienced in computing can easily be overwhelmed by the complex functions of AutoCAD and the cumbersome volume of most "complete" or "one-stop" AutoCAD books. Tutorials on how to create machine parts can very easily bore interior designers. To meet the special need of interior design students and professional interior designers, this book simplifies learning AutoCAD, and relates it as closely as possible to interior design applications.

About This Book

Basic AutoCAD® for Interior Designers Using AutoCAD® 2002 is a textbook for interior design students and is designed as their first AutoCAD book. It is an easy-to-understand tutorial with step-by-step instructions. It may also be used as a tutorial for interior design professionals with a need to catch up with the technological advancements of the field. This very pragmatic and focused book combines explanations of commands with practical and systematic drafting procedures to teach students an adequate set of skills that they can use immediately while in school and in the profession after graduation.

This book has the following unique features:

1. A humanistic philosophy that respects the interior designer as an AutoCAD user.

2. A focus on what an interior designer can do with AutoCAD rather than on what AutoCAD can do.

3. An emphasis on drafting task procedures using appropriate AutoCAD commands rather than functions of individual AutoCAD commands.

4. A careful selection of commands to simplify the learning process.

In this book, exercises with step-by-step instructions and comments are the primary format of instruction. These exercises can also be used as a practical how-to guide for future reference.

This book is for readers with minimal computing experience. Only basic knowledge and experience of Windows are expected. Upon finishing the tutorials in this book, the reader will have adequate skills to start as a CAD drafter in the design profession. This book is limited in scope. It treats AutoCAD as basically a drafting and presentation tool. Although AutoCAD can surely be used as a design tool, the creative design process is beyond the intended scope of this book. Meanwhile, the reader should remember that since this book is an introductory text, it does not cover all the AutoCAD skills and procedures that are used in the field of interior design.

How to Use This Book

This book is organized around the task of presenting a simple designed space in both 2D drawings and 3D modeling. The task is divided into chapters. Although the space is extremely simple, the presentational tasks require almost all the basic Auto-CAD skills frequently used in the design profession. The chapters are sequential, so the reader can simply follow the chapters in order. Learning AutoCAD is similar to learning to play the piano; just as a pianist must know the keyboard and memorize the music, the user needs to know the AutoCAD functions and commands by heart. The simple exercises in this tutorial can be seen as piano studies in the training of a pianist. If these exercises are "practiced" repeatedly, the reader can become fluent in AutoCAD in a short period of time. While practicing the exercises, the reader needs to reflect on what he or she is doing and on what the potential usage for a certain command or procedure might be.

The Tutorial Format

In this tutorial, instructions of operation are presented using the following conventions.

1. Each chapter consists of major tasks. Each task is divided into steps that are procedures for finishing the task and each step may be divided into sub-steps that utilize certain commands.

2. The sub-steps are listed with numbers and in bold type. These numbers correspond to the bold numbers in the illustrations.

3. When a command is used in a sub-step for the first time the interaction between AutoCAD and the operator is presented. AutoCAD command prompt output (what AutoCAD says) and input (what the operator replies) are printed in a special typeface (**Helvetica**). The output is printed in plain type and the operator's actions or inputs are printed in bold type. Descriptions and explanations are placed in the right-hand column.

4. AutoCAD commands are in all uppercase letters.

5. Explanatory notes are all preceded with a circular bullet point.

For example:

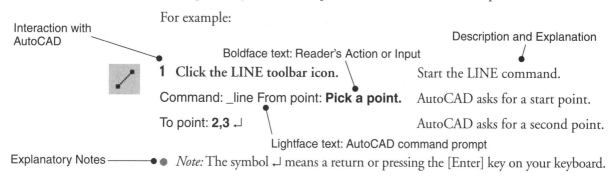

Interaction with AutoCAD

Description and Explanation

Boldface text: Reader's Action or Input

1 Click the LINE toolbar icon.   Start the LINE command.

Command: _line From point: **Pick a point.**   AutoCAD asks for a start point.

To point: **2,3** ↵   AutoCAD asks for a second point.

Lightface text: AutoCAD command prompt

Explanatory Notes ————● *Note:* The symbol ↵ means a return or pressing the [Enter] key on your keyboard.

Note on the Software and Hardware

AutoCAD has different releases prior to 2002 that used different platforms (or operating systems) including DOS, Mac, Unix, and Windows. In the design profession, AutoCAD releases prior to 14 have become obsolete, and Windows95, Windows98, WindowsNT, and Windows2000 have replaced other platforms. Therefore, this tutorial is based on the AutoCAD 2002 for Windows version. In order to make this book applicable to most readers, the tutorials are written based on the minimal hardware configuration required by AutoCAD: a WindowNT/95/98/2000-based personal computer with a two-button mouse.

Basic Terms

Certain terms are used throughout this book to describe the actions you need to take in operating the AutoCAD system. These terms are clarified as follows.

CHECK—click a check box in dialog boxes to make a check mark or cross appear in that box. It means that the option associated with the check box is taken.

CHOOSE (an item from a list or menu)—left-click on an item from a list.

CLEAR (a check box)—click a check box to make the check mark or cross disappear. It means that the option associated with the check box is not taken.

CLICK—click the left button of a mouse or equivalent button of another pointing device.

DOUBLE-CLICK—quickly click the left mouse button or equivalent button of another pointing device twice to open a drawing or to highlight an existing text string.

DRAG—move your mouse while holding down the left button. It is usually used in moving windows by the title bar or in a drag-and-drop operation.

ENTER—type an input (a command, a number, or any kind of data) from the keyboard and finish by pressing the [Enter] key (symbolized by ↵) at a command prompt or in a text window in a dialog box.

PICK (a point)—use your mouse to click at a point in the drawing area to identify the point. The *x,y* coordinate of the point will be entered into the system.

POINT TO (a menu item)—move your cursor with your mouse over a menu item without clicking. The item is usually highlighted.

PULL—move your mouse without holding down any button. It is used to create selection windows.

RIGHT-CLICK—click the right mouse button or equivalent button of another pointing device. It usually equals pressing the [Enter] key, and it sometimes brings out a menu.

SELECT—use your pointing device to pick a drawing entity, or entities, as required by certain AutoCAD commands. Usually, you signal the selection process to end by pressing the [Enter] key.

SHIFT-SELECT (an object)—hold down the [Shift] key while clicking on the object you want to select.

Acknowledgments

This book is an update from my previous book, *Basic AutoCAD® for Interior Designers Using Release 14*. When working on the update, the previous version kept reminding me of those people who had assisted me in the publication of that book. I still feel grateful to them. Therefore, I would like to mention their names here and thank them again for their help and support: Reed Benhamou and Olivia Snyder of Indiana University, Carol Bormann of Oklahoma State University, Ann Girand of North Dakota State University, Ron Mowat of West Virginia University, and Stephen Helba, Louise Sette, Karen Fortgang, Priscilla Mullins, Mary Storm-Baranyai, and Margaret Anderson of Prentice Hall and associated editorial services. For the current book, I want to thank my former colleague Olivia Snyder, and my former students Pauline Bothwell and Barbra Bennett Young who had used my manuscript in the classes they taught and provided me with valuable feedback. I also want to thank Debbie Yarnell of Prentice Hall for her support on this project. Patricia Wilson for her copyediting the manuscript, and Lisa Garboski of bookworks for her effective coordination of the production team. Mary Maxine Browne of Purdue University helped me with the editing of Chapter 13. Paul Eiff of Purdue University helped me resolve many hardware and software issues while testing the new release of Auto-CAD. Without him, this project could never have been completed.

I would also like to acknowledge the reviewers of this text: Nancy G. Miller, West Virginia University, and Thea Ellenberg, University of Georgia.

Contents

Chapter 5   Finishing the Floor Plan   79

Chapter 6   Dimensions   107

Chapter 7   Plotting   131

Chapter 8   Drawing an Elevation   157

Chapter 9   Drawing a Detail   179

Chapter 10   Assembling the Finished Drawing   199

Chapter 11   Building a 3D Model   223

Chapter 12   Rendering   259

Chapter 13   Posting the Drawings to the Web   283

Appendices

Index   305

Basic AutoCAD® for Interior Designers Using AutoCAD® 2002

Basic AutoCAD Knowledge

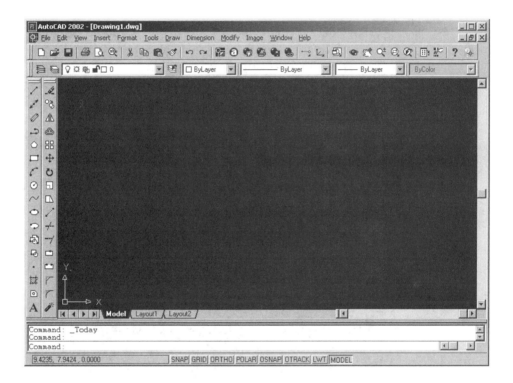

- Start AutoCAD
- Find your way around the AutoCAD program window
- Communicate with AutoCAD
- Look around an AutoCAD drawing using ZOOM
- Use commands to correct your mistakes: CANCEL, UNDO, REDO, ERASE, and OOPS
- Handle files

This chapter provides an illustrated description of AutoCAD's drawing environment. You will be guided through a virtual adventure as you communicate and work with AutoCAD.

Starting AutoCAD

Before you start the following tutorial, you should have some basic Windows environment computing skills. If you are unsure of your skills, you may find a tutorial such as the *Windows for Dummies* books helpful.

The exact location of the AutoCAD program in your computer system depends on how it was installed. Usually, it can be found in the Start menu.

1 Click the Start button at the lower-left corner of the screen. (Figure 1.1)

2 Point to Programs. A list of program folders appears.

3 Point to the AutoCAD 2002 program folder. A submenu appears.

4 Point to and click the AutoCAD 2002 program. Your computer boots the AutoCAD program.

● If the Shortcut icon is displayed on your Windows desktop, simply double-click it to start AutoCAD.

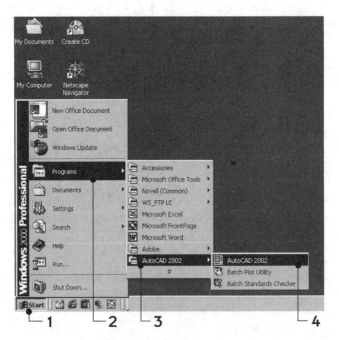

Figure 1.1
Starting AutoCAD in a typical Windows NT/95/98/2000 environment.

Getting to Know the AutoCAD Program Window

After successfully launching the AutoCAD program, the AutoCAD program window opens, and the AutoCAD 2002 Today window pops up (Figure 1.2). Click the Close button to exit the window. Although this new AutoCAD feature (since version 2000i) can help a designer organize his or her work and obtain information from the Internet, it may be quite overwhelming at this moment since you don't know much about AutoCAD, yet. How to use the tools in AutoCAD 2002 Today will be discussed in a later chapter.

The typical AutoCAD program window without customization contains many parts, as shown in Figure 1.3. You will understand these parts more fully after doing the tutorials. If you later encounter these terms and can't recall their functions, you can always come back to this section for exact definitions.

Note: If your AutoCAD program window looks different, it likely has been customized by others. To return the screen to its default settings, follow the procedures in Appendix A.

Title bar   Shows the current drawing name. In Figure 1.3, the drawing name is Drawing1.dwg. Window control buttons for closing, maximizing, or minimizing the AutoCAD window are located at the right end. You can also move the AutoCAD window by dragging the title bar.

Menu bar   Contains a row of menu names that are similar to all other Windows programs. Clicking on any of them brings out a pop-up menu, which lists commands to choose from. A second set of window control buttons that control the current drawing is located at the right end.

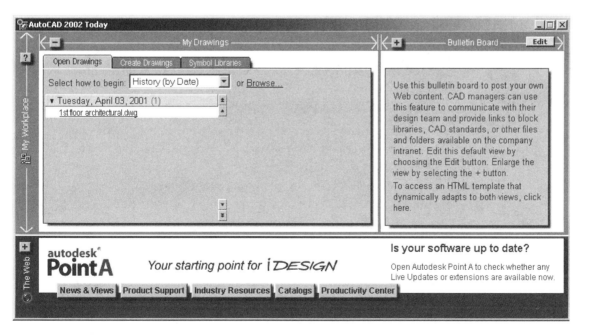

Figure 1.2
AutoCAD 2002 Today window.

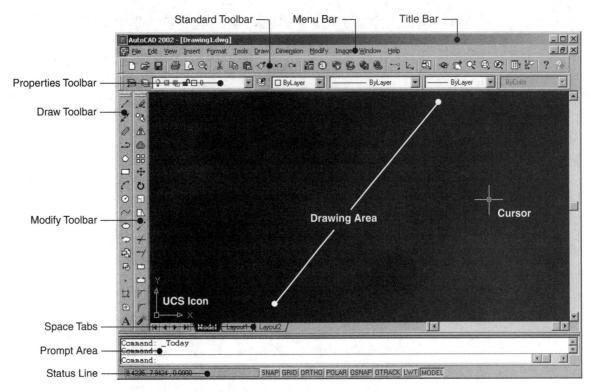

Figure 1.2
AutoCAD drawing window.

Standard toolbar   Contains a row of toolbar icons, including some of the standard Windows tools such as print, cut, copy, and paste.

Properties toolbar   Shows the properties of the current layer or selected objects. You can manipulate the properties through the lists and tools.

Draw toolbar   A collection of icons that activate some frequently used drawing commands.

Modify toolbar   A collection of icons that activate some frequently used editing commands.

Drawing area   Where you create and view your drawing.

Cursor   A pointer on the screen controlled by a digitizer, such as a mouse. The cursor may change to a small box when AutoCAD prompts you to pick objects.

Prompt area   The place you "talk" with AutoCAD; when you key in your command, AutoCAD talks back with questions and requests.

Status line   Provides some important information about your drawing environment, including the coordinates of the cursor in the drawing area and modes of drawing aides.

Space tabs   Switches between model space and layout space. The concept of spaces will be discussed in Chapter 6.

UCS icon   Shows the positive directions of the *x*, *y*, and *z* axes of the coordinate system.

Communicating with AutoCAD

Working with AutoCAD is very much like working with an assistant. You give an order, he or she talks back to ask for specific information needed to finish the task, you provide the information, and he or she finishes the job. Good communication is critical in this process: (1) You must use a language that AutoCAD understands, (2) you must pay attention to what AutoCAD says, and (3) you must provide Auto-CAD with the exact type of information it requests in the correct sequence. Once you have mastered this routine, AutoCAD will be happy to work for you.

Now, let's begin to experiment with different ways to give AutoCAD a command and see how AutoCAD responds.

Keyboard Command

Entering a keyboard command is the traditional way of "talking" to a computer. It will be the quickest and easiest way to give commands to AutoCAD *if* you memorize all the needed commands. This approach also allows you to "talk" to previous Auto-CAD versions that do not have the toolbar interface, since many key-in commands still work with previous releases.

Experiment 1: Keyboard Command

Command: **LINE** ↵	Enter (type in the word) LINE at the command prompt.
Specify first point: **Pick a point.**	AutoCAD asks for a start point.
	Pick a first point (anywhere in the drawing area).
Specify next point or [Undo]: **Pick a second point.**	AutoCAD asks for a second point.
	Pick a second point (anywhere away from the first point).
	AutoCAD draws the first line segment and asks for a third point.
Specify next point or [Undo]:↵	Press [Enter]to tell AutoCAD you don't want to continue.
Command:	AutoCAD terminates this command and is ready for the next command.

- If you pick a third point, the second line segment will be drawn; you can continue infinitely if you wish.

A common problem among beginner AutoCAD users is ignoring the AutoCAD command prompt line or entering an input that does not respond to AutoCAD's request. You *must* pay close attention to what AutoCAD says to you, and feed back the expected response. Otherwise, AutoCAD will never understand you and work for you.

Menu Commands

Another method of entering a command is by using the menus in the menu bar. The advantage of this method is that you don't have to know all the commands by heart. You can begin with a general task category and then select the appropriate command from a set of tasks in that category. This method is especially good for novices, since it is easier to learn.

Experiment 2: Menu Commands

1 Click Draw on the menu bar. The Draw menu pops up.

2 Point to Line and click. Start the LINE command.

Command: _line Specify first point:
Pick a point.   AutoCAD issues the same command (_line) as if you had typed it and asks for a start point.

                                          Pick a first point (anywhere in the drawing area).

Specify next point or [Undo]:
Pick a second point.   AutoCAD asks for a second point.

                                          Pick a second point (anywhere away from the first point).

                                          AutoCAD draws the first line segment and asks for a third point.

Specify next point or [Undo]: ↵   Press [Enter] to terminate the task.

Command: AutoCAD is ready for the next command.

Toolbar Icon Commands

Yet another method of entering a command is by using the toolbar icons. To use this method effectively, you must remember the meaning of the icon and its location. If you cannot remember the meaning of an icon, place your cursor over the unknown icon and in a few seconds a description will pop up.

Experiment 3: Toolbar Icon Commands

 Click the LINE icon.   Start the LINE command.

 • The LINE toolbar icon is the first one in the Draw toolbar, which is located in the left frame of the AutoCAD window.

Command: _line Specify first point:
Pick a point.   AutoCAD issues the command and asks for a start point.

                                          Pick a first point (anywhere in the drawing area).

Specify next point or [Undo]:

Pick a second point.   AutoCAD asks for a second point.

                                            Pick a second point (anywhere away from
                                            the first point).

                                            AutoCAD draws the first line segment and
                                            asks for a third point.

Specify next point or [Undo]: ↵   Press [Enter] to terminate the task.

Command: AutoCAD is ready for the next command.

Dialog Box

Certain AutoCAD commands use a pop-up dialog box to present information and
to request information input. You can respond easily and correctly within these
boxes. Let's try a simple one using the SAVE command.

Experiment 4: Bringing up a Dialog Box

Command: **SAVE** ↵   Enter the keyboard command.

                                            The Save Drawing As dialog box pops up
                                            (Figure 1.4).

                                            Prompt area stops output.

This is a very simple dialog box that contains only a few buttons and text fields.

Title bar   Shows the title of the dialog box.

Text box   Allows you to type text input.

List box   Shows a list from which to choose.

Shortcut window   Allows you to take a shortcut to get to frequently used
        folders.

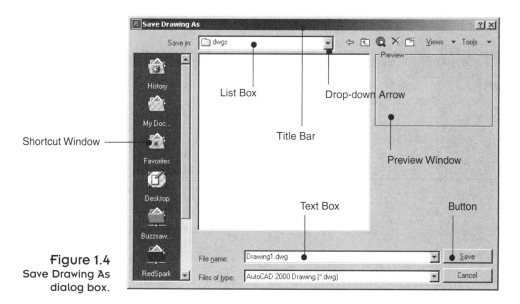

Figure 1.4
Save Drawing As
dialog box.

Preview window   Shows a thumbnail image of a selected drawing.

Drop-down arrow   Triggers a long drop-down list.

Button   Invokes certain functions. If a button has dark shadows, it can be invoked by using the [Enter] key.

Click [Cancel] to close the dialog box.

AutoCAD Text Window Report

Certain commands may cause AutoCAD to pop up a text window that lists long textual information. Let's try the LIST command to see how it works.

Experiment 5: Text window

Command: **LIST** ↵	Enter the command.
Select objects:**Click on a line.**	AutoCAD asks you to select objects.
	Select a line.
Select objects: 1 found	AutoCAD reports that it found 1.
Select objects: ↵	AutoCAD asks you to pick more.
	Press [Enter] to tell AutoCAD that you have finished the selection, or you can keep selecting additional objects.
	AutoCAD displays all the information about the line on the text window (Figure 1.5).

☒ **Click the Close button** (at the upper-right corner of the text window) to close the screen.

● If you enter a new command, the text window will automatically turn off.

● The LIST command is very useful when you need to find information about drawing entities. You will use it more when you begin to work on complicated

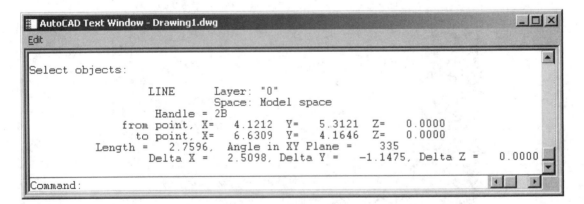

Figure 1.5
AutoCAD text window.

jobs. At this point, the information in the text window may not make much sense to you, but you will understand the listed information more fully once you have learned more about AutoCAD.

Canceling a Command

You can cancel a command at any time by simply pressing the Esc key. (Esc means "escape"; it also "kills" dialog boxes.)

Looking Around an AutoCAD Drawing

To work on an AutoCAD drawing on a monitor of limited size, you need to be able to zoom in and out to see both tiny details and the entire sheet. The ZOOM command allows you to look around in the drawing. Although ZOOM is a complex command with many subcommands, you only need to learn three of the subcommands to navigate freely in a large drawing: ZOOM-All, ZOOM-Window, and ZOOM-Previous.

ZOOM-Window

This subcommand allows you to define the area that you want to zoom into. Since it is the most frequently used option, it has been set as the "default," that is, AutoCAD automatically chooses this option unless you make a different choice. You can start to pick the window definition point right after the ZOOM command is entered. The ZOOM command also has a shortcut alias, as do many AutoCAD commands. When entering the command from the keyboard, you can enter its shortcut alias, Z, instead of the whole word, ZOOM. For a cross-reference list of commands, aliases, and toolbar icons see Appendix B.

Experiment 6: ZOOM-Window

The task of this experiment is to Zoom in to see the end of a line.

Command: **Z** ↵ | Enter the shortcut alias of the command.

ZOOM | AutoCAD interprets the alias as the ZOOM command and lists possible actions and subcommands for you to choose from.

Specify corner of window,
enter a scale factor (nX or nXP),
or [All/Center/Dynamic/Extents/
Previous/Scale/Window]
<real time>: **Pick point (1).** | (Figure 1.6a)

| Choose the first action by picking a point close to one end of a line.

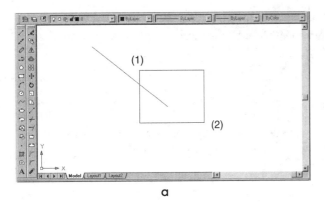 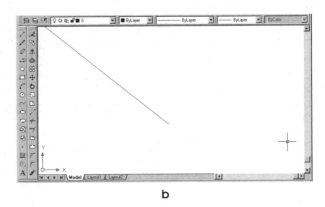

a   b

Figure 1.6
Zoom in.

(continued)   AutoCAD shows a rubber band window
                                       that stretches with the movement of your
                                       mouse, and asks you to pick the opposite
                                       corner of the window.

Specify opposite corner:
Pick point (2).   (Figure 1.6a)

Command: AutoCAD zooms into the window you just
                                       defined (Figure 1.6b).

- Your line doesn't have to look exactly like the one in the figure (in length and orientation) for this experiment. The background color of the AutoCAD drawing
  window in this book is changed to white for better printing effect; your drawing,
  however, should still have the black background.

ZOOM-Previous

This ZOOM function allows you to step back to a previous view. You can keep
repeating this subcommand until you get back to the very beginning if needed.

Experiment 7: ZOOM-Previous

The task of this experiment is to see what we were looking at previously.

Command: ↵   Press [Enter] to make AutoCAD repeat the
                                       last command.

- Pressing the [Enter] key to repeat the last command is fast and convenient. However, be careful, an accidental extra hit on the [Enter] key will throw you into a
  command you don't need.

ZOOM

Specify corner of window,
enter a scale factor (nX or nXP),
or [All/Center/Dynamic/Extents/
Previous/Scale/Window]
<real time>: **P** ↵

(continued)	Choose the subcommand Previous by entering P.
Command:	AutoCAD zooms to the previous view (Figure 1.6a).

- When choosing from a list of subcommands, you don't have to type in the whole word. Entering the capital letter(s) in each word will work. Usually the capital letter(s) is the first letter(s) of the subcommand, but not always.

ZOOM-All

The ZOOM-All command means "zoom out to see all the drawing." It allows you to see the drawing you are working on to its outermost limits. During a drawing session, you may zoom in and zoom out so many times that you get lost. The easiest way to get out of this uncertainty is to ZOOM-All to see the whole picture. Then you can jump in again.

Experiment 8: ZOOM-All

Command: ⏎	Press [Enter] to make AutoCAD repeat the last command.
ZOOM	
Specify corner of window, enter a scale factor (nX or nXP), or [All/Center/Dynamic/Extents/ Previous/Scale/Window] <real time>: **A** ⏎	Choose the subcommand All by entering A.
Command:	AutoCAD zooms to the outermost limits.

Correcting Your Mistakes: Cancel, Undo, Redo, Erase, Oops

As a novice, you cannot avoid making mistakes. AutoCAD provides a few commands to help you correct common mistakes during AutoCAD sessions. In the following "mini-exercise" you will practice how to correct your mistakes. Fairly speaking, Auto-CAD is very forgiving.

Let's assume that you want to draw a series of lines.

Scenario One: "I typed it wrong!"

Command: **K**	You accidentally typed a K instead of an L for LINE.

Rescue One:
You may either use the [Backspace] key to erase the K and type an L, or simply press [Esc] to cancel the command even before it is entered.

Command: **K [Esc]** *Cancel*   Use [Esc] to cancel the wrong command.

Command: **L** ↵   Start LINE command with its alias "L."

LINE Specify first point:
Pick a point.

Specify next point or [Undo]:
Pick a point.   The first segment of line is drawn.

Specify next point or [Undo]:
Pick a point.   The second segment of line is drawn.

Scenario Two: "This step doesn't look right!"

Let's assume that at this moment you discover that the second line segment was not correctly drawn.

Rescue Two:
You can back step without terminating the ongoing LINE command by entering U (alias for UNDO) at the prompt.

Specify next point
or [Close/Undo]: **U**   Second line segment disappears; first line segment remains.

Specify next point or [Undo]:
Pick a new point.   Second line segment is drawn to the new point.

Scenario Three: "I want to stop!"

You are still not sure about the second line segment, and you want to stop the ongoing LINE command.

Rescue Three:
Simply press [Esc] to escape from an ongoing command.

Specify next point or [Close/Undo]:
[Esc] *Cancel*   LINE command terminates; two line segments remain.

Scenario Four: "I messed it up! I need a new start."

You discover that the two line segments are both incorrect.

Rescue Four:

You can use the UNDO command to undo the command and start over. UNDO can go back as many steps as you wish or until you reach the last point when you saved the drawing.

Command: **U**	Start UNDO command.
LINE	AutoCAD indicates the LINE command is undone; line segments disappear.

- Compared with the UNDO command used within the LINE command in Rescue Two, this UNDO command is used to undo the entire LINE command. As you can see, the same UNDO command can be used at different levels.

Scenario Five: "Can I get them back?"

You discover that the two line segments are not totally incorrect. Therefore, you want to bring them back.

Rescue Five:

You can use the REDO command to redo the undone command, however, you can only REDO one time!

Command: **REDO** ↵	Start REDO command; line segments reappear.

Scenario Six: "Get rid of the first segment."

You discover that the first line segment is wrong and you want to erase it.

Rescue Six:

You can use the ERASE command to erase any drawing entity.

Command: **E** ↵	Start the ERASE command with its shortcut alias E.
ERASE	AutoCAD interprets E as ERASE.
Select objects: **Pick the line segment** 1 found	AutoCAD reports 1 object found.

Select objects:

Tell AutoCAD you have finished the selection, or continue to select other object to erase.

AutoCAD erases the selected line segment.

Scenario Seven: "Oops! I erased the wrong one."

You suddenly realize that you should not have erased it, and you want to bring it back.

Rescue Seven:
You can use the OOPS command to bring back the last erased objects.

Command: **OOPS** ⏎

Start the OOPS command to bring the line back.

The line segment re-appears.

- You may also use the UNDO command to bring back erased objects (by UNDO-ING the ERASE command). OOPS, however, can "jump" back to bring back the erased objects even after other commands have been used since the last ERASE. Another difference between the two commands will be discussed in a later chapter.

Handling Files

As you work on your drawing, the results of your work session are being stored in electronic files. Handling these files is fundamental to your work with AutoCAD. When you first start your drawing, you need to create a name for your AutoCAD drawing. During a drawing session, you need to save the changes you make to the drawing file. When you finish a drawing session, you need to make sure you save your work before exiting the program. When you start again to continue your work on an unfinished drawing you saved in a previous session, you need to open an existing drawing file.

SAVE a New Drawing

After starting a new drawing from scratch, you will need to save it and give it a name. The command for this purpose is SAVE.

Experiment 9: Save and name a new file.

1 Enter SAVE. The Save Drawing As dialog box pops up (Figure 1.7).

2 Clear the text field File name.

3 Type in the drawing name: myfirst.

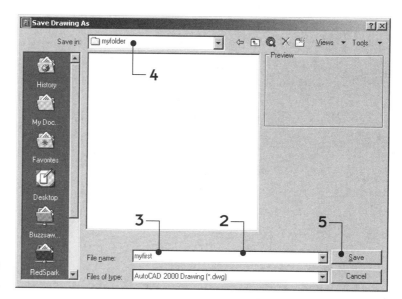

Figure 1.7
Save drawing.

4 Look at the Save in text box to see where the file will be saved (write yourself a note if you are not sure you can remember it). If that directory is not where you want to store your files, you may find the directory you want through the Save in drop-down list or the shortcut icons in the window on the left side of the dialog box, such as My Documents.

● A common problem for beginners is that they overlook this information and then cannot find their drawing files after saving them. If you have problems navigating in the Windows directory system, see your reference on basic Windows operations.

5 Click the [Save] button.

● The dialog disappears and the new drawing name appears in the title bar. A file is created with the name **myfirst.dwg**. The file name extension **.dwg**, which means drawing, is automatically added by AutoCAD.

Saving Changes Made to an Already Named Drawing in the Middle of a Drawing Session: QSAVE

 QSAVE, which means Quick Save, allows you to save the most updated changes to the named drawing file. It does not call up the Save Drawing As dialog box, unless you have not named your file. You may key in the command or click the icon in the standard toolbar.

Experiment 10: Save changes to a named drawing file.

Command: **QSAVE** ↵   Enter the command; AutoCAD updates the file.

● *Note:* When a file is updated, an old version of the file (as you saved last time) will be created with the same file name and the extension .bak, which means backup. In this experiment, a file named myfirst.bak is created in the same folder as the .dwg file.

Saving a Copy of the Current Drawing in a New Drawing File: SAVEAS

Sometimes you may want to save a copy of the current drawing (the one displayed on the monitor screen) and give it a new name. In this case use the SAVEAS command. The SAVEAS command allows you to give the current drawing a new name and keep the original file with its original file name.

Experiment 11: Save the current drawing as a new file.

Use LINE command to draw a line to make a change to the drawing.

- The detailed instruction for drawing the line is omitted. If you forget how to draw a line, refer to Experiment 1.

Command: **SAVEAS** ↵   Enter the command; the Save Drawing As dialog box pops up (Figure 1.8).

1 Enter a new drawing name, mysecond, in the Filename text field.

2 Make sure you know the folder name in the Save in field.

3 Press[Enter] on the keyboard. This action remotely "hits" the highlighted Save button (with dark shadow). The dialog box disappears; a drawing file named "mysecond" is created and opened as the current drawing; and the file "myfirst" is closed and preserved as it was last saved (without the last line added to the drawing).

- The SAVEAS command is very similar to SAVE when used to save the current drawing under a name different from the original; they both use the same Save Drawing As dialog box. The difference between the two commands is that the SAVE command saves the contents (with changes) of the current drawing in a new file with the new name and puts it away, whereas the SAVEAS command saves the contents (with changes) of the current drawing in a new file with the new name, puts it in the current drawing window, and puts away the original drawing file (without changes).

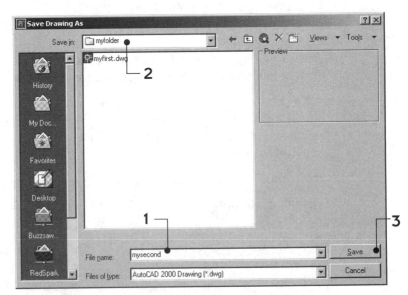

Figure 1.8
Save a file as a
new drawing.

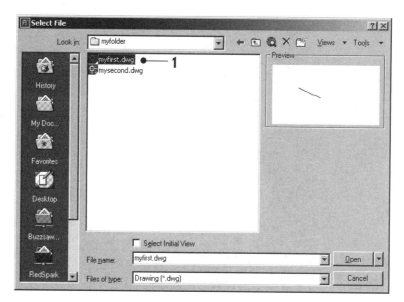

Figure 1.9
Open a file.

OPEN an Existing Drawing File

The OPEN command allows you to open existing files. When you enter a keyboard command or click on the standard toolbar icon, AutoCAD responds with a dialog box. You may select any drawing on the list and open it using the Open button. You can also go to different directories to locate your file and open it. When a new drawing is opened, the previously opened drawing recedes to the background but remains open. To support multiple drawing sessions, AutoCAD must divide the computing power to juggle the many tasks, which reduces the computer's performance. You should, therefore, close the previously opened drawings before opening a new drawing.

Experiment 12: Open a drawing file.

Command: **OPEN** ⏎   Enter the command; the Select File dialog
                                     pops up (Figure 1.9).

1 Click the myfirst file on the list. The file name appears in the File name field. You may see the image in the "Preview window."

2 Press [Enter].   The highlighted [Open] button is remotely hit; the selected drawing file opens.

Saving a Drawing to a Floppy Disk

At the end of a work session, you may want to save your drawing file to a floppy disk. You may need to turn in the file on a separate disk to your instructor; you may want to keep it on a separate disk as a backup file; or you may use another disk to move the file between different computers. The SAVE command can be used for this task. The procedure is similar to the one described in Experiment 9.

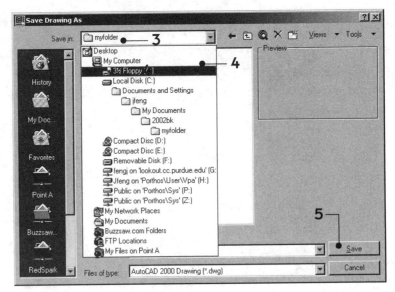

Figure 1.10
Save a drawing to a
floppy disk.

Experiment 13: SAVE a file to a floppy disk.

1 Insert a floppy disk into the floppy disk drive.

● The disk must have been formatted.

2 Enter SAVE. The Save Drawing As dialog box pops up (Figure 1.10).

**3 Click the drop-down arrow next to the Save in list box to find floppy disk
drive A: (for most personal computers drive A: is the floppy disk drive).**

4 Click floppy disk drive A: in the list. A: appears in the list box.

5 Click the Save button. AutoCAD will save the file to the floppy disk.

● If your floppy disk is already full, AutoCAD alerts you with a warning message
asking you to make space for the coming file or to save it to a different disk. You
should accept the warning and do as suggested. Since this warning may be quite
scary to a novice AutoCAD user, you may take a safer approach: Save your file to
the hard disk (drive C:) of your computer and use the Windows file management
program to copy it at a later time to your floppy disk.

● The procedure to save a file to a ZIP disk (or Removable Disk as it is called in
computer terminology) is essentially the same as saving a file to a floppy disk. The
only difference is the letter identification of the disk drive.

Saving a Drawing File in a Different Format

Since AutoCAD Releases 12, 13, and 14 are still in use, and they cannot open .dwg files
saved in Version 2002, you may need to save your file in the AutoCAD R12, R13, or
R14 format. This can be accomplished in the Save Drawing As dialog box where you
simply click the Save as type drop-down list and select the appropriate file type.

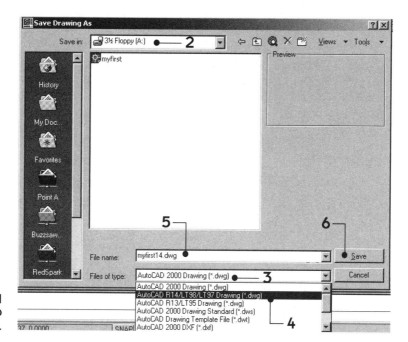

Figure 1.11
Save a file in the AutoCAD
R14 drawing format.

Experiment 14: SAVE a drawing file in AutoCAD R14 format.

1 Enter SAVE. The Save Drawing As dialog box pops up (Figure 1.11).

2 Click the drop-down arrow next to the Save in list box to find floppy disk drive A:, and click floppy disk drive A: in the list. A: appears in the list box.

3 Click the Save as type drop-down list. The list drops down.

4 Click AutoCAD R14/LT 98/LT 97 Drawing [*.dwg].

5 In the File name text box change the file name from "myfirst" to "myfirst14."

● Since some AutoCAD functions do not accept file names of more than 8 letters, it is a good idea to keep your file name within the limit. Naming the file with the number 14 may help you in the future to identify the file as an AutoCAD R14 drawing file.

6 Click the Save button. AutoCAD saves the file to the floppy disk.

Ending a Drawing Session: QUIT

The QUIT command terminates the AutoCAD program when you finish a drawing session. If you have not saved all the changes, a warning pops up. You may then choose to save or not to save.

Experiment 13: QUIT.

Use the LINE command to draw a line to make a change to the drawing.

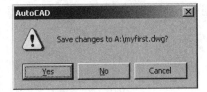

Figure 1.12
AutoCAD warning.

Command: **QUIT** ↵   Enter the command; a warning pops up (Figure 1.12).

Click [Yes].   Saves the newly added line.

● You may also end a drawing session by clicking the Close button.

Summary

In this chapter, you have learned the following concepts, procedures, and commands:

Knowledge/Concepts

● AutoCAD drawing window:

    Title bar
    Menu bar
    Standard toolbar
    Properties toolbar
    Drawing toolbar
    Modify toolbar
    UCS icon
    Drawing area
    Prompt area
    Space tab
    Status line
    Cursor

● Dialog box

    Title bar
    Text box
    List box
    Drop-down arrow
    Button

● Text window

● Alias

● File name extension: .dwg, .bak

Procedures

- Start AutoCAD program
- Cancel a command using [Esc]
- Start keyboard commands
- Pick a point
- Start menu commands
- Start toolbar icon commands
- Use a dialog box
- Use Close button to close a text window
- ZOOM in and out
- Pull out a (ZOOM) window
- Select a drawing element
- Save a drawing to a file (first time SAVE)
- Save changes to an existing file (QSAVE)
- Save changes to a new file and work on the new file (SAVEAS)
- Save changes to a new file and continue to work on the existing file (SAVE)
- Find a file directory and a file
- Save a drawing file in a particular format
- Save a file to a floppy disk
- End an AutoCAD drawing session

Commands

- SAVE/QSAVE

- OPEN

- Close button

- LINE (L)

- ZOOM (Z)

- UNDO (U)

- REDO

- ERASE (E)
- OOPS
- SAVE
- SAVEAS
- QSAVE
- LIST (LI or LS)
- QUIT

C h a p t e r **2**

Drawing a Floor Plan

- Set up a drawing
- Draw wall lines

In this chapter, as the starting point of your adventure into the world of AutoCAD drafting, a very simple method of drawing wall lines is introduced.

In the following tutorial you will draw a simple floor plan that includes door and window openings as shown in Figure 2.1. In the drawing process, you will learn a few of the frequently used commands. While you are practicing, reflect on what you are doing and memorize the commands and the corresponding responses from AutoCAD. If you are bogged down by mistakes, apply the rescue skills you practiced in the previous chapter.

Setting Up a Drawing

Three different approaches can be used to set up an AutoCAD drawing: a ready-made template, an automated wizard, or you can set it up yourself. This last approach requires a fundamental understanding of the drawing settings and, therefore, gives you total control of the procedure and the freedom to manipulate settings in the future. Although it is the hardest approach of the three, it is used in the following tutorial.

There are three major steps in the procedure of setting up a drawing: setting the units, setting the limits, and setting the drafting settings.

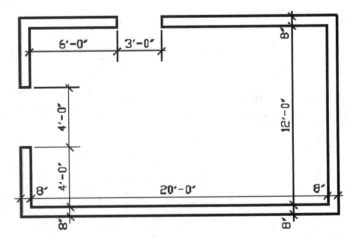

Figure 2.1
A simple floor plan.

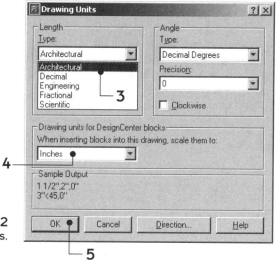

Figure 2.2
Set the drawing units.

Step 1: Set the drawing measurement units.

AutoCAD reports measurement output and accepts dimension input in a few different formats. Since the architectural style (feet and inches) is used in interior design drawings, we will tell AutoCAD of our preference.

1 Start AutoCAD and close the AutoCAD Today window.

2 Enter Command: UNITS. The Drawing Units dialog box pops up (Figure 2.2).

3 Click the Length-Type drop-down list and choose Architectural.

4 Click the Drawing Units for DesignCenter blocks list and select Inches.

5 Click [OK].

● From this point, AutoCAD begins to take in measurement input and to report measurement output in the architectural format (e.g., 2′-3″). Numerical inputs without foot or inch designators are taken as inches, therefore, you will never need to enter the inch mark when entering a dimension—unless, of course, you mind wasting a keystroke.

Step 2: Set the drawing limits.

Unlike drafting on paper, which is always limited in size, you virtually have unlimited space in AutoCAD. If you like, you can map the whole Earth in an AutoCAD drawing—in full scale! (Printing it out, however, is another matter.) Since space is unlimited in AutoCAD, we ALWAYS DRAW IN ACTUAL SIZE. If a door opening is three feet wide in reality, you draw it three feet wide in AutoCAD, too. Only when you start to think about printing out the drawing do you consider scale. (This will be discussed in a later chapter.) Although unlimited space is available in Auto-CAD, the space you will be working on is likely to be limited in size. A set of drawing limits helps AutoCAD to focus on the area of work. Some AutoCAD commands, such as ZOOM, also use the drawing limits as a guide. In setting up a drawing, therefore, you need to define the limits of your drawing area. For this tutorial, a 40′ × 25′ drawing area is more than adequate to contain the 20′ × 12′ floor plan. These limits are arbitrarily set based on a commonsense estimate. You may change it at any time if you need more or less space. To define the working area, use the LIMITS command, which defines a rectangular area by its lower-left and upper-right corners.

Command: **LIMITS** ↵	Enter the LIMITS command.
Reset Model space limits:	
Specify lower left corner or [ON/OFF] <0′-0″,0′-0″>: ↵	Accept the 0,0 default value.
Specify upper right corner <1′-0″,0′-9″>: **40′,25′** ↵	Enter the upper-right corner coordinate.
Command:	AutoCAD is ready for a new command.

- Usually, you always accept the point 0,0 as the lower-left corner.

Step 3: Turn ORTHO on.

In manual drafting, tools such as a T-square and triangles are used to draw horizontal and vertical lines. In AutoCAD drafting, the ORTHO (orthogonal) mode is turned on to restrain the cursor to horizontal or vertical movement. ORTHO mode's status is indicated on the status line at the bottom of the AutoCAD drawing window. If the ORTHO button on the status line is not depressed, it indicates the ORTHO mode is off. Click its button to turn it on. If you click it again, it will turn off.

Click the [ORTHO] button.	The button is depressed.

Note: The ORTHO mode can also be toggled by using the [F8] function key.

Step 4: Set up GRID.

In manual drafting we have a good sense of space and dimension because we know how big the paper is. In CAD drafting it is easy to lose this sense of space and dimension after zooming in and zooming out a few times. The GRID setting allows AutoCAD to display a grid in the drawing area, which gives a sense of space and dimension.

Command: **GRID** ↵	Enter the GRID command.
Specify grid spacing(X) or [ON/OFF/Snap/Aspect] <0′-0 1/2″>: **12** ↵	Set the grid spacing.

● Entering 12 at the prompt not only sets the grid spacing, but also turns on the grid. Since the current drawing window only displays an area of 12 inches wide by 9 inches high (by default), the grid is not visible until you ZOOM out to look at a greater area of the drawing.

Command: **Z** ↵

ZOOM

Specify corner of window,
enter a scale factor (nX or nXP),
or [All/Center/Dynamic/Extents/
Previous/Scale/Window]
<real time>: **A** ↵

Regenerating model.   Grid appears.

● The grid display can be toggled off and on by hitting the [F7] function key, or by clicking the [GRID] button embedded in the status line at the bottom of the AutoCAD window.

Step 5: Set up SNAP.

In CAD drafting, the drawing elements are generated in a coordinate system. A random pick of a point may result in coordinates of fractional values, such as 13/16″. This makes reading the coordinates very difficult. The SNAP setting restricts cursor movement to specified intervals and, therefore, controls the accuracy of the points picked. You can use the SNAP command to set the snap settings.

Command: **SNAP** ↵   Enter the SNAP command.

Specify snap spacing
or [ON/OFF/Aspect/Rotate/
Style/Type] <0′-0 1/2″>: **1** ↵

● As in setting the grid, entering 1 at the prompt sets the snap spacing and turns on the snap function. The effect of this command can be seen on the status line where the cursor position coordinates are reported. Now you no longer have the fractional measurements. The snap mode can be toggled off and on by pressing the [F9] function key or clicking the [SNAP] button embedded in the status line at the bottom of the AutoCAD window.

It is important to know the difference between the grid shown in the drawing area and the snap grid. The grid controlled by the GRID setting is a visual aid and does not restrict cursor movements. The visual grid may have a different spacing from that of the snap grid. The two can be turned on or off independently.

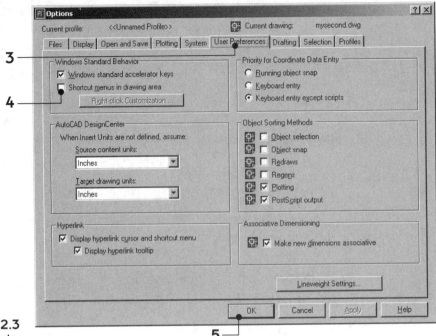

3 ——

4 ——

5 ——

Step 6: Set up right-click mode.

To speed up your operation, set the right-click equal to pressing the [Enter] key.

1 Click Tool on the menu bar. A list of options pops up.

2 Select Options at the bottom of the list. The "Options" dialog box pops up
   (Figure 2.3).

● You may access the Options dialog box by using the OPTIONS command or its
   alias OP.

3 Click the User Preferences tab. The User Preferences page opens.

4 Click to clear the check box in front of Shortcut menus in drawing area.

5 Click [OK] to apply the change.

From now on, a right-click equals an [Enter]. The ↵ symbol, which represents pressing the [Enter] key, may be entered with a right-click.

Drawing Wall Lines

Step 1: Create base wall lines using LINE.

LINE is the most fundamental command in AutoCAD. It is used for creating almost
all the lines in a design drawing. The easiest way to launch the LINE command is to
type L (the shortcut alias for LINE) and then press the [Enter] key. You may also
start the LINE command by clicking the LINE toolbar icon. After the command is
entered, AutoCAD prompts for a starting point. There are many ways to enter a

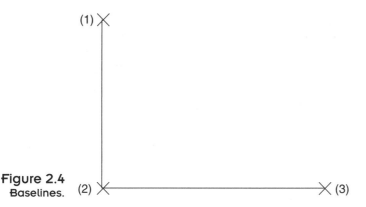

Figure 2.4
Baselines.

point, but the easiest is to "eyeball" and "pick" a point by clicking the left mouse button when the crosshair cursor moves to an appropriate place on the screen. Once the starting point is picked, a rubber band line stretching from the starting point to the cursor appears. Another pick turns the rubber band into a static solid line. A new rubber band line will start from the second point when you pick the next point. The LINE command continues to prompt you for a new segment until you press [Enter] to signal the end of the command.

Command: **L** ↵	Start the LINE command.
LINE Specify first point: **Pick point (1).**	(Figure 2.4)

Note: Point location does not need to be exact.

Specify next point or [Undo]: **Pick point (2).**	
Specify next point or [Undo]: **Pick point (3).**	
Specify next point or [Close/Undo]: ↵	Terminate the command.
Command:	AutoCAD is ready for the next command.

- This "eyeball" approach is obviously not a precise way of drawing lines when specific start or end points are required. This approach only works for the first two lines, since their whereabouts are not restricted by other drawing elements.

Step 2: Create interior wall lines using OFFSET.

The OFFSET command allows you to create another line or other linear element that is offset from the original. The offset line runs parallel to the original line. After launching the command by entering OFFSET from the keyboard, you will be prompted for the distance between the original line and the offset line. Type in the value of the distance. (This key-in operation saves you effort in maneuvering the mouse and it guarantees accuracy.) Next, you will be prompted to pick the original line. After picking the line, you will be prompted to indicate on which side of the original line you want the offset line to be. Pick any point that is to the side of the original line. To terminate the command, press [Enter] or right-click. This command may also be cancelled by clicking the OFFSET toolbar icon.

While drawing the two baselines in the previous step, you may have noticed that a small yellow-colored square appeared at the end of the lines. This is the Object Snap function, which snaps to certain critical points on an object, and will be discussed later. For now, when using the OFFSET command, make sure the object snap mode (OSNAP) is off to avoid unwanted snapping. Click [OSNAP] on the status line, or press [F3] to toggle the OSNAP off.

Command: **O** ↵	Start the OFFSET command with its shortcut alias.
Specify offset distance or [Through] <0'-1">: **20'** ↵	Input distance.
Select object to offset or <exit>: **Pick line (A).**	Pick original line (Figure 2.5).
Specify point on side to offset: **Pick point (4).**	Indicate side of offset and the offset line (C) is created.
Select object to offset or <exit>: ↵	Terminate the command.
Command: ↵	Restart the last command to enter a different distance.
OFFSET	
Specify offset distance or [Through] <20'-0">: **12'** ↵	Input distance.
Select object to offset or <exit>: **Pick line (B).**	Pick original line.
Specify point on side to offset: **Pick point (5).**	Indicate side of offset and offset line (D) is created.
Select object to offset or <exit>: ↵	Terminate the command.
Command:	

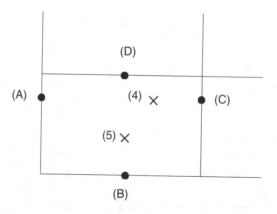

Figure 2.5
Interior wall lines created by using OFFSET.

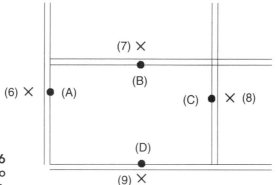

Figure 2.6
Using **OFFSET** to
create wall lines.

Step 3: Create exterior wall lines using OFFSET (Figure 2.6).

Command: ↵	Restart the last command to enter a different distance.
OFFSET	
Specify offset distance or [Through] <12′-0″>: **8** ↵	8 is taken as 8 inches.
Select object to offset or <exit>: **Pick line (A).**	Pick original line.
Specify point on side to offset: **Pick point (6).**	Indicate side of offset.
Select object to offset or <exit>: **Pick line (B).**	Pick original line.
Specify point on side to offset: **Pick point (7).**	Indicate side of offset.
Select object to offset or <exit>: **Pick line (C).**	Pick original line.
Specify point on side to offset: **Pick point (8).**	Indicate side of offset.
Select object to offset or <exit>: **Pick line (D).**	Pick original line.
Specify point on side to offset: **Pick point (9).**	Indicate side of offset.
Select object to offset or <exit>: ↵	Terminate the command.

Step 4: Create wall opening lines using OFFSET.

Command: ↵	Restart the last command to enter a different distance.

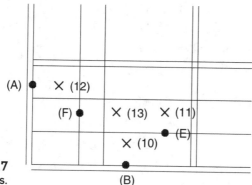

Figure 2.7
Create wall opening lines.

OFFSET	
Specify offset distance or [Through] <0'-8">: **4'** ⏎	For window opening.
Select object to offset or <exit>: **Pick line (B).**	Pick original line (Figure 2.7).
Specify point on side to offset: **Pick point (10).**	Indicate side of offset.
Select object to offset or <exit>: **Pick line (E).**	Pick original line.
Specify point on side to offset: **Pick point (11).**	Indicate side of offset.
Select object to offset or <exit>: ⏎	Terminate the command.
Command:	Restart the last command to enter a different distance.

OFFSET	
Specify offset distance or [Through] <4'-0">: **6'** ⏎	
Select object to offset or <exit>: **Pick line (A).**	Pick original line.
Specify point on side to offset: **Pick point (12).**	Indicate side of offset.
Select object to offset or <exit>: ⏎	Terminate the command.
Command:	Restart the last command to enter a different distance.

OFFSET	
Specify offset distance or [Through] <6'-0">: **3'** ⏎	
Select object to offset or <exit>: **Pick line (F).**	Pick original line.

Specify point on side
to offset: **Pick point (13).**   Indicate side of offset.

Select object to offset or <exit>: ↵   Terminate the command.

Step 5: Move wall opening lines to cross wall lines using MOVE.

This step is a preparation for creating a window opening in the wall. The lines that define the window opening need to be moved to cross the wall lines so that the TRIM command (to be discussed later) can work properly when removing lines and thereby creating the opening.

Command: **M** ↵   Start the MOVE command by its alias "M." (You may also use the toolbar icon to start the MOVE command.)

MOVE

Select objects:
Pick line (E) 1 found   Select the objects you want to move (Figure 2.8).

Select objects:
Pick line (G) 1 found, 2 total

Select objects: ↵   Terminate selection.

● In many commands, the Select objects prompt will not stop until you press the [Enter] key or right-click. (Forgetting to terminate the selection prompt has been a major problem among novice AutoCAD users.)

Specify base point
of displacement:
Pick point (14).   Pick base point.

Specify second point
of displacement or <use
first point as displacement>:
Pick point (15).   Pick second point.

● Movement is controlled by the relative position of the second point to the base point. The selected objects move in the direction from the base point to the second point; they also move the same distance as that between the two points. Because

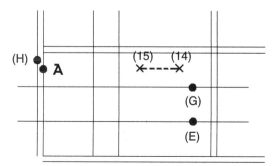

Figure 2.8
Move the lines.

what matters is the relative position of the two points, the location of the base point can be anywhere you want as long as you have the space for the second point.

For this step, these two points should be on a horizontal line. To ensure this, turn the ORTHO mode on.

Lines (E) and (G) are now crossing lines (A) and (H).

Step 6: Fix corner joints of wall lines using FILLET.

The FILLET command is intended to link two lines with an arc. The default value for the radius of the arc is 0.5. When this value is changed to 0, the command can be used to join two lines at the actual or implied intersection. The easiest way to launch the FILLET command is to enter its alias, F, from the keyboard. AutoCAD then prompts you to pick two lines. The picked lines will be perfectly connected. If the two lines intersect, a section of each line will be "cut off." It is important to remember that the picked section will remain while the section beyond the intersection will be removed.

Command: **F** ↵

Start the FILLET command using its alias.

FILLET

Current settings: Mode = TRIM, Radius = 0'-0 1/2"

Select first object
or [Polyline/Radius/Trim]: **R** ↵

Change radius.

AutoCAD has an initial default value of 1/2" for the radius.

Specify fillet radius <0'-0 1/2">: **0** ↵   For new radius.

Select first object
or [Polyline/Radius/Trim]:
Pick point (1).

(Figure 2.9)

Pick the part of the line that will remain.

Select second object:
Pick point (2).

The inside upper-left corner has a perfect connection.

Command: ↵

Restart FILLET command.

FILLET
Polyline/Radius/<Select first object>:
**Continue to pick points
from (3) to (14).**

The result should look like Figure 2.10.

- The FILLET command terminates after working on a pair of lines. You need to right-click to restart the command for each pair of lines.

- The toolbar icon for FILLET is shown here.

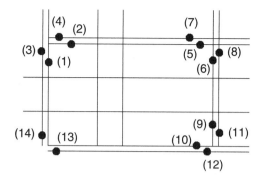

Figure 2.9
Use FILLET to connect
the corners.

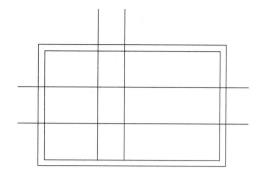

Figure 2.10
After FILLET commands.

Step 7: Make the door opening using TRIM.

When lines intersect, the TRIM command allows you to trim off the unwanted portion of the lines beyond the intersection. (You cannot use this command if the lines do not intersect.) In this operation, one line (or a group of lines) is selected as the cutting edge(s), and can be used to trim off other lines. If the selected cutting edges intersect, they can also be used to trim off each other.

Command: **TRIM** ↵	Start TRIM command to make door opening.
Current settings: Projection=UCS Edge=None	
Select cutting edges:	
Select objects: **Click point (1)** Specify opposite corner: **Drag and click point (2)** 4 found	Drags out a rubber band window (Figure 2.11).
Select objects: ↵	Terminate selection.

● In previous steps, you selected objects by clicking each individual object. In this step, you used an implied crossing-window to select a group of objects all at once. When AutoCAD prompted you to select objects, you clicked at an empty spot in the drawing area. AutoCAD interpreted this action as an implied request to create a selection

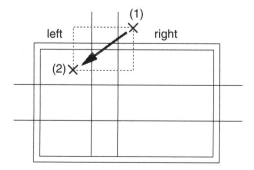

Figure 2.11
Select cutting edges.

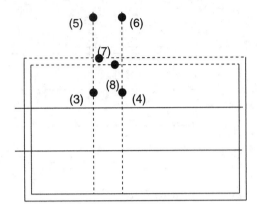

Figure 2.12
Select objects to trim.

window to catch a group of objects and a rubber band window that can be dragged out. If you pull the window out from right to left, it is a crossing-window that catches and selects both the objects that are entirely enclosed in the window and the objects crossed by the window frame. If you pull the window out from left to right, it is a selection-window that catches only the objects that are entirely enclosed in the window. Before using these selection methods, you must carefully plan the first picking point, which is used to drag out the type of window you need. The crossing-window is made of dotted lines and the selection-window of solid lines.

Select object to trim
or [Project/Edge/Undo]:
Pick point (3).   (Figure 2.12)

Pick unwanted line segment.

Select object to trim
or [Project/Edge/Undo]:
Pick point (4).

Select object to trim
or [Project/Edge/Undo]:
Pick point (5).

Select object to trim
or [Project/Edge/Undo]:
Pick point (6).

Select object to trim
or [Project/Edge/Undo]:
Pick point (7).

Select object to trim
or [Project/Edge/Undo]:
Pick point (8).

Select object to trim
or [Project/Edge/Undo]:   Terminate the command.

Command:

● The alias for TRIM is TR and its toolbar icon is shown in the margin. You may want to try it the next time.

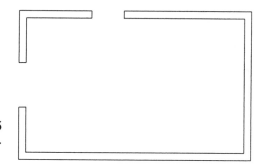

Figure 2.13
Finished wall lines.

Step 8: Make the window opening using TRIM.

Following the example in step 7, use the TRIM command to create the window opening in the left wall. The result should look like Figure 2.13.

Step 9: Make a quick print of your drawing (Optional).

If you have a laser or inkjet printer linked to your computer, you may want to print out your drawing.

1 ZOOM to create a good view of your plan.

2 Click the printer icon in the standard toolbar. The Plot dialog box pops up.

3 Click [OK]. Check your printed drawing.

Step 10: Save your file and end AutoCAD session.

Save your drawing as ch02.dwg.

Exit AutoCAD.

Summary

A Systematic Approach

A floor plan is made primarily of lines, mainly wall lines. There are many different ways to draw wall lines. They differ in speed, accuracy, and information processing. In this chapter, you have learned a systematic way to draw the wall lines of a floor plan. This specific approach, the first step toward high-quality AutoCAD drafting, is a systematic combination of four simple commands: LINE, OFFSET, FILLET, and TRIM. Compared with other approaches, this system: requires the least amount of information processing and the least effort for eye-cursor coordination; allows you to deal with one thing (the length of one segment of a wall) at a time; and does not rely on your fatigued eyes and hands to catch critical points in the drawing area. This makes it easy to learn and use and is appropriate in the interior design field, since interior space is usually measured in surface-to-surface dimensions.

This systematic approach begins with a pair of perpendicular lines located in a corner of the plan. The OFFSET command produces offset lines from the two original lines according to the dimensions of the plan. The FILLET and TRIM commands make perfect line connections at each corner, and make door and window openings in walls. You will appreciate this system when you apply it to a more complex, large-scale project.

In this chapter, you have learned the following concepts, procedures, and commands:

Knowledge/Concepts

- Drawing units
- Drawing limits
- Drawing scale
- Drafting settings: GRID, SNAP, ORTHO
- Object snap

Procedures

- Set up a new drawing
- Set up right-click mode
- Turn off OSNAP
- Repeat a command
- Define movement by picking 2 points
- Select by implied window: selection-window, crossing-window
- Make a print

Commands

- UNITS
- LIMITS
- GRID
- SNAP
- ORTHO
 - LINE (L)

 - OFFSET (O)

 - MOVE (M)

 - FILLET (F)

 - TRIM (TR)

 - PLOT

Adding to the Floor Plan

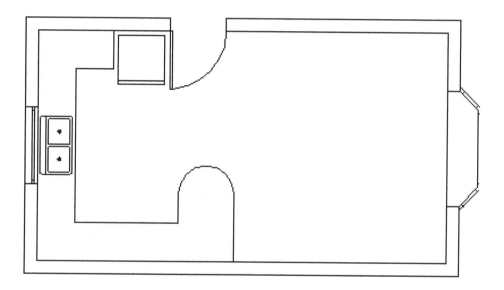

- Make changes using the STRETCH command
- Add to the floor plan

This chapter continues from the last chapter, adding on to the simple floor plan to make it a kitchen/dining space according to a designer's sketch (Figure 3.1). In the process, you will continue to learn more drawing and editing commands, as well as basic object snap functions.

Making Changes Using the STRETCH Command

In the design process, changes are inevitable and in manual drafting, making these changes is hard: it means erasures, dust, smudges, and repeated drafting of the same drawing elements. In CAD drafting, making changes is easy. You can erase, move, rotate, scale, and stretch drawing elements freely.

1 **Start an AutoCAD session** and **OPEN** the unfinished floor plan you created in the previous tutorial.

2 **Use the SAVEAS command to save it (to the hard disk of your computer) as a new drawing and name it Ch03.**

● If you just opened the file from a floppy disk, it is a good idea to save the new drawing to the hard disk of your computer. You should avoid working on a drawing opened from a floppy disk, because the speed of a floppy disk drive is relatively slow and the limited disk space can be easily filled up with the .bak files created by the SAVE or QSAVE command.

● Since the drawing settings you set in previous working sessions were usually saved, you don't have to set them again when you re-open an existing drawing.

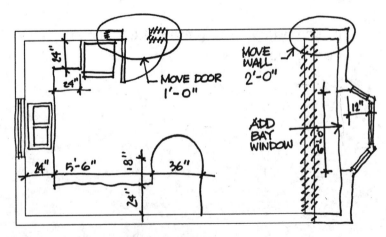

Figure 3.1
Designer's sketch.

3 Stretch the wall 24″ to the right using STRETCH.

● STRETCH is a wonderful tool to make changes in an existing drawing. After starting the command, AutoCAD prompts you to select an object with crossing-window. As you have done in Chapter 2, you can call out an implied crossing-window by clicking on an empty area and pulling from right to left. The selected portion of the drawing then can be stretched in the direction defined by you.

Command: **Click the STRETCH icon.**

Command: _stretch

Select objects to stretch
by crossing-window
or crossing-polygon...

Select objects: **Pick point (1)**
Other corner: **Pick point (2)**
6 found   (Figure 3.2)

Select objects: ⏎   End selection.

Specify base point
or displacement: **24,0** ⏎

● A drastic stretch of the wall may take place in the drawing window. Don't be scared.

Specify second point
of displacement: ⏎   The wall is stretched out 2′.

Command: The command terminates.

● The displacement coordinate (24,0) you entered at the prompt defines the movement 24″ in the direction of the *x* axis and 0″ in the direction of the *y* axis. Pressing the [Enter] key at the following prompt tells AutoCAD the coordinate you just entered is a displacement vector, not a base point. Using the displacement input also works in other commands (such as MOVE and COPY). The reason why 24″ is used instead of 2′ is that the foot mark is away from the number keys on the keyboard. Entering 24 is faster than entering 2′. The difference becomes more significant when both feet and inches are involved; for example, entering 30 is much faster than entering 2′6.

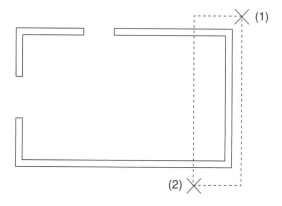

Figure 3.2
Selecting wall with implied
crossing-window.

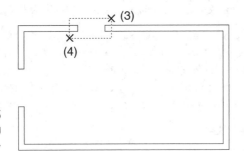

Figure 3.3
Selecting door opening
for **STRETCH**.

● In this example note that the lines entirely included in the selection window remain the same shape; the lines crossed by the selection window are stretched. By applying this rule when you make a selection with the crossing-window, you can predict what will be stretched and what will not.

4 Stretch the door opening to the right 12″ using STRETCH.

Command: ↵	Repeat the last STRETCH command.
STRETCH	
Select objects to stretch by crossing-window or crossing-polygon...	
Select objects: **Pick point (3)** Other corner: **Pick point (4)** 6 found	(Figure 3.3) Use implied crossing-window (right to left) to select the door opening.
Select objects: ↵	End selection.
Specify base point or displacement: **12,0** ↵	
Specify second point of displacement: ↵	Use the displacement method to define the stretching movement. The door opening is stretched 1′ to the right.

● The alias for STRETCH is S.

Adding to the Floor Plan

Step 1: Set the Object Snap toolbar.

Object Snap modes help you pick particular points (such as the endpoint and mid-point of a drawing element) in the drawing area. You can use any of these as a one-time-only service when you need help picking a particular point, or you can keep

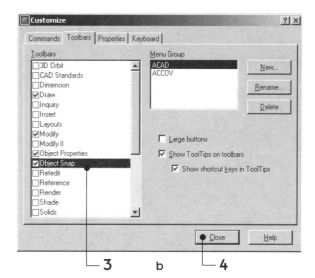

Figure 3.4
View menu and Toolbars
dialog box.

a   2   3   b   4

this service running all the time. For the one-time-only application, you can call up the function either through your keyboard or from the Object Snap toolbar. The latter is a better approach when you intend to use it frequently. Although the Running Object Snap mode can be very handy when used for the right task, it can easily get out of control, especially when you forget it is still on. Therefore, use it only when it is really needed, and turn it off after finishing the job.

1 Click the View menu. (Figure 3.4a)

2 Choose Toolbars... The Toolbars dialog box pops up (Figure 3.4b).

3 Check the Object Snap box. The Object Snap toolbar pops up (Figure 3.5).

● You can close a toolbar by clearing the check box in front of its name.

4 Click [Close].

5 Drag the title bar of the Object Snap toolbar to move it close to the right border of the drawing window until a dashed rectangle appears; release the held mouse button to embed the toolbar into the border.

● You can follow this procedure to set up other toolbars when needed. If you don't need them anymore, drag them from the border and close them.

● The Toolbar dialog box can also be accessed through the TOOLBAR command or its alias TO.

Step 2: Add the door using the direct-entry method.

1 Zoom in to look at the door opening. Be sure to leave space for the door. See Figure 3.1 for reference.

Figure 3.5
The Object Snap toolbar.

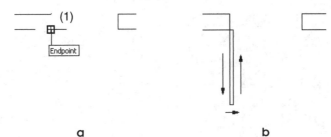

Figure 3.6
Drawing the door.   a   b

2 Turn ORTHO on if it is not already turned on. Use function key [F8].

3 Draw the door.

Command: **L** ↵   Start the LINE command.

LINE Specify first point:
Click Endpoint icon.   Use toolbar to activate the one-time-only
                                          Endpoint object snap mode.

● The Endpoint toolbar icon is very similar to the LINE command toolbar icon.
  The difference is that the LINE icon has solid points at the ends of the line
  image.

_end of **pick point (1)**   (Figure 3.6a)

● When you move your cursor close to point (1), a small, yellow-colored box
  appears and a "Tip" pops up to tell you it is an endpoint. If you click when the
  colored box appears, you are guaranteed a perfect catch of that endpoint.

Specify next point or [Undo]:
**(Move mouse to make the rubber
band line go straight down.) 36** ↵   A 3′ line is drawn down vertically, and the
                                          rubber band is anchored at the new endpoint
                                          of the line segment.

● In this direct-entry method, inputting the next point is accomplished by keying
  in the length of the line segment (36″), and controlling the rubber band direction
  with the mouse. Turning the ORTHO mode on assures accurate direction of the
  line. This method can also be used to specify a next point in other commands
  such as MOVE and STRETCH.

Specify next point or [Undo]:
**(Move mouse to make the rubber
band line go right.) 2** ↵   A 2″ line is drawn horizontally to the right.

Specify next point or [Close/Undo]:
**(Move mouse to make the rubber
band line go up.) 36** ↵   A 3′ line is drawn up vertically.

Specify next point
or [Close/Undo]: **C** ↵   A line is drawn toward point (1) to close the
                                          rectangle.

Command: The LINE command terminates (Figure
                                          3.6b).

- "C" means to "close" the shape. It makes the last line segment go to the beginning point, and automatically terminates the command.

4 Draw the door swing using ARC.

Command: **A** ↵	Start ARC command with its alias A.
ARC Specify start point of arc or [Center]: **END** ↵	

- You can call for the Endpoint object snap mode from the keyboard by typing the object snap mode you want (END for endpoint, MID for midpoint, CEN for center of circle or arc, or INT for intersection).

of **pick point (1)**	Pick the start point of the arc (Figure 3.7).
Specify second point of arc or [Center/End]: **C** ↵	"C" means Center.
Specify center point of arc: **END** ↵	Activate Endpoint object snap.
of **pick point (2)**	Pick the center point of the arc.
Specify end point of arc or [Angle/chord Length]: **END** ↵	Activate Endpoint object snap.
of **pick point (3)**	Pick the endpoint of the arc.
Command:	The ARC command terminates.

- The ARC command generates arcs in a counterclockwise direction. For the above example, if you select point (3) as the starting point and point (1) as the end, AutoCAD will not draw the arc as you expect. Instead, it creates a $^3/_4$ circle in the opposite direction. Therefore, when you use the ARC command you need to plan the sequence of point picking before you start to pick points.

Step 3: Draw the window.

1 Zoom to the previous view to see the whole plan.

2 Zoom in to see the window opening in detail.

3 Draw the windowsill lines.

Command: **L** ↵

LINE Specify first point: **END** ↵

Of **pick point (1)**   (Figure 3.8a)

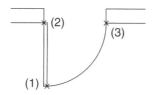

Figure 3.7
Draw the door swing.

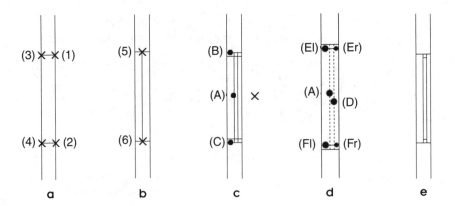

Figure 3.8
Drawing the window.

a   b   c   d   e

Specify next point or [Undo]: **END** ↵

Of **pick point (2)**

To point: ↵

Command: ↵

LINE Specify first point: **END** ↵

Of **pick point (3)**

Specify next point or [Undo]: **END** ↵

Of **pick point (4)**

Specify next point or [Undo]: ↵

4 Draw the window lines.

Command: ↵

LINE Specify first point: **MID** ↵   Activate MIDpoint object snap.

Of **pick point (5)**   Midpoint identified by colored triangle (Figure 3.8b).

Specify next point or [Undo]: **MID** ↵

Of **pick point (6)**

Specify next point or [Undo]: ↵

Command: **O** ↵   Start the OFFSET command by its alias.

OFFSET

Specify offset distance or [Through] <Through>: **2** ↵

Select object to offset or <exit>: **Pick window line (A).**   (Figure 3.8c)

Specify point on side to offset: **Click inside the room.**

Select object to offset or <exit>:
Pick window opening line (B).

Specify point on side to offset: **Click near
the midpoint of the window.**

Select object to offset or <exit>:
Pick window opening line (C).

Specify point on side to offset: **Click near
the midpoint of the window.**

Select object to offset or <exit>: ↵

Command: **TR** ↵   Start the TRIM command by its
                                                       alias.

TRIM

Current settings: Projection=UCS Edge=None

Select cutting edges ...

Select objects: **Pick line (A)** 1 found   (Figure 3.8d)

Select objects: **Pick line (D)** 1 found, 2 total

Select objects: ↵

Select object to trim or [Project/Edge/Undo]:
Pick the left end of line (E).

Select object to trim or [Project/Edge/Undo]:
Pick the right end of line (E).

Select object to trim or [Project/Edge/Undo]:
Pick the left end of line (F).

Select object to trim or [Project/Edge/Undo]:
Pick the right end of line (F).

Select object to trim or [Project/Edge/Undo]: ↵   (Figure 3.8e)

Command:

Step 4: Draw the bay window.

Adjust the view.

1 Zoom out to the previous view to see the whole room plan.

2 Zoom in to look at the right-side wall.

Draw the window opening lines in the wall.

According to the designer's sketch, the opening of the bay window is 6′ wide and we
can assume that it is located on center. Since the wall is 12′ long, the window opening line is 3′ from the ends of the walls at the corners. To start a line 3′ from the

corner, use the Snap From object snap tool. This tool allows you to use an anchor point to locate a point required by an AutoCAD command.

Command: **L** ↵	Start a LINE command.

LINE Specify first point:
Click the Snap From icon.

_from Base point: **END** ↵	Use Endpoint object snap to catch the anchor point (Figure 3.9).
of **pick point (1)** <Offset>: **@0,36** ↵	Locate the start point of the line relative to the anchor point.
	A rubber band line stretches out from a point 36″ above the anchor point.

- @*x,y* inputs relative coordinates for the next point from the last point you have just picked. @0,36 means the next point is 36″ up from the last point. This method can also be used in commands such as MOVE, COPY, STRETCH, and any other command that requires an input of a second point.

Specify next point or [Undo]: **PER** ↵	Use Perpendicular object snap to ensure a good connection to the outside wall line.
	A yellow-colored right angle symbol appears when the cursor is over a line.
to **pick the outside wall line** Specify next point or [Undo]: ↵	End the command.

Draw the 45° line.

There are many ways to instruct AutoCAD to draw a line. An easy way to draw a line in a particular angle is to use the polar coordinates that are defined by the length of the line segment and the angle of the line. Since the length of the line segment is not directly given in the designer's sketch, we can tentatively draw a 12″ line in a 45° angle, and later link it to the side of the bay window that is parallel to the wall.

Command: ↵	Repeat the last command.

Figure 3.9
Using temporary tracking to draw the window opening line.

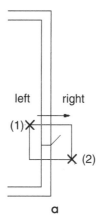

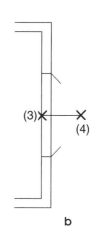

Figure 3.10
Draw the 45° line.

Figure 3.11
Use the MIRROR command.

LINE Specify first point: ↵

This second Enter starts a new line segment from the last point of the object you worked on with the last command.

Specify next point or [Undo]:
@12<45 ↵

Enter the length and angle of the line segment.

● In this expression, @ means "from last point"; 12 is the length; "<" means angle; and 45 is the degree value of the angle. The whole expression means drawing a 12″ line in a 45° angle from the last point.

Specify next point or [Undo]: ↵   End the LINE command (Figure 3.10).

Create the other side of the bay window using the MIRROR command.

The MIRROR command creates a flipped copy of selected objects on the other side of a mirror line defined by two points. You need to figure out how to locate the mirror line to make best use of this command. You can also use this command as a flipping tool by opting to delete the old set of objects.

Command: **MIRROR** ↵

Select objects: **Pick point (1)**
Specify opposite corner:
Pick point (2) 2 found   (Figure 3.11a)

Use an implied selection-window (left to right) to select the two lines without picking up the wall lines.

Select objects: ↵   End selection.

Specify first point of mirror line:
MID ↵   Activate MIDpoint object snap mode.

A small, yellow-colored triangle appears when the cursor is over a line.

of **pick point (3)** Specify second point
of mirror line: **Pick point (4).**   (Figure 3.11b)

Define the mirror line.

● Hint: Turning ORTHO mode on helps to make the mirror line perfectly horizontal.

Delete source objects? [Yes/No]<N>: ↵   Accept the No default value.

● When you face a multiple-choice prompt like this, the item in the angular brack-
ets < > is the "default." Simply press [Enter] to accept the default choice.

● The MIRROR icon is in the Modify toolbar.

Create the outline of the bay window.

According to the designer's sketch, the vertical portion of the bay window is 12″ off
the outside wall line. You can use the OFFSET command to create a line and use the
FILLET command to connect it to the two angled lines.

Command: **O** ↵   Start the OFFSET command.

OFFSET

Specify offset distance or [Through] <0′-2″>:
12 ↵   Enter offset distance.

Select object to offset or <exit>:
Pick line (A).   (Figure 3.12a)

Specify point on side to offset:
Pick a point to the right.   The line is created.

Select object to offset or <exit>: ↵   End the OFFSET command.

Command: **F** ↵

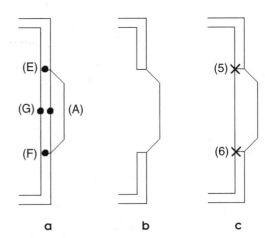

Figure 3.12
Create the bay window
outline.

Figure 3.13
TRIM the wall lines.

FILLET

Current settings: Mode = TRIM, Radius = 0'-0"

Select first object or [Polyline/Radius/Trim]:
Pick line (B).

Select second object: **Pick line (C).**

Command: ⏎

FILLET

Current settings: Mode = TRIM, Radius = 0'-0"

Select first object or [Polyline/Radius/Trim]:
Pick line (C).

Select second object:
Pick line (D).   (Figure 3.12b)

Create the window opening using the TRIM command.

Since the windowsill line and the wall line need to be differentiated in the future with different line weights, they have to be separated. In this step, you will use the TRIM command to delete the windowsill portion of the line and draw it with the LINE command.

Command: **TR** ⏎   Start the TRIM command.

Current settings: Projection=UCS Edge=None

Select cutting edges ...

Select objects: **Pick line (E)** 1 found   (Figure 3.13a)

Select objects: **Pick line (F)** 1 found, 2 total

Select objects: ⏎   End selection.

Select object to trim or shift-select to extend
or [Project/Edge/Undo]: **Pick line (A).**

Select object to trim or shift-select to extend
or [Project/Edge/Undo]: **Pick line (G).**

Select object to trim or shift-select to extend
or [Project/Edge/Undo]: ⏎   End TRIM command.

Command: (Figure 3.13b)

Command: **L** ⏎   Start the LINE command.

LINE Specify first point: **END** ⏎

Of **pick point (5)**   (Figure 3.13c)

Specify next point or [Undo]: **END** ⏎

Of **pick point (6)**

Specify next point or [Undo]: ⏎

Double-line the bay window.

Based on the outline of the bay window you just created, use the OFFSET command to create the exterior lines, and then connect them using the FILLET command.

Command: **O** ↵	Start the OFFSET command.

OFFSET

Specify offset distance or [Through] <1'-0">: **2** ↵	Enter offset distance.

Select object to offset or <exit>: **Pick line (H).**   (Figure 3.14)

Specify point on side to offset:
Pick a point to the right.

Select object to offset or <exit>: **Pick line (J).**

Specify point on side to offset:
Pick a point to the right.

Select object to offset or <exit>: **Pick line (K).**

Specify point on side to offset:
Pick a point to the right.

Select object to offset or <exit>: ↵	End the command.
Command: **F** ↵	Start the FILLET command.

FILLET

Current settings: Mode = TRIM, Radius = 0'-0"

Select first object or [Polyline/Radius/Trim]:
Pick line (L).   (Figure 3.15)

Select second object: **Pick line (M).**

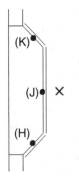

Figure 3.14
Double-line the window.

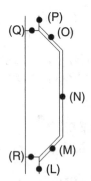

Figure 3.15
Connect the lines.

Command: ↵   Repeat the FILLET command.

FILLET

Current settings: Mode = TRIM, Radius = 0'-0"

Select first object or [Polyline/Radius/Trim]:
Pick line (M).

Select second object: **Pick line (N).**

Command: ↵   Repeat the FILLET command.

FILLET

Current settings: Mode = TRIM, Radius = 0'-0"

Select first object or [Polyline/Radius/Trim]:
Pick line (N).

Select second object: **Pick line (O).**

Command: ↵   Repeat the FILLET command.

FILLET

Current settings: Mode = TRIM, Radius = 0'-0"

Select first object or [Polyline/Radius/Trim]:
Pick line (O).

Select second object: **Pick line (P).**

Command: ↵   Repeat the FILLET command.

FILLET

Current settings: Mode = TRIM, Radius = 0'-0"

Select first object or [Polyline/Radius/Trim]:
Pick line (P).

Select second object: **Pick line (Q).**

Command: ↵   Repeat the FILLET command.

FILLET

Current settings: Mode = TRIM, Radius = 0'-0"

Select first object or [Polyline/Radius/Trim]:
Pick line (R).

Select second object: **Pick line (L).**

Draw the mullions.

In a bay window the mullions are no longer simple rectangles. The challenge is to accurately create the angled short lines on the slanting sections. Use the MIRROR command to tackle this problem.

1 ZOOM in to look at the connections of the vertical and the 45° sections.

2 Draw the first mullion line on the vertical section of the window, using the Snap From object snap tool to start the line 2″ from the corner.

Command: **L** ↵

LINE Specify first point: **FROM** ↵	Activite the Snap From object snap from the keyboard.
_from Base point: **END** ↵	Activate Endpoint object snap to catch the anchor point.
of **pick point (1)** <Offset>: **@0,2** ↵	(Figure 3.16)
	Define a point 2″ straight up (x=0, y=2) from the anchor point.
Specify next point or [Undo]: **PER** ↵	Activate the PERpendicular object snap to pick line (N).
Specify next point or [Undo]: ↵	End the command.

3 Use MIRROR command to create the mullion line on the 45° section.

Command: **MI** ↵	Use alias MI to start the MIRROR command.
MIRROR	
Select objects: **Pick line (S)** 1 found	(Figure 3.17)
Select objects: ↵	
Specify first point of mirror line: **END** ↵	Activate the Endpoint object snap.
of **Pick point (2)**	
Specify second point of mirror line: **END**	
of **Pick point (3)**	

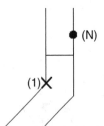

Figure 3.16
Draw the first mullion line.

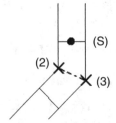

Figure 3.17
Create the mullion line on the slanting section.

Delete source objects?
[Yes/No] <N>: ⏎   The line is created.

4 ZOOM out to look at the entire bay window.

5 ZOOM in to look at the 45° section of the bay window.

6 Use the MIRROR command to create the windowframe line next to the wall.

Command: **MI** ⏎

MIRROR

Select objects: **Pick line (T)**
1 found   (Figure 3.18)

Select objects: ⏎

Specify first point of mirror line:
MID ⏎

of **pick the middle of line (H)**
Specify second point
of mirror line: **PER** ⏎

to **pick line (M)**

Delete source objects? [Yes/No] <N>: ⏎

7 ZOOM out to look at the entire bay window.

8 Use the MIRROR command to create the mullion and frame lines on the opposite side of the bay window.

Command: **MI** ⏎

MIRROR

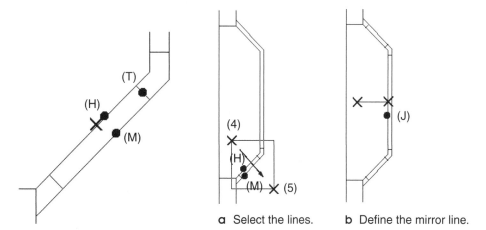

Figure 3.18
Create the window frame
line.

a Select the lines.   b Define the mirror line.

Figure 3.19
Finish the bay window.

Select objects: **Pick point (4)**
Specify opposite corner:
Pick point (5) 5 found

                                       Use selection window to catch the lines
                                       (Figure 3.19a).

● This window selection caught not only the short lines you want to mirror to the opposite side, but also the two window lines that you do not need. You can take out these items from a selection set by turning on the Remove mode of selection.

Select objects: **R** ↵   Turn the Remove mode on.

Remove objects: **Pick line (H)**
1 found, 1 removed, 4 total   (Figure 3.19a)

Remove objects: **Pick line (M)**
1 found, 1 removed, 3 total

Remove objects: ↵   End selection.

Specify first point of mirror line:
MID ↵   (Figure 3.19b)

of **pick the middle of line (J)**

Specify second point of mirror line:
**Move cursor left with ORTHO mode
on (use [F8] key to toggle it on if
needed) and click.**

Delete source objects? [Yes/No] <N>: ↵

9 ZOOM out to look at the entire floor plan.

Step 5: Draw the counter.

Since the counter is built against walls and the depth of the counter is 24″, you can use the OFFSET-FILLET combination to create all the counter lines.

1 Use OFFSET to create counter lines. See Figure 3.20 for offset distances.

2 Use FILLET to connect the counter lines. See Figure 3.21 for picking points and Figure 3.22 for the result.

● The two lines of the last pair are parallel. The FILLET command, therefore, connects the two lines with a half circle arc. When selecting the lines, you must pick the lines in the upper portion of each line to ensure that the arc is created above the lines.

3 ERASE the straight line in the arc.

Step 6: Draw the refrigerator outline using RECTANGLE.

According to the designer's sketch, the refrigerator is a 30″ × 30″ square. Simply use the RECTANGLE command to draw it. To carry out the command, AutoCAD

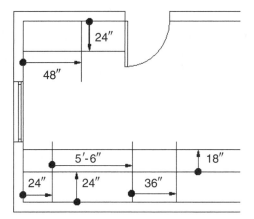

Figure 3.20
Lines for the counter
created using OFFSET.

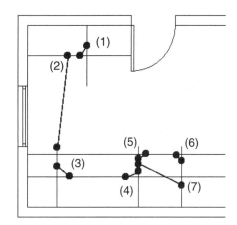

Figure 3.21
Pick points for FILLET.

needs inputs of two opposite corners of the rectangle. The relative coordinates @x,y can be used to define the second point. Since it is difficult to estimate the exact location of the refrigerator, pick a starting point on a clear spot on the drawing and move it into position later.

Command: **REC** ↵	Start the RECTANGLE command using its alias.
RECTANGLE	
Specify first corner point or [Chamfer/Elevation/Fillet/ Thickness/Width]: **Pick a point** (anywhere).	
Specify other corner point: **@30,30** ↵	Enter the relative position of the second corner point.
Command:	The rectangle is drawn.

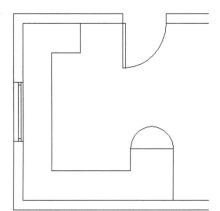

Figure 3.22
Countertop line.

- The rectangle drawn with the RECTANGLE command is made of polylines, a type of entity different from line. A polyline can have a width, and all segments form a connected whole. If you select one side of the rectangle, the whole rectangle is selected. The RECTANGLE command can also be launched by clicking the Drawing toolbar icon.

Step 7: Draw the refrigerator door using Snap From object snap.

This task entails drawing only one line, 2″ inside the refrigerator outline. Since the refrigerator outline is made of a polyline, the OFFSET command does not work in this situation because it will not create a line, but instead creates a smaller rectangle inside the original rectangle. Therefore, you need to use the Snap From object snap to locate the starting point of the line using the corner of the refrigerator as an anchor.

1 ZOOM in to look at the rectangle closely. The rectangle should fill the drawing window.

2 Start a LINE command.

Command: **L** ↵

LINE Specify first point:
Click the Snap From icon

_from Base point: **END** ↵   Activate Endpoint object snap to catch the anchor point.

of **pick point (1)** <Offset>: **@0,2** ↵   (Figure 3-23)

                                               Define a point 2″ straight up (x=0, y=2) from the anchor point.

Move cursor to the right (with ORTHO turned on).

Specify next point or [Undo]: **30** ↵   Use the direct-entry method.

Specify next point or [Undo]: ↵

Step 8: MOVE the refrigerator into position.

1 ZOOM out to see the whole floor plan.

2 Turn ORTHO mode off using the [F8] key.

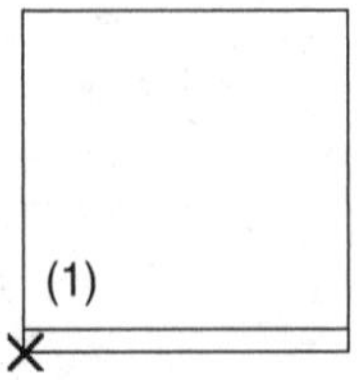

(1)

Figure 3.23
Draw the refrigerator.

3 Start the MOVE command (with alias M).

4 Select the refrigerator (by a crossing-window).

5 Use Endpoint object snap to pick the upper-left corner of the refrigerator as the base point for the move.

● The refrigerator is now attached to the cursor and moves along with your cursor. When you move the refrigerator to a place you like, click to "drop" the refrigerator at that spot. Compared with accurately controlled movement, this MOVE is more intuitive, tentative, and flexible.

6 Move the refrigerator to the space between the counter and the door, and click to drop it. You should leave a small space (1 to 2″) between the refrigerator and surrounding objects. (Figure 3.24)

● If you are not satisfied with your first move, you can repeat the MOVE command by pressing [Enter]. Instead of selecting the refrigerator again, you can enter a P (short for Previous) to reselect the last selection set that is still remembered by AutoCAD (until a new selection is made). Then you may select a new base point and adjust the location of the refrigerator.

Step 9: Draw the sink using the AutoCAD symbol library.

A symbol library is included in AutoCAD 2002. You can access it through the Auto-CAD Today window.

1 Click the AutoCAD Today icon on the standard toolbar to bring up the AutoCAD Today window. If you see the welcome page, click [Continue]. (Figure 3.25)

2 Click the Symbol libraries tab. The library page appears.

3 Click Kitchen. A side panel opens with symbols in it (Figure 3.26).

4 Use the scroll bar to find the Sink-double–36 in top symbol.

5 Drag it into the drawing window and release the mouse button to drop it.

6 Close the side panel by clicking its Close button.

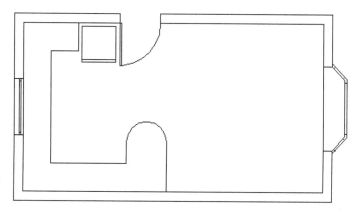

Figure 3.24
Place the refrigerator.

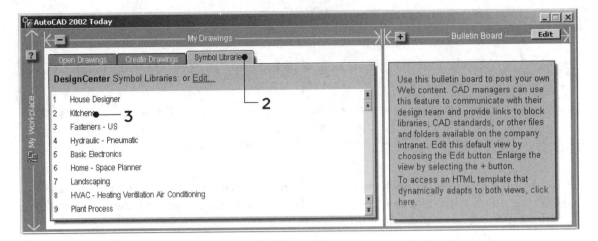

Figure 3.25
Access the symbol library.

Step 10: Locate the sink and ROTATE and MOVE it using object snap.

In this step, you will rotate the sink symbol and place it on the counter and align it with the centerline of the window.

1 Use the ROTATE command to rotate the sink.

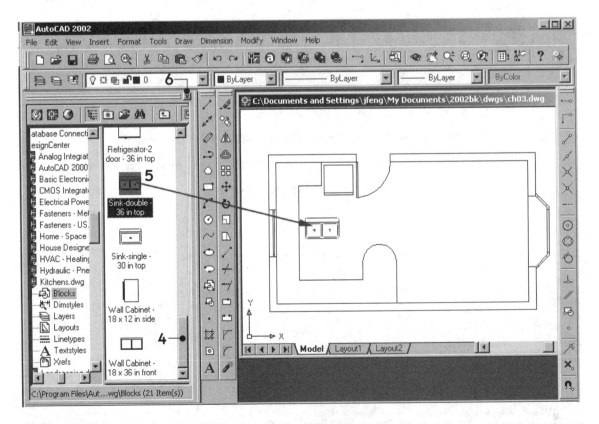

Figure 3.26
Drag-and-drop the refrigerator symbol.

● The ROTATE command rotates selected objects about a base point. You can either enter the angle of rotation or use your mouse to define the rotation angle on the screen.

Command: **ROTATE** ↵

Current positive angle in UCS:
ANGDIR=counterclockwise ANGBASE=0

Select objects: **Pick the sink symbol** 1 found

Select objects: ↵

Specify base point: **Pick a point inside the symbol.**

Specify rotation angle or [Reference]: **90** ↵

● The alias for ROTATE is RO and its icon is in the Modify toolbar.

● You may have noticed that although the sink is made of many lines and circles, it appears to be a single object. One click picks up the sink as a whole. This type of object is called a block. How to make blocks and insert blocks will be discussed in a later chapter.

2 ZOOM in to look at the window and the sink.

3 MOVE the sink onto the counter top and align it with the window.

● In this MOVE command, use Midpoint object snap to align the sink with the midpoint of the window.

Command: **M** ↵

MOVE

Select objects: **Pick the sink** 1 found

Select objects: ↵

Specify base point or displacement: **MID** ↵

of **pick the left side of the sink**   (Figure 3.27)

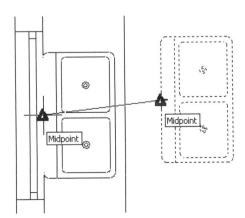

Figure 3.27
Move and align the sink.

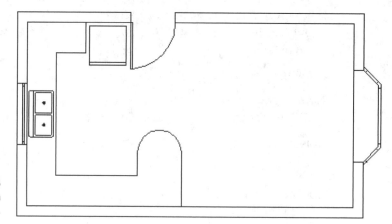

Figure 3.28
The finished floor plan
(for this chapter).

Specify second point of displacement
or <use first point as displacement>: **MID** ↵

of **pick the interior windowsill line**

Command:

● This midpoint-to-midpoint move is an example of accurate placement of objects. For future applications, different object snap modes in various combinations, such as endpoint to endpoint, or endpoint to midpoint, can be used.

4 MOVE the sink 1″ from the wall, using the direct-entry method.

Command: **M** ↵   Start the MOVE command.

MOVE

Select objects: **Pick the sink** 1 found

Select objects: ↵   End selection.

Specify base point or displacement:
Specify second point of displacement or
<use first point as displacement>:
Pick a point, press [F8].   Turn ORTHO on.

<Ortho on> **(move cursor to the right) 1** ↵   Use direct-entry method to
                                                         define movement.

Command:

5 ZOOM out to see the whole plan. (Figure 3.28)

6 QSAVE the drawing and QUIT AutoCAD.

Summary

In this chapter, you have learned the following concepts, procedures, and commands:

Knowledge/Concepts

- Object snap
- AutoCAD symbol library and block
- Polyline
- Direction of positive angle

Procedures

- Define movement by displacement coordinates
- Set a toolbar
- Use object snap: Endpoint, Midpoint, Perpendicular, Snap From
- Define next point by direct-entry method
- Define next point by relative coordinates: $@x,y$
- Use AutoCAD symbol library
- Define movement by direct-entry method
- Remove object from selection set

Commands

   • STRETCH (S)

   • RECTANGLE (REC)

   • ARC (A)

   • MIRROR (MI)

   • ROTATE (RO)

   • Endpoint object snap (END)

● Midpoint object snap (MID)

 ● Snap From object snap (FROM)

 ● Perpendicular object snap (PERP)

● TOOLBAR (TO)

Getting Organized Using Layers

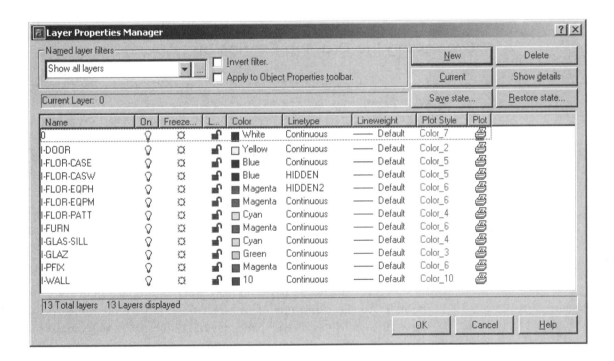

- Organize the drawing entities by layers
- Make a list of layer names for your floor plan
- Use colors
- Use linetype
- Create and set a layer
- Create more layers
- Put drawing entities on their appropriate layers

In the designer's second sketch (Figure 4.1) more details are added. Since the drawing is becoming more and more complicated with an increased number of objects and different types of lines, you need to use the "layer" feature, an important AutoCAD organizational device that gives the drawing objects a systematic order for better management. Meanwhile, you will learn more about the "properties" of drawing entities.

Organizing the Drawing Entities by Layers

In manual drafting all the drawing entities you put on a sheet stay together; it is extremely difficult to isolate any particular type of objects from the rest. In AutoCAD you can put different types of drawing entities on different "layers" to organize your drawing information more effectively. You can control the visibility of individual layers; you can control the activeness of layers when they are visible; and you can also use layer to control certain properties of the drawing entities, such as color and linetype.

In the design profession there are strict standards of layer control that were developed by individual design firms and space management departments of large institutions.

The AIA CAD Layer Guidelines

Most of the standards are based on the *CAD Layer Guidelines* that were developed by the AIA (American Institute of Architects) and other professional societies. According to AIA guidelines, a layer name may be composed of four components:

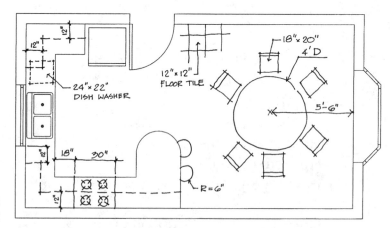

Figure 4.1
The designer's sketch

1. **Discipline Code:** One character standing for major discipline groups with a dash (e.g., I–for interior).

2. **Major Group:** Four characters standing for different types of building systems (e.g., WALL for walls).

3. **Minor Group:** Four characters for further differentiation within a major group (e.g., PRHT for partial height wall in the major group walls). This modifier is optional.

4. **Status Field:** Four characters to differentiate the drawing objects by their nature, such as new construction vs. existing. This modifier is also optional.

For example, the layer name **I-WALL-PRHT-NEWW** stands for Interior, Wall, Partial height, New construction.

The following is a list of the most commonly used group names that are related to interiors. You may use these names to compose your layer names. By combining the codes from different categories, you can create numerous layer names to fit your needs.

Discipline Code

A   Architectural, interiors, facilities management

I   Interior

E   Electrical

P   Plumbing

M   Mechanical

X   Others

Major Group

ANNO	Annotation
WALL	Wall
COLS	Columns
DOOR	Door
GLAZ	Windows
CLNG	Ceiling information
EQPM	Equipment
FURN	Furniture
LITE	Lighting
HVAC	HVAC
FLOR	Floor information
ELEV	Elevation
SECT	Sections
DETL	Detail

Minor Group

IDEN	Identification number
PRHT	Partial height
FULL	Full height
MOVE	Movable
PATT	Hatch patterns
MCUT	Material cut by section
MBND	Material beyond section cut
HEAD	Door and window headers (shown on reflected ceiling plan)
JAMB	Door and window jambs
SILL	Windowsill
LEVL	Level changes, ramps, etc.
STRS	Stair treads
RISR	Stair risers
HRAL	Hand rails
SPCL	Specialties (system furniture)
WDWK	Woodwork (field-built)
CASE	Casework (manufactured)
OVHD	Overhead skylight
FILE	File cabinets (used with furniture group)
FREE	Free standing (furniture)
CHAR	Chairs and seating
PNLS	Panels (system furniture)
WKSF	Work surface (system furniture)
STOR	Storage units (system furniture)
POWR	Power designations (system furniture)
PLNT	Plants
GRID	Ceiling grid
FNSH	Finishes, woodworks, and trim
SIGN	Signage
OTLN	Outline
SDFF	Supply diffuser
RDFF	Return diffuser
PFIX	Plumbing fixture
NOTE	Notes
TEXT	Text: general notes and specs
SYMB	Symbols, bubbles, etc.
DIMS	Dimensions
TTLB	Title block
NPLT	Nonplot information and construction lines
LEGN	Legends and schedules

Status Field

EXST	Existing to remain
DEMO	Existing to be demolished
NEWW	New or proposed work
MOVE	Items to be moved
RELO	Relocated items

● This is not a complete list. For more detailed information about layer naming conventions, see *CAD Layer Guidelines* edited by Michael Schley with others (Washington, D.C.: The American Institute of Architects Press, 1997).

Making a List of Layer Names for Your Floor Plan

Using the layer name guidelines described above, you can make a list of layers for your drawing by analyzing the designer's sketch. The list may be as follows:

Drawing Object	Layer Name	Meaning
wall	I-WALL	Interior-wall
door	I-DOOR	Interior-door
windows	I-GLAZ	Interior-glazing
windowsills	I-GLAZ-SILL	Interior-glazing-sill
counter	I-FLOR-CASE	Interior-floor information-casework
wall cabinets	I-FLOR-CASH	Interior-floor information-casework (hidden)
sink	I-FLOR-PFIX	Interior-plumbing-fixture
range, refrigerator	I-FLOR-EQPM	Interior-floor information-equipment
dishwasher	I-FLOR-EQPH	Interior-floor information-equipment (hidden)
furniture	I-FURN	Interior-furniture
floor tile	I-FLOR-PATT	Interior-floor information-pattern

● The codes CASW and EQPH are invented to meet our need to differentiate the objects drawn in hidden lines. The AIA guidelines allow you to invent codes at the Minor Group level, and such codes are called "user-defined."

Layers and Colors

After making the plan for layer names, we need to assign colors to the various layers. The difference in color for the different layers helps us to visually group the drawing entities, and it will also be used in plotting to control lineweights. Before we begin to assign colors to layers, we need a good understanding of the AutoCAD color system.

AutoCAD Colors

AutoCAD has a color pallet with 255 colors. Each color has an index number, which is referred to as ACI (AutoCAD Color Index). You can specify a color by its index number. The first nine colors in the index system are standard colors. Each of the first seven standard colors has both an index number and a color name. You may specify a standard color by either the color name or the index number. The color names and index numbers of the first seven standard colors are as follows:

Index	1	2	3	4	5	6	7
Color	red	yellow	green	cyan	blue	magenta	white/black

When you are prompted by AutoCAD to specify a color for layers or objects, the Select Color dialog box with the full color pallet usually pops up. You can pick whatever colors you like from that pallet. (You will do it later in this chapter.)

Assigning Colors to Layers

In the layer standards developed by individual design firms or institutions, a particular color is usually assigned to a layer. For this tutorial, let's make the color assignment for each layer as follows:

Drawing Object	Layer Name	Color
wall	I-WALL	1 (red)
door	I-DOOR	2 (yellow)
windows	I-GLAZ	3 (green)
windowsills	I-GLAZ-SILL	4 (cyan)
counter	I-FLOR-CASE	5 (blue)
wall cabinets	I-FLOR-CASH	5 (blue)
sink	I-PFIX	6 (magenta)
range, refrigerator	I-FLOR-EQPM	6 (magenta)
dishwasher	I-FLOR-EQPH	6 (magenta)
furniture	I-FURN	6 (magenta)
floor tile	I-FLOR-PATT	4 (cyan)

● This is an arbitrary assignment of colors. Standard colors are used for easy memoriza-tion; a single color is assigned to a group of layers with similar or related contents.

Layers and Linetype

Before we begin to create layers, we have to think about what types of lines should be assigned to each layer. In the designer's sketch, we find three different types of lines: continuous lines (the type of line you have been drawing so far), large segment hidden lines for wall cabinets, and small segment hidden lines for the dishwasher. In AutoCAD, there are many linetypes you can select and assign to layers and objects. We will make our selection in the process of creating individual layers.

Creating and Setting a Layer

When you create a new drawing from scratch, there is only one layer: layer 0. So far, you have been drawing on that layer and, therefore, all the drawing objects are on that layer. Now you need to create more layers in order to put the drawing objects into their appropriate layers according to our layer list. After creating more layers, only one of these layers is open at a time to receive newly created drawing elements. This open layer is called the "current layer." Its name and status are shown in the Layer list on the Properties toolbar. Up to this point, the current layer of your draw-ing is layer 0. How to change the current layer will be discussed in a later chapter.

Step 1: Create a new layer.

1 Start AutoCAD, OPEN ch03.dwg, and save it as ch04.dwg.

2 Click the LAYER icon in the Object Properties toolbar (Figure 4.2). The Layer Properties Manager dialog box pops up (Figure 4.3).

● You may also use the LAYER command or its alias LA to access the Layer Proper-ties Manager dialog box.

● On the layer list in the dialog box, you have only the 0 layer. The layer status is shown by icons and verbal information following the layer name. They are:

♀ / ♥   on/off

☼ / ❋   thaw/freeze

🔒 / 🔓   lock/unlock

Figure 4.2
Object Properties toolbar.

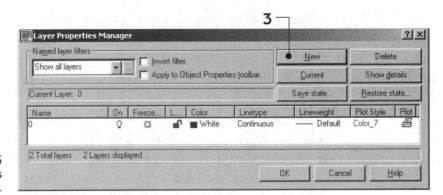

Figure 4.3
The Layer Properties
Manager dialog box.

■   color linetype (shown by name)

lineweight (shown by example line)

plot style

🖨 / 🖨   printable/nonprintable.

(The last two items will be discussed in a later chapter.) You may click the icons or the item name to change the status.

3 Click [New]. A new line appears on the list with the layer name "Layer1," which is highlighted with a rectangle over the layer name text (Figure 4.4).

● In dialog boxes, when texts are highlighted you can type a different name to replace them.

4 Type "I-FLOR-CASH" to replace "Layer1." The layer name changes.

● On our list the layer I-FLOR-CASH is for the wall cabinet and was assigned the color blue (5).

Step 2: Set layer color.

When a new layer is created, it usually copies the features of the current layer (in this case, layer 0). The new layer, therefore, inherited the color white. Now you need to change it to the blue color.

5 Click the Color icon to bring up the Select Color dialog box (Figure 4.5).

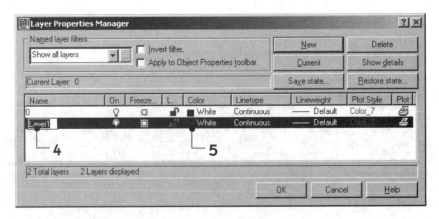

Figure 4.4
Create a new layer.

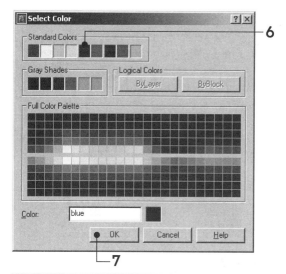

Figure 4.5
Select Color dialog box.

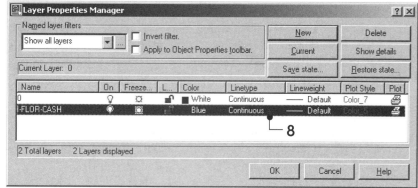

Figure 4.6
Layer color shows in
Color icon.

6 Click the blue color. The selected color shows in the Color field.

7 Click [OK]. The Select Color dialog box disappears, and the selected color appears in the layer status icon (Figure 4.6).

Step 3: Set layer linetype.

When the new layer is created, it also inherits the continuous linetype. Since the wall cabinet should be drawn with hidden lines, you need to set the linetype for the new layer to Hidden.

8 Click the current Continuous linetype. The Select Linetype dialog box pops up (Figure 4.7).

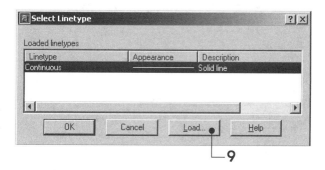

Figure 4.7
The Select Linetype
dialog box.

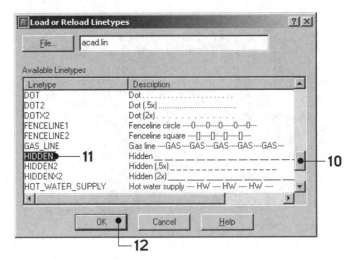

Figure 4.8
Load the linetype
"Hidden."

● There is only one type listed: continuous. Although AutoCAD has many line-types available, they are stored in the AutoCAD acad.lin linetype library file. You must load the needed linetypes from that file into your drawing to make them available for selection.

Step 4: Load a linetype.

9 **Click the [Load...] button.** The Load or Reload Linetypes dialog box pops up. It contains a long list of linetypes that are stored in the AutoCAD linetype library file (Figure 4.8).

● You may directly access the Linetype Manager and the Load or Reload Linetypes dialog boxes through the LINETYPE command or its alias LT.

10 **Scroll down the list to find HIDDEN.**

11 **Click HIDDEN to highlight it.**

12 **Click [OK].** The Select Linetype dialog box comes to the front, with the HID-DEN linetype added to the list (Figure 4.9).

● You may have noticed the two linetypes—HIDDEN2 and HIDDENX2 —next to HIDDEN. Conventionally, when the number 2 is added to a linetype, it is a

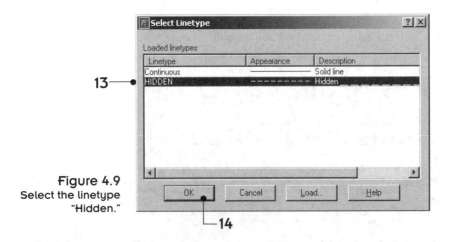

Figure 4.9
Select the linetype
"Hidden."

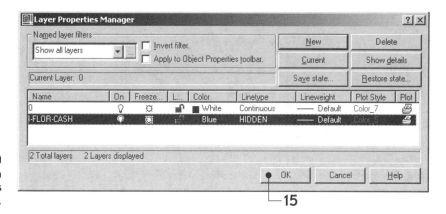

Figure 4.10
HIDDEN linetype shows in the Layer Properties Manager dialog box.

half-sized version of the regular linetype (of the same name); when X2 is added, it is a double-sized version of the regular linetype.

13 **Click HIDDEN to select it.**

14 **Click [OK]** to close the Select Linetype dialog box. The Layers Properties Manager dialog box comes to the front and the I-FLOR-CASH linetype layer has been changed to HIDDEN (Figure 4.10).

15 **Click [OK]** to close the dialog box.

Creating More Layers

Follow the same procedure as shown from step 1 to step 4 to create more layers according to our layer list (on page 70). Set the linetype HIDDEN2 for layer I-FLOR-EQPH. (All other new layers should have Continuous linetype.)

NOTE: You may have noticed while loading the linetype that there are many linetypes with names starting with "ISO." These linetypes have a very different scale from the non-ISO linetypes. Using the ISO linetype and the non-ISO linetype at the same time will cause difficulties in controlling the linetype scale, which we will discuss later.

Putting Drawing Entities on Their Appropriate Layers

If a drawing entity is created when a particular layer is the current layer, the entity is usually on that layer, unless it is a duplication of an existing entity of a different layer. Up to this point, all the drawing entities have been created in layer 0, and will need to be put into appropriate layers. Now, let's try to change the layer of the door from layer 0 to layer I-DOOR.

Step 1: Put the door and swing on the I-DOOR layer.

1 **Select the door and the door swing using an implied selection-window.**

● When you select drawing entities before you start a command, blue-colored boxes appear along the objects being selected. These blue boxes are called "grips." How to use these grips to manipulate the objects will be discussed in later chapters. You can now see them as selection indicators.

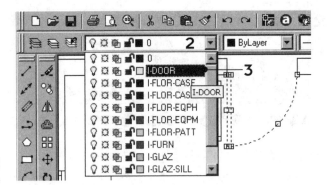

Figure 4.11
Change layers.

2 Click the Layers list in the Properties toolbar to unfold the Layer List.

3 Click the I-DOOR layer. The selected objects turn to yellow. The I-DOOR layer appears in the Layer list window (Figure 4.11).

4 Press [Esc] to cancel the selection of the door. The grips disappear. The layer 0 reappears in the Layer list window and continues to be the current layer.

● If the selection of the door is not cancelled by pressing [Esc] and a new command is launched, the previous current layer (layer 0 in this case) will not be reset as the current layer. If this happens, you can reset the current layer by clicking on the Layer drop-down list the layer you want to be current.

Step 2: Freeze the I-DOOR layer to simplify the view.

1 Click the Layer list to see the drop-down list.

 2 Click the "Freeze/Thaw" icon in front of the I-DOOR layer to freeze that layer. The icon changes into a snowflake indicating the layer is now frozen.

3 Click the drawing area to close the Layer drop-down list and to make the layer status change take effect. The door and swing disappear.

● Freezing the I-DOOR layer visually puts the door and swing away to simplify the drawing and to make your future selection of objects easier. We are actually taking advantage of the AutoCAD layer control functions to make our job easier.

Step 3: Put the refrigerator on the I-FLOR-EQPM layer and freeze it.

1 Select the refrigerator.

2 Click the Layer drop-down list.

3 Click the I-FLOR-EQPM layer. The refrigerator changes color and the Layer list rolls up.

4 Press [Esc] to cancel the refrigerator selection.

5 Click in the Layer drop-down list.

6 Click the Freeze/Thaw icon in front of the I-FLOR-EQPM layer. It changes into a snowflake.

7 Click the drawing area. The refrigerator disappears.

● In this step, you may freeze a layer before you put the object on that layer, so that you don't need to re-open the layer drop-down list. However, a warning will pop up requesting your confirmation for putting an object into a frozen layer. Click [OK] to proceed.

Step 4: Put the rest of the drawing entities onto appropriate layers.

To simplify the task, freeze the layers you finish. Think about how to best use the selection windows to catch the drawing entities you want to select.

Step 5: Thaw the frozen layers to see all the drawing entities.

1 Click the Layer icon.   The Layer Properties Manager dialog box pops up.

● The key-in command for layer control is LAYER; its alias is LA.

2 Right-click (anywhere in the dialog box). A menu pops up at the cursor (Figure 4.12).

3 Click Select All. All the layers are highlighted (selected).

4 Click any snowflake. All the snowflakes change into a shining sun.

● Using this Select All menu in the Layer Properties Manager dialog box, you can also freeze all layers. There is one exception. AutoCAD does not allow you to freeze the current layer; therefore, what you can do is to freeze all the layers but the current layer.

5 Click [OK]. The dialog box closes and all the drawing entities appear.

6 Save your drawing and exit AutoCAD.

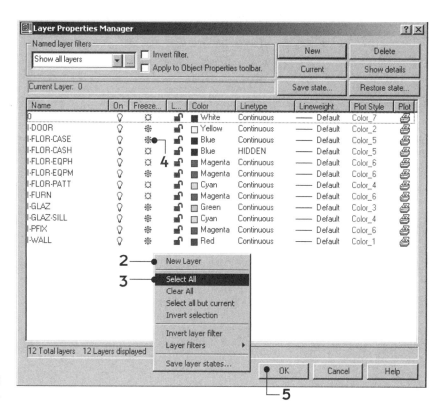

Figure 4.12
Thaw all the layers.

Summary

In this chapter, you have learned the following concepts, procedures, and commands:

Knowledge/Concepts

- Layer
- Current layer
- Layer name standards
- Layer status
- Linetype
- Linetype library
- Color system: color name and color index number
- Properties of drawing entities
- Grips

Procedures

- Set up layers
- Freeze a layer
- Thaw a layer
- Load linetypes
- Assign linetype to layers
- Change layers of drawing entity
- Select all layers
- Preselect object prior to command

Commands

- LAYER (LA)

- LINETYPE (LT)

Finishing the Floor Plan

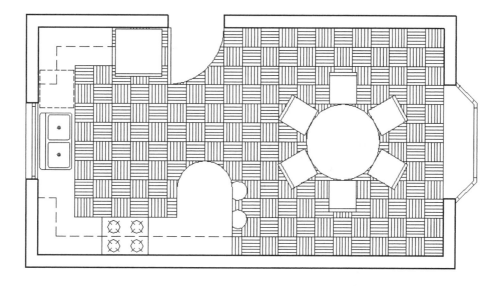

FLOOR PLAN
SCALE: 1/ 4" = 1'-O"

- Draw the range outline
- Draw the burners
- Draw the wall cabinet
- Draw the dishwasher
- Draw the furniture
- Draw the floor tile using **BHATCH**
- Create a drawing title
- Change the floor tile pattern and alignment

In this chapter, you will continue to work on the floor plan according to the designer's second sketch (Figure 5.1). By finishing this floor plan, you will learn more drawing editing commands and learn various ways to draw accurately.

Drawing the Range Outline

Step 1: Measure up using OFFSET.

1 **Open your ch04.dwg drawing and save it as ch05.dwg.** (Command: SAVEAS)

2 **Use OFFSET to create two lines to mark the location of the range.** (Figure 5.2)

Step 2: EXTEND and trim the lines.

EXTEND is a command used to extend linear objects toward selected boundary objects. These boundary objects can also be used as cutting edges to trim objects crossed by them. In this step, you will first extend the marking lines of the range to the wall, and then trim them.

1 **Start the EXTEND command.**

Command: **EXTEND** ↵   The alias for EXTEND is EX.

Current settings: Projection=UCS,
Edge=None

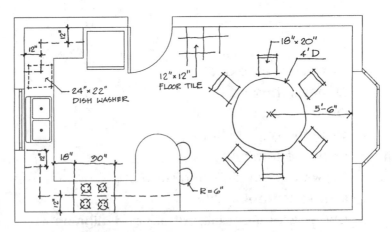

Figure 5.1
The designer's sketch.

80

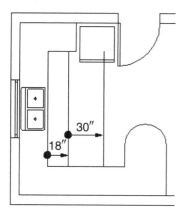

Figure 5.2
Locate the range.

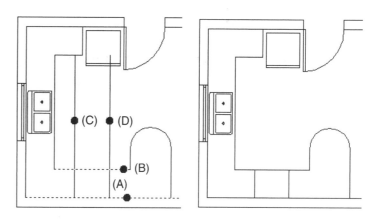

Figure 5.3
Extend and trim lines.

Select boundary edges ...

Select objects: **Select line (A)**
1 found

Select objects: 1 found,   Select boundary edge to extend to (Figure 5.3).
select line (B) 2 total   Select cutting edge to trim the lines later.

Select objects: ⏎   End selection.

Select object to extend
or shift-select to trim
or [Project/Edge/Undo]:
Select line (C)   Extend line (C) to (A).

Select object to extend
or shift-select to trim
or [Project/Edge/Undo]:
Select line (D)   Extend line (D) to (A).

Select object to extend
or shift-select to trim
or [Project/Edge/Undo]:
Shift-select line (C)   Trim line (C) above line (B).

Select object to extend
or shift-select to trim
or [Project/Edge/Undo]:
Shift-select line (D)

Select object to extend
or shift-select to trim or
Project/Edge/Undo]: ⏎   End command.

Command:

2 ZOOM in to look at the cook-top area.

Drawing the Burners

Step 1: Draw the first circle.

The burners on the cook top are made of circles and short lines that represent grates. Let's assume that the burners are located precisely at the center of each quarter of the cook top. The relative coordinate of the center of the first circle, therefore, is 7 1/2″, 6″. To locate the first burner, use the Snap From object snap.

Command: **C** ↵	Start the CIRCLE command using its alias C.
CIRCLE Specify center point for circle or [3P/2P/Ttr (tan tan radius)]:	
Click the Snap From object snap tool _from Base point: **END** ↵	
of **pick point (1)** <Offset>: **@7.5,6** ↵	(Figure 5.4)
Specify radius of circle or [Diameter]: **4** ↵	
Command:	AutoCAD draws the circle and terminates the command.

● *Note:* There are many other ways to define a circle in the CIRCLE command. The center–radius combination is the most frequently used.

Step 2: Set polar tracking.

The first grate line is 3″ long, in a 45° angle, and 2″ from the center of the circle. Although this looks complicated, you can simplify it by completing the task in two steps; (1) Draw a 3″ line in a 45° angle starting from the center of the circle, and (2) move the line 2″ in the 45° direction. In order to constrain the movement in the 45° direction, you need to set the Polar Tracking, which allows you to define an angular increment to control the cursor movements. For example, if the angular increment is set as 45°, the cursor movement for picking the next point will be constrained in the directions of 0°, 45°, 90°, 135°, 180°, and so on.

1 **Click the Tools pull-down menu** (Figure 5.5).

2 **Choose Drafting Settings.** The Drafting Settings dialog box pops up (Figure 5.6).

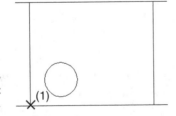

Figure 5.4
Track the center point of the circle.

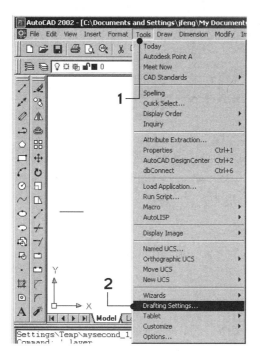

Figure 5.5
Set the Drafting Settings.

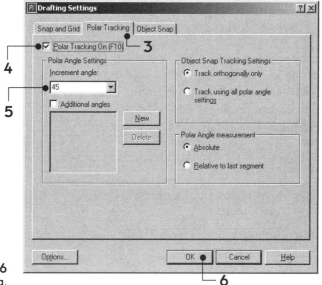

Figure 5.6
Set the Polar Tracking.

3 Click the Polar Tracking tab. The Polar Tracking page opens.

4 Check the Polar Tracking On box to turn it on.

● The Polar Tracking mode can be toggled by pressing [F10] as well as by clicking the [POLAR] button in the status line (at the bottom of the AutoCAD window).

5 Click the Increment Angle list and select 45.

6 Click [OK].

7 Set the snap spacing to 0.5.

Command: **SNAP** ↵

Specify snap spacing or [ON/OFF/Aspect/
Rotate/Style/Type] <0'-1">: **0.5** ↵

- Since the center point of the circle is not on the 1" × 1" snap grid (due to the 7 1/2" measurement from the corner), setting the SNAP spacing to 0.5 allows the cursor to snap to points on the 45° axis from the center point of the circle so that the polar tracking can function properly.

Step 3: Create the first grate line.

- Draw the grate line from the center point.

Command: **L** ↵

LINE Specify first point: **CEN** ↵   Use Center object snap.

of **click the circle**   A rubber band line stretches out from the center of the circle.

- When the cursor is on the circle, the center point of the circle is marked by a small colored (yellow) circle. Clicking while the colored circle is on allows you to catch the center point of the circle.

Specify next point or [Undo]: **Move cursor to stretch the rubber band line approximately at a 45° angle until the line snaps to the 45° angle indicated by a dotted axis and a small hint tag (Figure 5.7).**   The mouse movement defines the angle.

Then, enter 3.   Key in the length of the line.

- This operation is an application of the Direct-Distance Entry method combined with Polar Tracking.

Specify next point or [Undo]: ↵

2 Move the line 2" in the 45° direction.

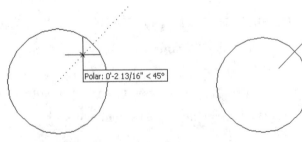

Polar: 0'-2 13/16" < 45°

Figure 5.7
Using polar snap.

Figure 5.8
The first grate line.

Command: **M** ↵

MOVE

Select objects: **Pick the line** 1 found

Select objects: ↵

Specify base point or displacement: **CEN** ↵

of **pick the circle**

Specify second point of displacement
or <use first point as displacement>:
**(Move cursor to allow the rubber band
line to snap to the 45° angle) 2** ↵   Use Direct-Distance Entry
                                                        method.

Command: (Figure 5.8)

Step 4: Duplicate the grate lines with ARRAY (polar).

The ARRAY command works on two types of array: polar and rectangular. The polar ARRAY function creates an array of selected objects around a center point according to your number input and the angle in which the objects are to be evenly arranged; the rectangular ARRAY function creates an array in columns and rows. In this step, you will use the polar ARRAY function to duplicate the first grate line and place them evenly around the circle.

Command: **ARRAY** ↵   The alias for ARRAY is AR.

                                                        The Array dialog box pops up
                                                        (Figure 5.9).

1   Check the button in front of Polar. The dialog box changes (Figure 5.10).

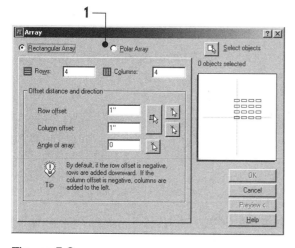

Figure 5.9
The Array dialog box.

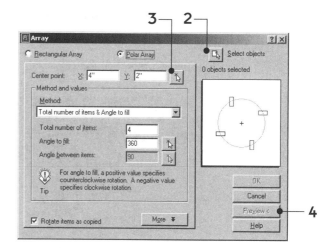

Figure 5.10
The Array dialog box changes.

Figure 5.11
The confirmation dialog box.

Figure 5.12
The first grate line is duplicated.

2 Click the Select Objects button. The dialog box disappears.

Select objects: **Pick the first grate line** 1 found

Select objects: ↵   End selection. The dialog box reappears.

3 Click the pick point button to define the Center point. The dialog box disappears.

Specify center point of array: **CEN** ↵   Activate Center object snap.

of **pick the circle**   Select the circle to snap to its center.

4 Click the Preview button. Preview displays a confirmation dialog box (Figure 5.11).

5 **Click [Accept].** Command terminates after creating the array (Figure 5.12).

● In this step, three default settings are used. The first is the Total number of items (4); the second is the Angle to fill (360°); and the third is Rotate items as copied. You may need to change these settings as future tasks require.

Step 5: Duplicate the burner with ARRAY (rectangular).

After creating the first burner, you are ready to duplicate it with the ARRAY (rectangular) command.

1 ZOOM to the previous view to look at the whole cook top.

2 Use ARRAY to duplicate the first burner.

Command: **AR** ↵   The Array dialog box pops up (Figure 5.13).

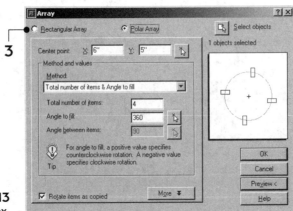

Figure 5.13
The Array dialog box.

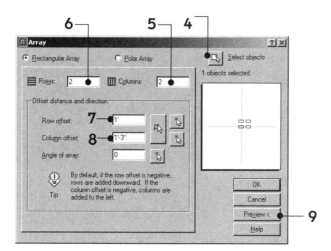

Figure 5.14
The Array (rectangular) dialog box.

3 Check the button in front of Rectangular Array. The Array dialog changes (Figure 5.14).

4 Click the Select Objects button.

Select objects: **Pick point**
Specify opposite corner:
Pick point 5 found   Select the first burner with implied window.

Select objects: ⏎   End selection. The dialog box returns.

5 Change the number of rows to 2.

6 Change the number of columns to 2.

7 Change the row offset to 12.

8 Change the column offset to 15.

9 Click [Preview].

10 Click [Accept]. Command terminates after creating the array (Figure 5.15).

● Negative values for the distance between rows and columns can be used to place the array below and to the left of the original.

11 ZOOM out to look at the entire counter.

Step 6: Put the range into the I-FLOR-EQPM layer.

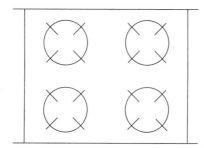

Figure 5.15
The completed cook top.

Drawing the Wall Cabinet

1 Use OFFSET to create wall cabinet lines based on wall lines (Figure 5.16).

2 Use TRIM to trim the lines (Figure 5.17).

● In this step, the order in which the objects are picked and trimmed does not matter except for point (1) and point (2). If point (2) is picked before point (1), the portion of the line where point (1) is located can no longer be trimmed in the same command, because the cutting edge no longer crosses the line. If this happens, you need an additional ERASE command to erase that portion of the line. Therefore, a little thinking before picking objects may save you extra steps when multiple cutting edges are selected.

3 Put the wall cabinet lines into the I-FLOR-CASH layer. The color of the line changes (from red to blue), but the linetype appears to be the same.

● Why does the hidden line not show? It is a problem of scale. Since the linetypes are usually defined by fractions of the basic drawing unit (inch), they are visible only when you look at them very closely. In this particular case, the hidden line is made of 1/8″ spaces between 1/4″ dashes. When the image of the drawing is reduced on the screen, it appears to be continuous. To make it visible for a normal view on the screen, or on a printout, a linetype scale factor needs to be set.

4 Set the linetype scale: LTSCALE.

● The linetype scale is controlled at two different levels by two variables. (The operation of AutoCAD is actually controlled by many of these variables.) The first variable, LTSCALE (meaning LineType SCALE), is a *global* scale factor for all linetypes in a drawing. Changing it will change the appearance of all linetypes. The second variable, CELTSCALE (meaning Current Entity LineType SCALE), gives a *local* scale factor to individual drawing objects. The appearance of a draw-

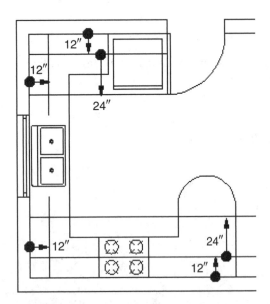

Figure 5.16
Draw the wall cabinet lines.

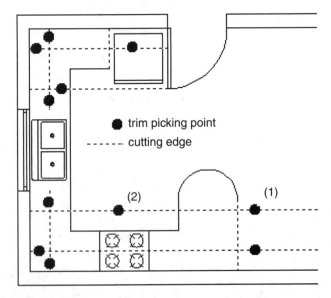

Figure 5.17
Trim the cabinet lines.

ing object is decided by the result of LTSCALE × CELTSCALE. The default value for both variables is 1. The value of LTSCALE can be defined by entering LTSCALE as a command. According to many AutoCAD tutorials, the value of the scale should be the same as the drawing scale factor. That means that the linetype scale should be 48 if we want to print out the drawing at 1/4″=1′-0″ scale. (It is 48 because 1/4″=1′-0″ can be converted to 1″=4′, or 1″=48″.) However, the segments of linetypes set by such a rule usually look too large. One half of the scale factor seems to be a better choice.

Command: **LTSCALE** ↵

Enter new linetype scale factor <1.0000>: **24** ↵

Regenerating model.

Command: The hidden linetype shows in dashes.

● This LTSCALE value is now set for you to see the linetype on your screen. You need to reset it when you want to apply a different drawing scale.

Drawing the Dishwasher

The dishwasher is represented by a rectangle. You can simply use the RECTANGLE command you learned in the previous chapter to draw it, and move it to its position. This time we are going to generate a new drawing entity without copying existing objects. We can, therefore, directly "draw" it on the right layer. To do that, you need to set I-FLOR-EQPH as the current layer.

Step 1: Set current layer (through Layer list).

1 Click the Layers icon. The Layer Properties Manager dialog box pops up (Figure 5.18).

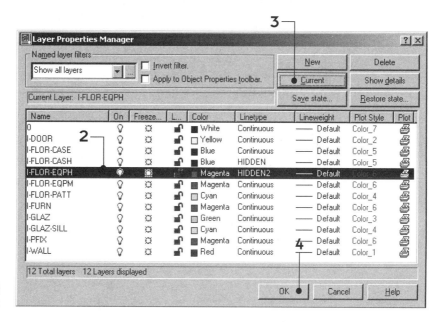

Figure 5.18
Set current layer.

2 Click the I-FLOR-EQPH layer to highlight it.

3 Click [Current]. The current layer name next to the Current button changes to I-FLOR-EQPH.

4 Click [OK].

Step 2: Draw the rectangle.

Although we can figure out where the exact location of the dishwasher is relative to the sink, and we can use the Snap From object to help us locate the starting point of the rectangle to finish the task in one step, most of us usually do not want to over-load our brain with multiple information-processing jobs. Therefore, we will finish this task in two easy steps; (1) Create the rectangle at an easily located known point, and (2) move the rectangle into its correct position.

1 Draw the rectangle.

Command: **REC** ↵

RECTANGLE

Specify first corner point
or [Chamfer/Elevation/Fillet/
Thickness/Width]: **MID** ↵

Of **pick the counter line**	Start the rectangle at the midpoint of the counter.

● Putting the corner of the rectangle at a specific known point allows you to use this point as a reference point for moving it into position in the future.

Specify other corner point: **@22,24** ↵	The rectangle is drawn.

2 ZOOM to look at the area you are working on more closely.

3 MOVE the dishwasher to its location.

Command: **M** ↵

MOVE

Select objects:
Pick the dishwasher 1 found

Select objects: ↵	End selection.

Specify base point
or displacement: −**23,21** ↵

Specify second point of displacement or <use first point as displacement>: ↵	Assume that the base cabinet has a 42″ sink unit and the dishwasher is next to it (Figure 5.19).

Command:

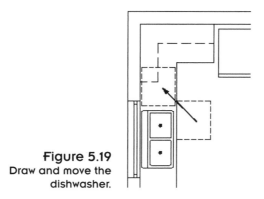

Figure 5.19
Draw and move the
dishwasher.

Drawing the Furniture

Step 1: Set the current layer (through Layer list).

You may set the current layer through the Layer control drop-down list window instead of the Layers tool and the Layer Properties Manager dialog box.

1 **Click the Layer Control list window.** The list drops down (Figure 5.20).

2 **Click the I-FURN layer.** The list closes and the I-FURN layer appears in the Layer Control drop-down list window as the current layer. (The current layer is always shown in that window.)

Step 2: Draw the dining table.

Taking a similar approach as you did when creating the dishwasher, first create the table at a known point, and then locate it by moving it 5′6″ to the left.

1 **ZOOM to look at the right side of the floor plan.**

2 **Use the CIRCLE command to draw the table (r =24).** To align the table with the window, use the midpoint of the windowsill line as the center of the circle for the dining table (Figure 5.21).

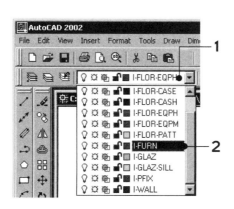

Figure 5.20
Set the current layer.

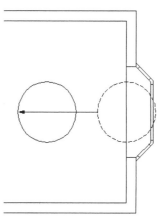

Figure 5.21
Create the dining table.

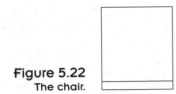

Figure 5.22
The chair.

3 MOVE the circle 5′6″ to the left (displacement = −5′6, 0).

Step 3: Draw the chair.

Let's assume the chair has an 18″ × 18″ seat and a 2″ back. Use the LINE command to draw the chair (Figure 5.22). Don't worry about the location of the chair for now.

Step 4: Make the chair a block.

Since the chair will be used in different places around the table, you need to consider how to duplicate the chair and how to put the duplicates into place. You could use ARRAY, but after duplicating the chair with the ARRAY command, the many individual lines of all the chairs will not only be difficult to handle for future revision but also take a lot of disk space. Further grouping is needed. AutoCAD provides the BLOCK command for this purpose. The BLOCK command makes a collection of drawing objects into an associated whole that can be named; you can then recall that name and insert it into the drawing with the INSERT command. In the process of inserting a block, you have control over the scale and orientation of the block. Through the DesignCenter, blocks can be shared by many drawings. As a principle, you should use blocks whenever possible. Anything that will be used repeatedly in a drawing should be converted to a block before duplication.

1 Put the chair on layer 0.

- A block keeps the color of the layer in which it is created and it is difficult to change it later. However, if the block is made on layer 0, the color of the block will be the same as the color of the layer in which the block is inserted, and can be changed by using the Properties tool. Therefore, it would be a good idea to put the drawing objects on layer 0 before you make them a block.

2 Start the BLOCK command.

Command: **BLOCK** ↵   The Block Definition dialog box pops up
                                       (Figure 5.23).

3 Enter the CHAIR block name. A descriptive name should be used for easy future identification.

4 Click the Pick Point button. The dialog box closes. You are prompted to pick the insertion base point.

Insertion base point: **MID** ↵

of **pick point**   Catch the midpoint of the seat's front edge
                                       (Figure 5.24).

                                       The dialog box returns with the point
                                       coordinate (x, y, z) fields filled in.

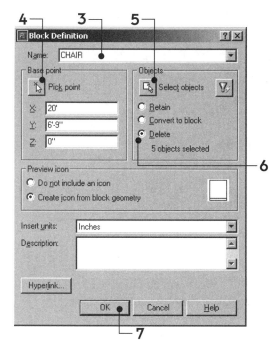

Figure 5.23
The Block Definition dialog box.

Figure 5.24
Insertion point.

● When you define the insertion base point, you need to imagine how this block will be used. If a particular point could help you locate the block in future insertions, you should make that point the insertion base point. A well-planned insertion base point saves time and makes your drawing more accurate. Since this chair will be placed around the dining table, the front midpoint of the chair can be used to align the chair with a quadrant point of the circle. Therefore, make the front midpoint of the chair the insertion point of the block.

5 Click the Select Object button.   The dialog box closes.

Select objects: **Pick point**
Specify opposite corner:
Pick point 5 found   Use implied window.

Select objects: ⏎   End selection.

Command: The dialog box returns.

6 Check the button in front of Delete Object.

● Three options—Retain, Convert to block, and Delete object—control the status of the original object. Selecting the Delete Object option deletes the original chair made of individual lines. In this case, Delete Object is chosen because we want to re-insert the chair block instead of moving the converted original so that you can learn more about the INSERT command. In the future, you may make your own choice according to your needs.

7 Click [OK]. The chair disappears.

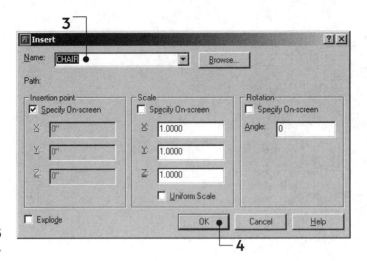

Figure 5.25
The Insert dialog box.

Step 5: Insert the chair block.

The INSERT command allows you to insert blocks into the drawing.

1 Make sure I-furn is the current layer, so that the inserted chair will be in the right layer.

2 Insert the chair.

Command: **INSERT** ↵   The Insert dialog box pops up
                                                        (Figure 5.25).

3 Make sure the CHAIR block name shows in the Name list.

4 Click [OK]. The dialog box closes. You are prompted to pick an insertion point.

Specify insertion point or [Scale/X/Y/Z/
Rotate/PScale/PX/PY/PZ/PRotate]: **QUA** ↵   Activate Quadrant object snap
                                                 (Figure 5.26).

of **pick point (on the circle near
the lowest point)**

● Quadrant object snap snaps to the nearest quadrant point when the cursor touches a circle. You may also use the icon to activate the Quadrant object snap.

Command: The chair is fixed in the drawing.

5 Duplicate the chair using the ARRAY (polar) command. (Figure 5.27) (Use Center object snap to catch the center of the table.)

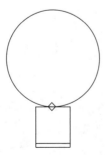

Figure 5.26
Insert the chair block.

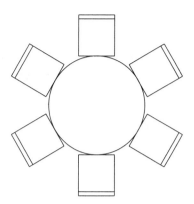

Figure 5.27
Duplicate the chair.

Step 6: Draw the stools.

1 Use the CIRCLE command to draw a circle (*R*=6) **near the snap bar.**

2 Use the COPY command to make a copy of the first stool and place it beside the first (as shown in the designer's sketch).

Command: **COPY** ↵

Select objects: **Pick the stool**
1 found

Select objects: ↵

Specify base point
or displacement,
or [Multiple]: **Pick a point
and move the cursor straight
down or up.**

Use the direct-entry method to direct movement.

Specify second point of
displacement or <use first point
as displacement>: **18** ↵

Command:

● The alias for the COPY command is CP, and the icon is located in the Modify toolbar.

3 Use TRIM command to trim off the portion of the circles under the table (Figure 5.28).

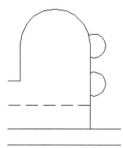

Figure 5.28
Trim the stools.

Drawing the Floor Tile with BHATCH

The BHATCH (boundary hatch) command fills an enclosed drawing area with patterns. BHATCH detects the enclosed area before filling it with a pattern. The User Defined pattern is simply parallel lines with direction and spacing defined by you. When the Double Hatch option is selected, it generates a grid. You can use this function to draw simple floor tiles.

1 ZOOM to show the entire floor plan.

2 Set the I-FLOR-PATT layer as the current layer.

3 Enter the BHATCH command (or alias BH). The Boundary Hatch dialog box pops up (Figure 5.29).

4 Click the pull-down list (currently showing Predefined) **and select User-defined.**   Some items on the dialog box turn gray.

5 Double-click the field after Spacing, and type 12 (the size of tile).

6 Check the box before Double.

7 Click the Pick Points button. The dialog box disappears and AutoCAD prompts you to pick internal point.

8 Pick a point in the room. Then press [Enter] to end selection. The dialog box re-appears.

9 Click [Preview]. The pattern appears in the space.

10 Press [Enter]. The dialog box returns.

11 Click [OK] to apply the pattern on the drawing and end the command (Figure 5.30).

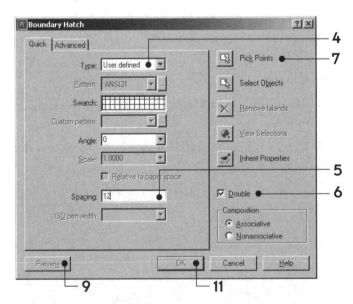

Figure 5.29
The Boundary Hatch
dialog box.

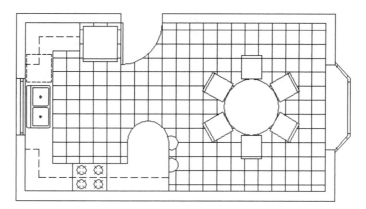

Figure 5.30
Hatch pattern applied.

Creating a Drawing Title

Every drawing needs a title. A drawing title is composed of texts, an underline, and a north arrow. Before you put text into a drawing, you need to set the text style. Otherwise, the Standard style will be used by default.

Step 1: Set a text style.

An AutoCAD text style defines the text font, text size, orientation, proportion, and so on. It can be used in dimension styles, and it can be shared through the AutoCAD DesignCenter.

1 **Click the Format menu in the menu bar, and choose Text Style...** (Figure 5.31). The Text Style dialog box pops up (Figure 5.32).

2 **Click [New].** The New Text Style dialog box pops up.

3 **Type Notes in the Style Name field.**

4 **Click [OK].**

5 **Click the list under Font Name; find and select CityBlueprint.** A sample shows in the preview window.

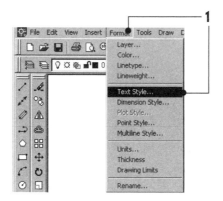

Figure 5.31
Set text style.

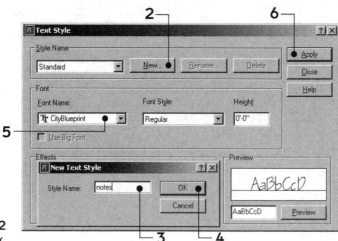

Figure 5.32
The Text Style dialog box.

- The CityBlueprint font looks very much like the architectural style lettering commonly used on interior design drawings. If this font is not available in your computer, you may choose a comparable alternative.

6 Click [Apply] and [Close] to exit. The Notes text style has been set.

Step 2: Enter text.

The DTEXT (Dynamic TEXT) command allows you to type directly in the drawing. Because the height of your text style is 0, you will be requested to input a text height every time you start the command. This gives you flexibility to enter texts of different heights.

1 Zoom out to see the whole drawing.

- You may need to move your floor plan (using the MOVE command) to make space for the drawing title. Before you start the MOVE command, it is very important to make sure you do not have frozen layers, because frozen layers will be left behind.

2 Create a layer and name it I-ANON-NOTE. Set the layer as the current layer.

3 Enter text.

Command: **DTEXT** ↵	The alias for DTEXT is DT.
Current text style: "NOTES" Text height: 0'-2 3/16"	
Specify start point of text or [Justify/Style]: **Pick point**	(below the lower-left corner of the plan)
Specify height <0'-2 3/16">: **12** ↵	This value makes the text 1/4" high on printed sheet.
Specify rotation angle of text <0>: ↵	Accept the default value.

Figure 5.33
North arrow.

Figure 5.34
North arrow.

Enter text: **FLOOR PLAN** ↵

Enter text: ↵   End text entry.

Command:

4 Adjust the placement of the text if necessary. Use MOVE.

5 Draw a line under the text.

6 Use DTEXT to enter the drawing scale under the line (text height = 6″).

Step 3: Draw a simple north arrow.

1 Draw a vertical line near the right end of the line under the drawing title (Figure 5.33).

2 Draw a circle centered at the intersection (R=10″) (Figure 5.34).

● You may use the Intersection object snap to catch the intersection. Before you pick the point, enter INT to activate the Intersection object snap. An "X" appears when you move your cursor near an intersection.

3 Draw a short vertical line near the top of the circle to indicate the north direction (Figure 5.35).

4 Adjust line length.

● If you need to adjust the length of the vertical line, a simple way to do this is to use "grips" to stretch the line. When you are not using any command, click at the line. Three blue boxes (called grips) appear at the ends and midpoint of the line (Figure 5.36a). Click the box at the end and the box turns solid and red (called "hot") (Figure 5.36b). You can now stretch the line by picking a new endpoint. Press [Esc] to clear the grip.

● Using the grips to make changes to drawing entities is called "Autoediting." Stretching is only one of its functions; you can use it to do other tasks such as moving, copying, and so on.

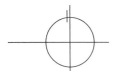

Figure 5.35
North arrow.

a   b

Figure 5.36
Use grips to sketch a line.

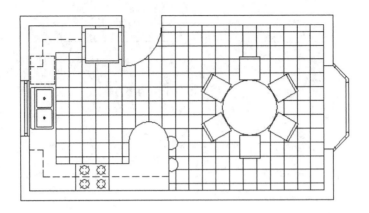

Figure 5.37
Finished drawing.

5 **Zoom out** to see the whole drawing (Figure 5-37).

Changing the Floor Tile Pattern and Alignment

After reviewing your floor plan, the designer wants to use a patternned floor tile (Figure 5.38) and a perfect alignment of the tile to the center of the space.

Step 1: Change the pattern.

1 **Click the Modify menu** (Figure 5.39).

2 **Choose Object.**

3 **Choose Hatch.** You are prompted to pick hatch object.

4 **Pick the floor tile.** The Hatch Edit dialog pops up (Figure 5.40).

5 **Click the Type list and choose Predefined.** The Patterns list and button become active.

6 **Click the button next to the Pattern list.** The Hatch Pattern Palette pops up (Figure 5.41).

7 **Click the Other Predefined tab, if it is not already open.**

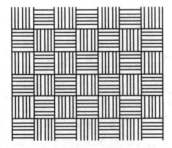

Figure 5.38
The new floor tile pattern.

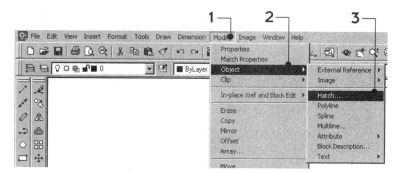

Figure 5.39
Start Hatch edit.

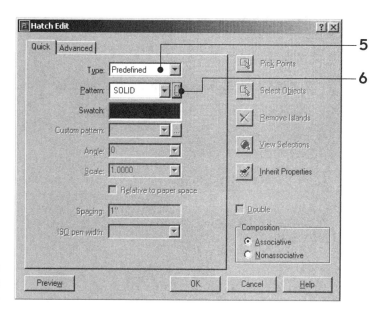

Figure 5.40
The Hatch Edit
dialog box.

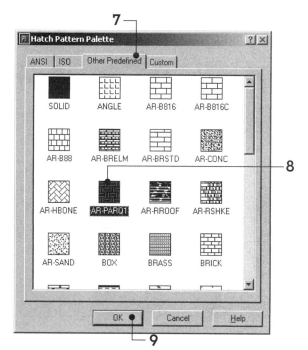

Figure 5.41
The Hatch Pattern
Palette.

8 **Click the pattern that looks like the designer's choice. (The pattern name is AR-PARQ1.)**

9 **Click [OK].** The Hatch Pattern Palette closes.

10 **Click [Preview] to check the effect.**

11 **Press [Enter] to exit the Preview mode.**

12 **Click [OK] to end the command.** The tile changes (Figure 5.42).

Step 2: Measure the size of the new tile.

The designer wants the tile to be the same size as the previous one. Although the new tile looks fine, you still need to make sure the size of the pattern is correct. To measure a distance, you use the DIST command.

1 ZOOM in to look closely at the tile pattern.

2 Measure a tile with the DIST command.

Command: **DI** ↵	Start the DIST command by using its alias DI.
DIST Specify first point: **INT** ↵	Use Intersection object snap to catch a corner of a tile.
of **pick an intersection point**	
Specify second point: **INT** ↵	Use Intersection object snap to catch another corner of the tile.
of **pick an intersection point**	AutoCAD reports the result.

Distance = 1′-0″,
Angle in XY Plane = 9″,
Angle from XY Plane = 0

Delta X = 0′-0″, Delta Y = 1′-0″,
Delta Z = 0′-0″

Command:

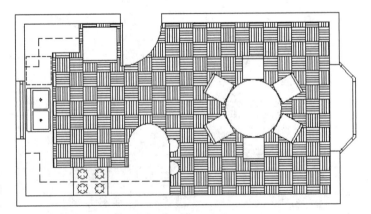

Figure 5.42
Change the tile pattern.

- If the size is not 1′-0″, you need to go back to the HATCHEDIT command to change the scale of the hatch pattern to make it the right size.

3 ZOOM out to look at the whole plan.

Step 3: Align the tiles to the center of the space.

By default, the hatch pattern you created is Associative. That means the hatch pattern has a dynamic relationship to the boundary objects. We can use this dynamic relationship to move everything but the tile pattern to change their relative position.

1 Draw a pair of diagonal lines to locate the center of the space (Figure 5.43).

- When placing floor tiles, you usually start from the center of the space.

2 Thaw all frozen layers (if any).

3 Start the MOVE command.

Command: **M** ↵

MOVE

Select objects: **Pick a point.**	Use implied selection window to select the whole drawing.
Specify opposite corner: **Pick a second point** 95 found	
Select objects: **R** ↵	"R" means to remove from selection.
Remove objects: **Pick the tile pattern** 1 found, 1 removed, 94 total	
Remove objects: ↵	Finish removing.

Specify base point or displacement:
**Click the ZOOM icon
in the standard toolbar** ′_zoom

- This ZOOM command does not terminate the ongoing MOVE command; it is called "transparent."

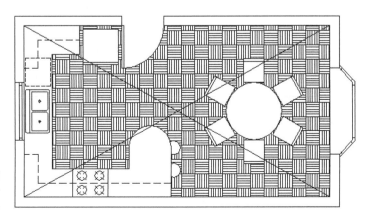

Figure 5.43
Locate the center
of the space.

>>Specify corner of window, enter a scale factor (nX or nXP), or [All/Center/Dynamic/Extents/Previous/Scale/Window] : _w

>>Specify first corner: **Pick a point near the intersection of diagonal lines.**

Define the Zoom window.

>>Specify opposite corner:
Pick another point.

Define the Zoom window.

You now have a close view of the intersection.

Resuming MOVE command.

Specify base point or displacement: **INT ↵**

Activate Intersection object snap.

of **pick the intersection of the two diagonal lines**

Specify second point of displacement or <use first point as displacement>: **INT ↵**

Activate Intersection object snap.

Of **pick the nearest corner of a tile**

(Figure 5.44)

The intersection point of the diagonal lines falls on the corner of a tile.

Command:

● You may also use the icon to activate the Intersection object snap.

4 ZOOM out to see the whole plan (Figure 5.45).

5 ERASE the diagonal lines.

6 Save your drawing and exit AutoCAD.

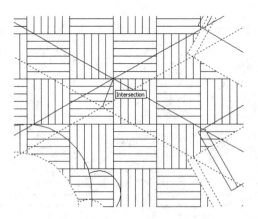

Figure 5.44
Align the tiles.

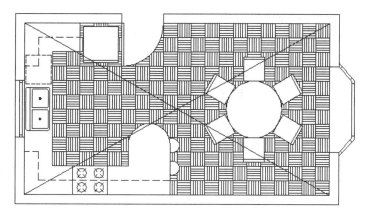

Figure 5.45
Floor tiles aligned to the center of the space.

Summary

In this chapter, you have learned the following concepts, procedures, and commands:

Knowledge/Concepts

- Block
- Special feature of layer 0
- Hatch
- Text style
- Grip
- Autoediting
- Linetype scale
- Associative hatch
- Transparent command
- Polar tracking

Procedures

- Use Center object snap
- Use Quadrant object snap
- Use Intersection object snap
- Set polar tracking
- Use polar tracking
- Set text style
- Enter texts
- Adjust drawing entity by using grips

- Set linetype scale
- Set current layer
- Make and insert block
- Move hatch boundary objects
- Edit hatch pattern
- Measure distance

Commands

 • EXTEND (EX)

 • CIRCLE (C)

 • ARRAY–polar (AR)

 • ARRAY–rectangular (AR)

 • BLOCK (B)

 • INSERT (I)

 • COPY (CP)

 • BHATCH (BH)

 • Quadrant (QUA)

 • Intersection (INT)

- DTEXT (DT)

- LTSCALE

- DIST (DI)

Dimensions

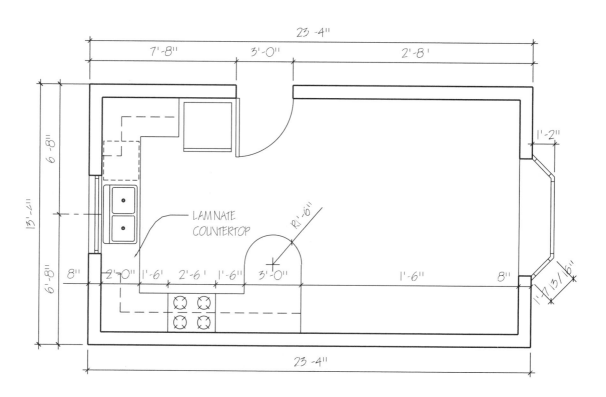

23 -4"

7'-8"   3'-0"   2'-8'

6 -8"

15'-2"

6'-8"

1'-2"

LAMINATE
COUNTERTOP

R1'-6"

8"   2'-0"   1'-6'   2'-6'   1'-6"   3'-0"   1'-6"   8"

1'-7 3/16"

23 -4"

FLOOR PLAN

SCALE: 1/ 4" = 1'-0"

- ● Set a dimension style
- ● Use dimension commands
- ● Troubleshoot

This chapter will guide you to dimension the finished floor plan. In this process, you will learn how to set up an architectural dimension style and how to use the dimension style.

Setting a Dimension Style

Before you begin to dimension an AutoCAD drawing, you need to set your dimension styles. AutoCAD's dimension style controls all the features from the size and format of architectural ticks to text font. Since the Standard dimension style is not one used in architectural drawings, you need to define an architectural style yourself.

The terminology of dimension features used in AutoCAD is illustrated in Figure 6.1. The dimension feature sizes for a typical architectural drawing are also given in the drawing. When setting your dimension style, you may need to refer to this drawing for a better understanding of dimension settings.

- The dimension feature sizes given in Figure 6.1 are decided by aesthetic judgment and practical concerns for visual clarity.

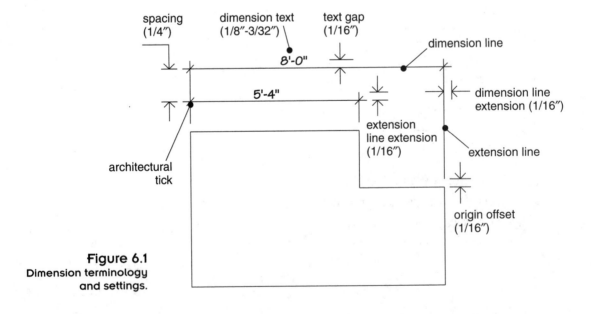

Figure 6.1
Dimension terminology and settings.

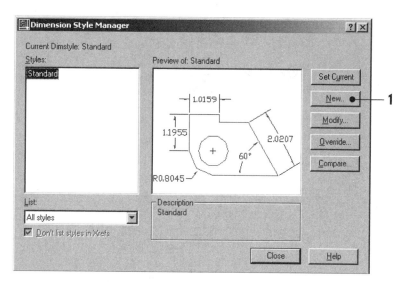

Figure 6.2
Dimension Style Manager
dialog box.

Step 1: Start with the DDIM command.

To set a dimension style, use the DDIM (D means dialog; DIM stands for dimension) command.

1 **Open the floor plan drawing Ch05.dwg, and save it as Ch06.dwg.**

2 **Enter DDIM.** The Dimension Style dialog box pops up (Figure 6.2). The alias for the DDIM command is D.

● This dialog box leads you to more dialog boxes to set your dimension styles. At this moment, there is only one existing style: Standard. Similar to the Standard text style, it is a basic dimension style that serves as the default.

Step 2: Create and name your style.

1 **Click [New].** The Create New Dimension Style dialog box pops up (Figure 6.3).

2 **Type in a name (archi48) for your first architectural style.**

3 **Click [Continue].** The Create New Dimension Style: ARCHI48 dialog box pops up (Figure 6.4). AutoCAD creates a style called archi48 based on the Standard style.

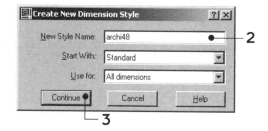

Figure 6.3
Create New Dimension
Style dialog box.

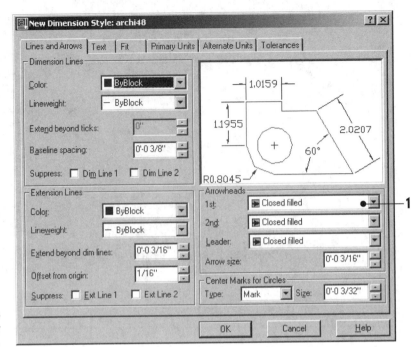

Figure 6.4
Set up a new
dimension style.

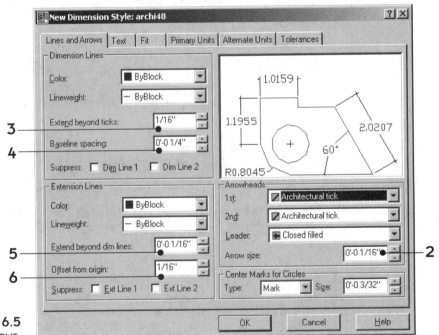

Figure 6.5
Set lines and arrows.

Step 3: Set Lines and Arrows.

1 Click the 1st list in the Arrowheads section and choose Architectural tick.
The second arrowhead changes automatically (Figure 6.5).

2 Change Arrow size to 1/16″.

3 Change Extend beyond ticks to 1/16″.

4 Change Baseline spacing to 1/4″.

5 Change Extend beyond dim lines to 1/16″.

6 Change Offset from origin to 1/16″.

● The settings on this page control the geometric features of the dimension line, extension lines, architectural ticks, and arrowhead. All the values and settings in this dialog box are inherited from the Standard style. You need to look at them one by one and change them if necessary. The principle of setting the sizes of dimension features is to set it to its real size on paper. For example, if you want the arrowhead to be 1/16″, you set the value for the arrowhead size as 1/16″.

Step 4: Set Dimension Text.

1 Click the Text tab. The Text page opens (Figure 6.6).

2 Click the Text style list and choose Notes.

3 Change Text height to 1/8″.

4 Change Vertical text placement to Above.

5 Change Offset from dim line to 1/16″.

6 Check Aligned with dimension line.

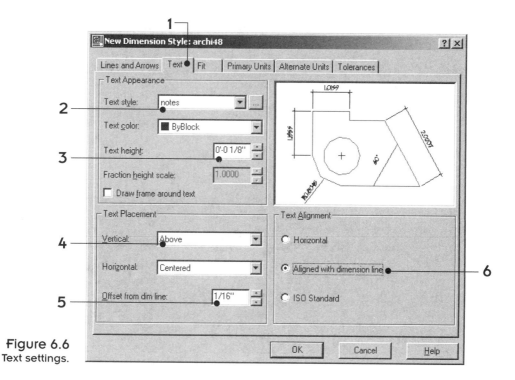

Figure 6.6
Text settings.

Step 5: Set Fit settings.

1   Click the Fit tab. The Fit setting page opens (Figure 6.7).

2   Check Always keep text between ext lines in Fit Options.

3   Check Beside the extension line in Text Placement. This ensures the dimension line runs through the space between extension lines.

4   Change the Scale for Dimension Features to 48.

● This value has to be decided by a drawing scale in which you want to print out your drawing. Since 1/4″=1′-0″ is a frequently used scale in our field, let us use it as the scale for the final presentation of this drawing. The value of this Overall Scale should equal the scale factor. Therefore, it is 48. If you need to present the drawing in a different scale, you may change this value according to the scale you will use.

5   Check Always draw dim line between ext lines in the Fine Tuning section.

Step 6: Set Dimension Units.

1   Click the Primary Units tab. The Primary Units page opens (Figure 6.8). The settings on this page control the measuring unit.

2   Click the Units format list and select Architectural.

3   Click the Fraction format list and select Not Stacked.

4   Clear 0 Inches in the Zero Suppression check box to have 0 inch shown in the dimension text.

5   Click [OK]. The Primary Units dialog box closes.

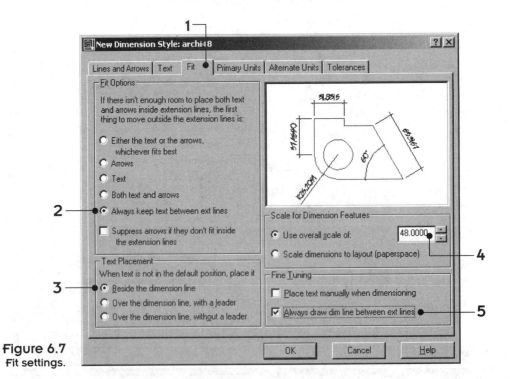

Figure 6.7
Fit settings.

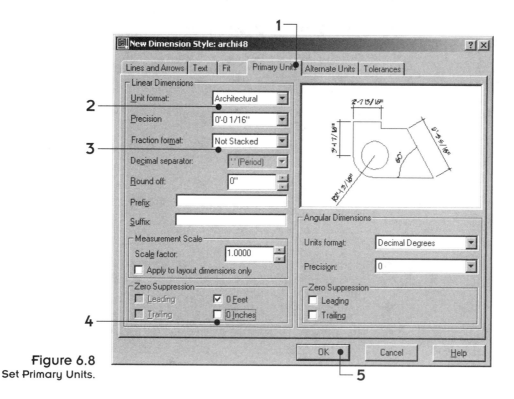

Figure 6.8
Set Primary Units.

Step 7: Set the "nofirst" style.

In order to make your drawing look perfect both on monitors and prints, you need three more dimension styles to suppress the first, second, or both extension lines. Otherwise, the extension lines that overlap the wall lines will put extra weight on the spot and destroy the smoothness of a line.

The Nofirst dimension style allows you to create dimensions without the first extension line. You may need this style to start a dimension directly from an object such as the surface of a wall (Figure 6.9).

1 **Click [New] in the Dimension Styles Manager dialog box.** The Create New Dimension Style dialog box pops up (Figure 6.10). The default name for the new layer is "copy of archi48."

● After creating the archi48 style, it becomes the highlighted style. Since a new style is always a copy of the highlighted style, the current new style is a copy of arch48.

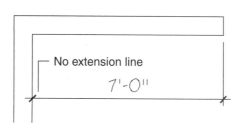

Figure 6.9
Application of the Nofirst style.

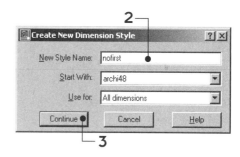

Figure 6.10
Name the new style "nofirst."

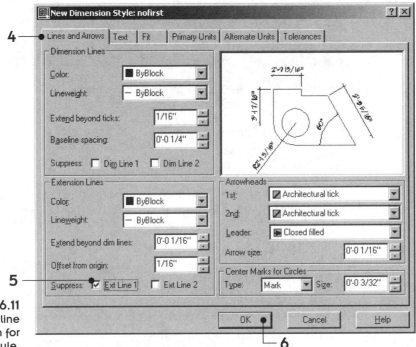

4 → Lines and Arrows

5 →

6

After nofirst is set up, it will become the highlighted style, and it will be copied for the next new style. If you want to create a new style based on another style, you may highlight that style by clicking the name before setting up the new style.

2 Change the New Style Name from "copy of archi48" to "nofirst."

3 Click [Continue]. The New Dimension Style dialog box pops up (Figure 6.11).

4 Click the Lines and Arrows tab.

5 Check the Ext. Line 1 box to suppress the first extension line.

6 Click [OK]. You are back to the Dimension Style Manager.

Step 8: Set the "nosecond" style.

This dimension style allows you to create dimensions without the second extension line. You may need this style to end a dimension directly on an object, such as the surface of a wall (Figure 6.12).

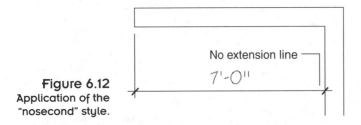

No extension line

7'-0"

Figure 6.12
Application of the
"nosecond" style.

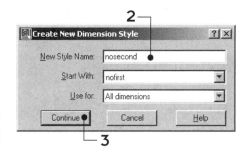

Figure 6.13
Name the new style
"nosecond."

1 **Click [New] in the Dimension Styles Manager dialog box.** The Create New Dimension Style dialog box pops up (Figure 6.13).

2 **Change the New Style Name from "copy of nofirst" to "nosecond."**

3 **Click [Continue].** The New Dimension Style dialog box pops up (Figure 6.14).

4 **Check the Ext. Line 2 box** to suppress the second extension line.

5 **Clear the check Ext. Line 1 box.**

6 **Click [OK].** You are back to the Dimension Style Manager.

Step 9: Set the "noboth" style.

This dimension style allows you to create dimensions without both extension lines. You may need this style to create a dimension in-between objects (Figure 6.15).

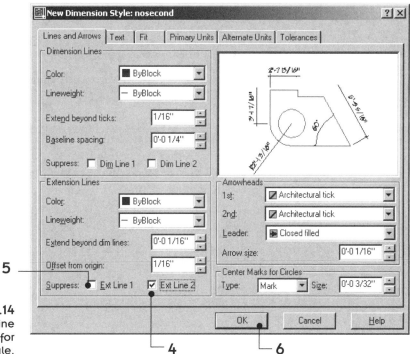

Figure 6.14
Setting the extension line
suppression for
"nosecond" style.

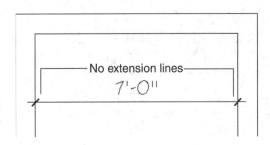

Figure 6.15
Application of the
"noboth" style.

1 **Click [New] in the Dimension Styles Manager dialog box.** The Create New Dimension Style dialog box pops up.

2 **Change the New Style Name from "copy of nosecond" to "noboth."**

3 **Click [Continue].** The New Dimension Style dialog box pops up.

4 **Check the Ext. Line 1 box.**

5 **Click [OK].** You are back to the Dimension Style Manager.

6 **Click [Close]** to exit the Dimension Styles Manager dialog box.

Using Dimension Commands

In this section, you will dimension the floor plan.

Step 1: Set the Dimension toolbar.

The best way to use the dimension commands is through the Dimension toolbar.

1 **Click the View menu in the menu bar.**

2 **Select Toolbars from the menu.** The Toolbars dialog box pops up.

3 **Check the box before Dimension.** The Dimension toolbar pops up.

4 **Click [Close].** The Toolbars dialog box closes.

5 **Drag the Dimension toolbar by its title bar over the bottom frame of the AutoCAD drawing window; release it when the phantom box becomes thin near the frame.** The Dimension toolbar is embedded into the frame.

Step 2: Set the running object snap.

Since catching exact points is critical for accurate dimensioning, object snap should be used to pick every point. The Object Snap toolbar makes this procedure easier.

1 **Set the Object Snap toolbar** (if not already set).   (See step 1 in Chapter 3 for instruction.)

2 **Click the Object Snap Settings icon** to set the running object snap mode. The Drafting Settings dialog box pops up (Figure 6.16).

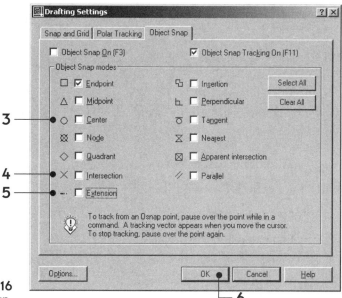

Figure 6.16
Set running object snap.

- From this dialog box, we can see that a few object snap modes are already checked by default. To avoid confusion and misfire, we want to check off all modes except Endpoint (although more than one type of object snap can run simultaneously).

3 Clear the Center box.

4 Clear the Intersection box.

5 Clear the Extension box.

6 Click [OK] to close the dialog box.

7 Click the [OSNAP] button in the status line to turn on the Object Snap mode.   The button should look depressed.

Step 3: Prepare the drawing.

1 ZOOM out to look at the whole plan (leaving space for dimensions around it).

2 Create a new layer, I-ANON-DIMS, for dimensions and set as current.

3 Create a new layer, I-ANON-CTLN, for center lines used for on-center dimensions. Set the center2 linetype as the linetype for this new layer.

4 Freeze the I-FLOR-PATT (floor tiles) and I-FURN (furniture) layers to simplify the floor plan.

Step 4: Set "archi48" as the current dimension style.

The concept of current dimension is similar to that of current layer or the current text style. The dimensions you create will be in the current style. In the same way as you can change an object's layer after its creation, you can change the style of a dimension (that will be discussed later in this chapter). The current dimension style is shown in the window of the drop-down list in the Dimension toolbar (Figure 6.17).

Figure 6.17
The current dimension style as shown in the Dimension toolbar.

If you don't see archi48 in the window, click the list and select it from the drop-down list.

Step 5: Create your first external dimension.

 Click the Linear Dimension icon.

Command: _dimlinear

Specify first extension line origin
or <select object>: **Pick point (1).**   (Figure 6.18)

Specify second extension line origin:
Pick point (2).

Specify dimension line location
or [Mtext/Text/Angle/Horizontal/
Vertical/Rotated]: **Pick point (3).**

● The location of point (3) defines the distance between the dimension line and the wall. This distance needs to be "eyeballed" based on your experience.

Dimension text = 23'-4"   AutoCAD reports the measured
                                           dimension.

Command: Command ends and the dimen-
                                           sion is automatically entered.

Step 6: Create continued dimensions.

 1 Click the Linear Dimension toolbar icon.

2 Pick point (1), point (2) (Figure 6.19a).

3 Pick point (3) to locate the dimension line.

 4 Click Continue Dimension icon.

Specify a second extension line origin
or (Undo/<Select>): **Pick point (4).**

Specify a second extension line origin
or (Undo/<Select>): **Pick point (5).**

Specify a second extension line origin
or (Undo/<Select>): ↵

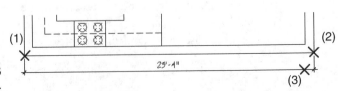

Figure 6.18
Create the first dimension.

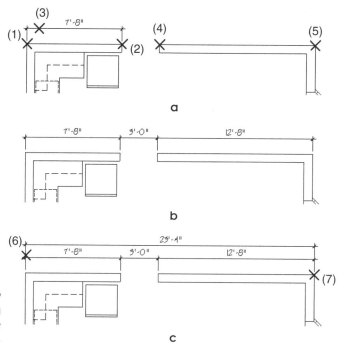

Figure 6.19
Continuous dimensioning
and baseline
dimensioning.

Select continued dimension: ↵

Command: Command ends (Figure 6.19b).

Step 7: Use Baseline Dimension tool to create an overall dimension.

An architectural plan usually has three levels of dimensions from detailed dimension to the overall dimension. The Baseline Dimension tool allows you to create larger dimensions based on smaller dimensions. The new higher-level dimension is automatically placed according to the "spacing" defined in the dimension style.

 Click the Baseline Dimension icon.

Command: _dimbaseline   A rubber band dimension
                                                               stretches out from the first point
                                                               of the last dimension.

● Don't be scared by the rubber band dimension. (You did not do anything wrong!) By default, the baseline command assumes that you want to start the new baseline dimension from the first origin point of the last dimension you created. In this case, however, we want to start from the first dimension above the floor plan. Therefore, we need to choose Select so that AutoCAD knows where to start.

Specify a second extension line origin
or [Undo/Select] <Select>: ↵   For Select.

Select base dimension: **Pick the end
of the first extension line (point 6).**   (Figure 6.19c)

Specify a second extension line origin
or [Undo/Select] <Select>:
Pick the corner of the wall (point 7)

Dimension text = 23'-4"

Specify a second extension line origin
or [Undo/Select] <Select>: ↵

Select base dimension: ↵

Command: Command ends.

Step 8: Create the on-center dimension of the window.

Sometimes on-center dimensions are required for windows. Since you cannot change the linetype of individual extension lines in a dimension, you need to draw a centerline over the window and use the dimension styles with suppressed extension lines to create the dimension.

Draw the centerline of the window

1 Draw a line from the midpoint of the interior windowsill (Figure 6.20a).

2 Change the layer of the line to I-ANON-CTLN.

Set current dimension style

Click the Dimension Style list in Dimension toolbar and select Nosecond.

● This substep will be used to switch dimension styles while creating dimensions.

Create dimensions

1 Click the Linear Dimension toolbar icon.

2 Pick point (1) (Figure 6.20b).

3 Pick point (2).

● Because point (1) and point (2) are not on a vertical line, there are two possible dimensions to present: the horizontal differential between the two points and the vertical differential between the two points. AutoCAD will make a choice based on the cursor position relative to the two points. You need to guide AutoCAD to make the right decision by moving the cursor in the direction perpendicular to the distance you want to dimension. (In this case, move cursor to the left of points (1) and (2), and then back to (3).)

4 Locate the dimension line by point (3).

5 Switch dimension style to "nofirst." See the previous substep for reference.

6 Click the Continue Dimension icon.

7 Pick point (4).

8 Press [Enter] twice to end the command.

9 Switch dimension style to "archi48." See the previous substep for reference.

10 Click the Baseline Dimension icon and create an overall dimension.

Command: _dimbaseline

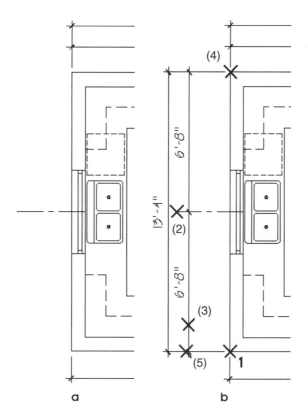

Figure 6.20
Centerline dimension.

a   b

Specify a second extension line origin
or [Undo/Select] <Select>: ↵   For Select.

Select base dimension: **Pick the end
of the first extension line (point 5).**

Specify a second extension line origin
or [Undo/Select] <Select>:
Pick point (4)

Dimension text = 13'-4"

Specify a second extension line origin
or [Undo/Select] <Select>: ↵

Select base dimension: ↵

Command:

Step 9: Create dimensions for angled lines.

Although we usually do not need to provide detailed dimensions for a bay window unless it is custom designed, we want to use the slanting lines of the bay window to practice dimensioning angled lines. For an angled line, you can provide two types of dimension: aligned or orthogonal.

Create an Aligned Dimension

1 ZOOM to look at the bay window (Figure 6.21a).

2 Click the Aligned Dimension icon.

Command: _dimaligned

Specify first extension line origin
or <select object>: **Pick point (1).**

Specify second extension line origin:
Pick point (2).

Specify dimension line location
or [Mtext/Text/Angle]: **Move mouse to
pull the rubber band dimension out
and pick point (3).**

Dimension text = 1'-7" 13/16"

Command:

Create an Orthogonal Dimension

Click the Linear Dimension icon.

Command: _dimlinear

Specify first extension line origin
or <select object>: **Pick point (4).**

Specify second extension line origin:
Pick point (5).

(Figure 6.21b)

Specify dimension line location
or [Mtext/Text/Angle/Horizontal/
Vertical/Rotated]: **Move mouse upward
and pick point (6).**

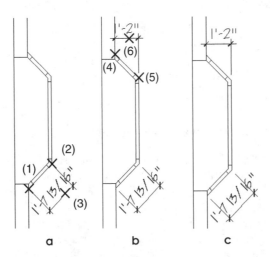

Figure 6.21
Dimensions of
the north wall.

a   b   c

Dimension text = 1'-2":

Command:

● A vertical dimension can be made by pulling the rubber band dimension to the right after picking the anchor points.

Adjust the Dimension Text Position

When we set the archi48 dimension style, we chose not to use the automatic function to relocate dimension text. When there is not enough space for the text, the automatic relocation is usually not aesthetically acceptable, so we need to use the Dimension Text Edit tool.

1 Use function key [F8] to turn off the ORTHO mode if it is on. (When ORTHO is on, cursor movements are restrained.)

 2 Click the Dimension Text Edit icon.

Select dimension: **Pick the 1'-2" text.**   (Figure 6.21c)

Enter text location (Left/Right/Home/Angle): **Move the text slightly to the right to avoid interference with the wall line and click to place the text.**

Command: Command ends.

Change the Dimension Style of a Dimension

You may have noticed that the 1'-2" dimension is in the archi48 style with extension lines on both sides of the dimension text. Since the left-side extension line is not needed because it overlaps with the wall line, you may want to hide it to make your drawing look better.

1 Click the dimension whose style you want to change. The grips appear.

2 Click the Dimension Style drop-down list and choose Nofirst.

3 Press [Esc] to cancel the grip.

Step 10: Create internal dimensions with Quick Dimension.

The Quick Dimension tool allows you to create dimensions by picking objects instead of points. This simplifies the process. Creating internal dimensions is basically the same as creating external dimensions. A major difference between the two is that dimension styles with extension line suppression are more often used for internal dimensions. To avoid frequent switching between dimension styles, which slows down the operation, first create the dimensions all in one style and change the dimension style of certain dimensions at a later time.

1 **ZOOM out to look at the entire floor plan** (Figure 6.22a).

2 **Set Noboth as the current dimension style.**

3 **Click the Quick Dimension icon.**

Command: _qdim

Select geometry to dimension:
Pick line [A] 1 found

Select geometry to dimension:
Pick line [B] 1 found, 2 total

Select geometry to dimension:
Pick line [C] 1 found, 3 total

Select geometry to dimension:
Pick line [D] 1 found, 4 total

Select geometry to dimension:
Pick line [E] 1 found, 5 total

Select geometry to dimension:
Pick line [F] 1 found, 6 total

Select geometry to dimension:
Pick line [G] 1 found, 7 total

Select geometry to dimension:
Pick line [H] 1 found, 8 total

Select geometry to dimension:
Pick line [I] 1 found, 9 total

Select geometry to dimension: ↵

Specify dimension line position, or
[Continuous/Staggered/Baseline/
Ordinate/Radius/Diameter/datumPoint/Edit]
<Continuous>: **Pick point (1)**

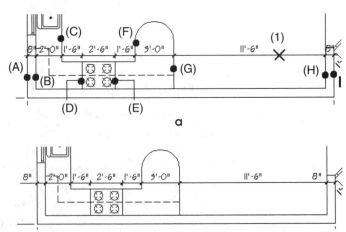

Figure 6.22
Use Quick Dimension to
create internal
dimensions.

4 Turn off running object snap.

5 Use the Dimension Text Edit tool to relocate the dimensions for the wall thickness. (Pull the texts out of the wall and keep the dimension line alignment.)

6 Change the dimension style of the 2'-6" segment to archi48 (Figure 6.22b).

Step 11: Create a radius dimension.

For shapes made of circles and arcs, radius dimensions and their center points may need to be marked. In this step, you will create the radius dimension for the curved countertop and mark its center point.

1 ZOOM to look at the curved counter (Figure 6.23).

2 Click the Radius Dimension icon.

Command: _dimradius

Select arc or circle: **Pick the arc.**   A rubber band radius dimension
                                                     moves with the cursor.

Dimension text = 1'-6"

Specify dimension line location
or [Mtext/Text/Angle]: **Click at point (1).**

Command:

3 Click the Center Mark icon.

Command: _dimcenter

Select arc or circle:Select geometry
to dimension: **Pick the arc** 1 found

Command: The center point is marked with
                                                     a cross.

Step 12: Create a note with leader.

1 Turn ORTHO off (if it is on).

2 ZOOM out to look at the entire floor plan.

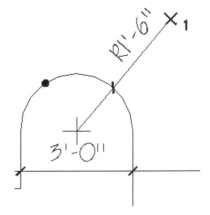

Figure 6.23
Dimension the arc.

3 Click the Quick Leader icon.

Command: _qleader

Specify first leader point,
or [Settings]<Settings>: **Pick point (1).**   (Figure 6.24)

Pick the point the arrowhead
points to.

Specify next point: <Ortho off>
Pick point (2)

This is the point where the
annotation starts.

Specify next point: <Ortho on> ↵

- You are prompted to enter a third point because the default leader setting sets the maximum definition point of the pointer line as 3. If you don't want an extended horizontal section in the pointer, simply press [Enter] to skip the third point. This will make later adjustment of the leader and the text easier.

Specify text width <0">: ↵

- If you enter a distance value at this prompt, the text you enter later will automatically wrap. Taking the default value 0" means that you don't want the text to be automatically wrapped; use the [Enter] key to control the line breaks of the text.

Enter first line of annotation text <Mtext>:
LAMINATE ↵

Enter next line of annotation text:
COUNTERTOP ↵

Enter next line of annotation text: ↵   The note text appears.

Command:

Move the annotation with grip

The annotation text can be moved by dragging the grip. The leader adjusts automatically.

1 Click the annotation. The text turns gray and a grip (small blue square) appears.

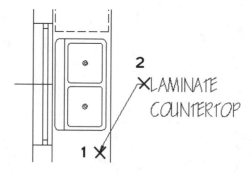

Figure 6.24
Leader and note.

2 Click the grip. It turns red (hot), and the texts moves with the cursor.

3 Pick a point. The text is relocated, and the leader lines stretch and maintain the connection between the reference point and the annotation.

● The leader can also be stretched using grips. When you stretch the leader, the annotation will not move with it; thus, you can adjust the relationship between the leader and the annotation.

Draw a curved leader

Sometimes to prevent interference you may need to use a curved leader, or you may simply prefer the curve for aesthetic reasons.

1 ERASE the note and leader.

2 Click the Quick Leader icon.

Command: _qleader

Specify first leader point,
or [Settings]<Settings>: ↵   Accept the Settings default value.

The "Leader Settings" dialog box pops up (Figure 6.25).

3 Click the Leader Lines & Arrow tab.

4 Check Spline in the Leader Line section.

● Spline is a natural-looking curve defined by anchor points.

5 Click [OK] to close the dialog box.

● AutoCAD keeps this setting effective until you reset it.

Specify first leader point, or [Settings]<Settings>:
Pick point (1).   Pick the point of reference (Figure 6.26).

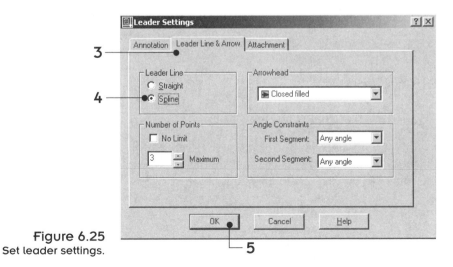

Figure 6.25
Set leader settings.

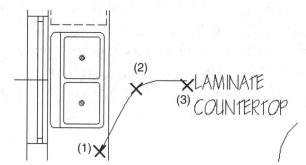

Figure 6.26
Draw a curved leader.

Specify next point: **Pick point (2).**

Pick a "pass through" point for the leader curve.

A straight line leader is drawn between the two points.

Specify next point: **Pick point (3).**

Pick the point where the curve ends. The leader turns into a curve.

Specify text width <0">: ↵

Enter first line of annotation text <Mtext>:
LAMINATE ↵

Enter next line of annotation text:
COUNTERTOP ↵

Enter next line of annotation text: ↵

Command:

● The shape of the curve can be easily adjusted by moving its grips. Click the curve, click the grip, move the cursor, and the curve will change.

6 ZOOM out to see the whole drawing.

7 Save your drawing and exit AutoCAD.

Troubleshooting

Problem 1: "I can't get the point I picked."

This is a common problem when you use running object snap with dimension commands. You are actually overserved by the Object Snap function. Turning off the running Object Snap mode solves this problem.

Problem 2: "My extension line goes the wrong way."

This problem indicates that the two points you picked for the dimension were not on the same side of the dimension line. An extension line always starts from the origin point. You need to redo it with a better choice of origin points.

Problem 3: "I don't have the arrowhead in front of my leader."

AutoCAD shows the arrowhead only when it measures enough space for it. If your arrowhead is too big, or the distance between your note and the point your leader points to is too short, AutoCAD omits the arrowhead. Check your arrowhead size, leaving adequate space for it.

Problem 4: "The dimension is not right."

The first possibility is that you did not pick the exact point you wanted to pick. You may have forgotten to use Object Snap. If this is the case, erase it and redo that dimension. The second possibility is that you did not draw the object correctly and the measured dimension is telling the truth. If this is the case, you should correct the problematic object and redo the dimension.

Problem 5: "I have a typo in the annotation text."

Use the DDEDIT command to edit the text.

Summary

In this chapter, you have learned the following concepts, procedures, and commands:

Knowledge/Concept

● Dimension styles

Procedures

● Set dimension styles

● Create linear dimensions

● Create continued dimensions

● Create baseline (overall) dimensions

● Create aligned dimensions of angled object

● Switch between dimension styles

● Change the style of an existing dimension

● Adjust dimension text location

● Create annotation with leader

● Create curved leader

● Adjust annotation and leader position

Commands

- Dimension styles (DDIM, D)

- Object Snap settings

- Linear dimension

- Dimension text edit

- Baseline dimension

- Continued dimension

- Aligned dimension

- Radius dimension

- Center mark

- Quick dimension

- Quick leader

Plotting

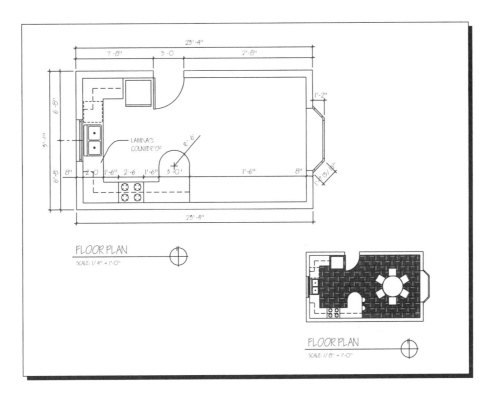

- Set plotter configurations
- Use model space and paper space
- Plot from model space
- Plot to a file
- Plot from a paper space layout

Now that you have finished the floor plan, you are ready for plotting. In the process of plotting, you need to do a few things. First, you will need to set up your printer or plotter; second, you need to set up the drawing as a presentable page by setting the paper size and orientation, the area of the drawing to be printed, the drawing scale, and so on; third, you need to set the lineweight and other plot style options. Only if all these things are set up correctly, can the drawing print out as you expect. In this chapter, we will go through the steps needed to print out the floor plan.

Plotter Configuration

In order to use a plotter, its configuration (the program that drives the plotter and the parameter settings for the program) needs to be loaded. This is usually done when the plotter is first connected to your computer, and you don't have to do it thereafter. Since the process of installing a printer driver differs from printer to printer, the following procedure is only an example, which may or may not be applicable in your situation. If you do not have a plotter, you can still follow this tutorial to learn the procedure; if you already have a plotter working with your computer, you may skip this section and go to the next section, which details how to make a plot of your drawing.

1 **Start AutoCAD and click the Tools menu in the menu bar and select Options.** The Options dialog box pops up (Figure 7.1).

2 **Click the Plotting tab.**

3 **Click [Add or Configure Plotters].** The Plotters window pops up (Figure 7.2).

4 **Double-click Add-A-Plotter Wizard.** The Add Plotter–Introduction page pops up (Figure 7.3).

5 **Click [Next >].** The Add plotter–Begin page pops up (Figure 7.4).

6 **Check an appropriate item according to your situation.**

● In this example, the My Computer default selection will be accepted. This is good for one plotter serving one computer.

7 **Click [Next >].** The Add Plotter–Plotter Model page pops up (Figure 7.5).

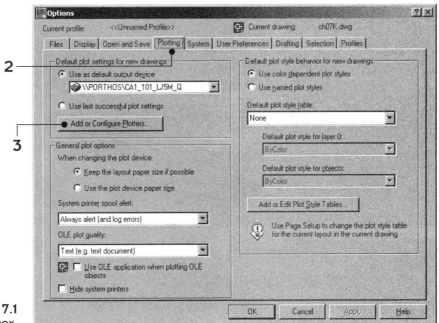

Figure 7.1
The Options dialog box.

2

3

Figure 7.2
The Plotters window.

4

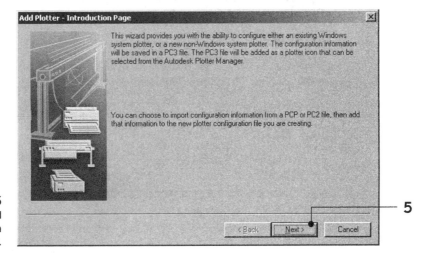

Figure 7.3
The Add
Plotter–Introduction
Page window.

5

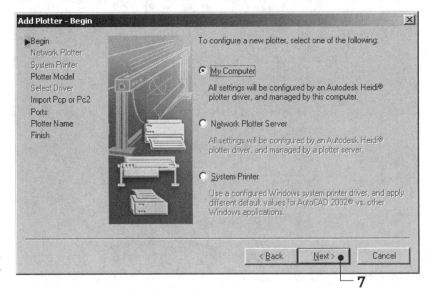

Figure 7.4
The Add Plotter–
Begin page.

8 Select a plotter brand name (such as Hewlett Packard) in the Manufacturers list. The model names appear in the Models list.

9 Select the model of your plotter.

10 Click [Next >]. The Add Plotter–Import Pcp or Pc2 page pops up (Figure 7.6).

● The Pcp and Pc2 files are previously saved plotter configuration files. Since this is the first time you are setting up a plotter, we can assume that you don't have these files.

11 Click [Next >]. The Add Plotter–Ports page pops up (Figure 7.7).

● This page sets the connection between the plotter and the computer. Make your selection according to your particular situation.

12 Click [Next >]. The Add Plotter–Plotter Name page pops up (Figure 7.8).

13 Enter a name of your choice or click [Next >] to accept the default name. The Add Plotter–Finish page pops up (Figure 7.9).

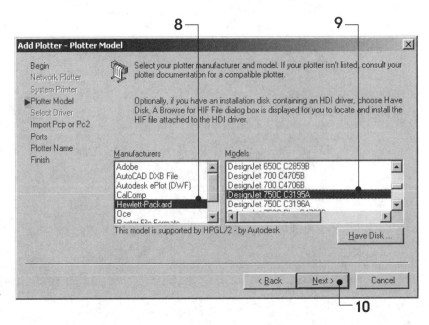

Figure 7.5
The Add Plotter–
Plotter Model page.

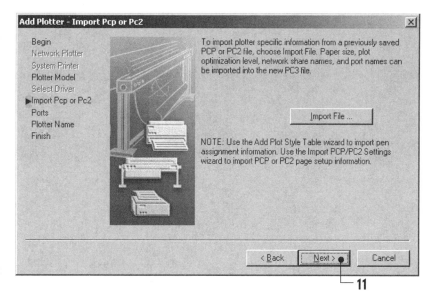

Figure 7.6
The Add Plotter–Import Pcp or Pc2 page.

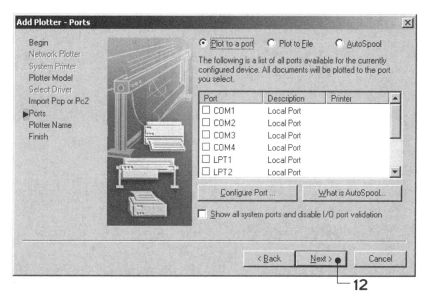

Figure 7.7
The Add Plotter–Ports page.

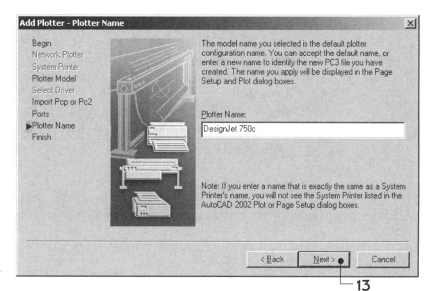

Figure 7.8
The Add Plotter–Plotter Name page.

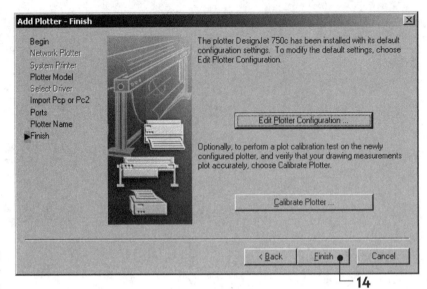

Figure 7.9
The Add Plotter–
Finish page.

● At this time, you can click [Edit Plotter Configuration...] to do the more detailed configuration required by the specific printer you chose. Since this step is case-specific, you have to work it out by yourself or get help from system support personnel at your institution.

14 **Click [Finish].** The dialog closes and the plotter is ready for use.

15 **Click [OK] to exit the Options dialog box.**

Model Space and Paper Space

In an AutoCAD drawing window, you have two default tabs: the Model tab and the Layout1 tab. In previous AutoCAD releases, the Model tab was called model space and the layout tab the paper space. Model space is where you create your drawing entities (such as lines), and paper space is where you assemble the drawing entities on a drawing sheet (for plotting) as a presentation. Although this concept seems to be rather confusing, it may help you to know that you have already been working in model space in the previous chapters. Before paper space was implemented in Auto-CAD, there had been only one world (equivalent to the present model space) for both drawing (modeling) and presenting (plotting). The problem with this approach is that it is very confusing and difficult to have drawings of different scales on the same sheet. (You would be forced to violate the principle of always drawing at full scale.) In addition, it was impossible to present 3D views along with 2D drawings. Paper space is the solution to these problems.

Paper space is like a piece of paper placed on top of your basic model space drawings. You can cut out holes (technically called viewports) to show, in different scales or view angles (for 3D models), the drawings in model space. The viewports can be resized and moved freely. In paper space, you also have control of layer visibility for individual viewports; thus, you can create different versions of the same model space drawing. Using all these paper space features, you can make the task of sheet composition much easier. For this reason, you should always use paper space for plotting. In the building industry, however, plotting from model space, as a tradition, is still a common practice. Therefore, you need to learn both.

Plotting from Model Space

In this section you will make a plot of your dimensioned floor plan from model space.

Step 1: Determine the drawing scale and drawing size.

In CAD drawings, you always create drawing entities in their true dimensions (or in full scale), and the drawing scale is decided by your presentation needs. Now, it's time to make decisions on some pertinent AutoCAD settings. As a designer, you may have to follow the conventions of the profession. Since the 1/4″=1′-0″ scale is usually used for floor plans in interior design drawings, we will simply follow this convention. Once the scale is determined, the question shifts to the sheet size. Similarly, you can follow the conventions of the profession, or you may have to consider available paper sizes for a certain type of printer. If you use a laser printer, your choice may be 11″ × 8.5″ (letter size), 14″ × 8.5″ (legal size), or 11″ × 17″ (tabloid). With a possible paper size in mind, you can then figure out whether it is large enough to hold the content. For example, if we considered a letter-sized sheet for our floor plan, at 1/4″ scale, an 11″ × 8.5″ paper represents a 44′ × 34′ space in reality. [Since 1/4″=1′-0″ can be converted to 1″=4′, 11″ (on paper) represents 44′ (=11×4).] This space seems to be large enough to hold our 23′-4″ by 13′-4″ room. To make sure that the sheet is indeed large enough to include the dimensions and the drawing title, draw a 44′×34′ rectangle to do a mock-up.

1 OPEN drawing ch06.dwg and save it as ch07.dwg.

- *Note:* You are now in model space. This is indicated by the Model tab beneath the drawing area.

2 ZOOM to show the entire drawing.

Step 2: Start the PLOT command and select the appropriate plotter.

1 Enter the PLOT command or click the printer icon in the standard toolbar. The Plot dialog box pops up (Figure 7.10).

2 Click the Plot Device tab if it is not already open.

- *Note:* Printer names shown in the illustration reflect a particular case in the author's computer. Yours may be different.

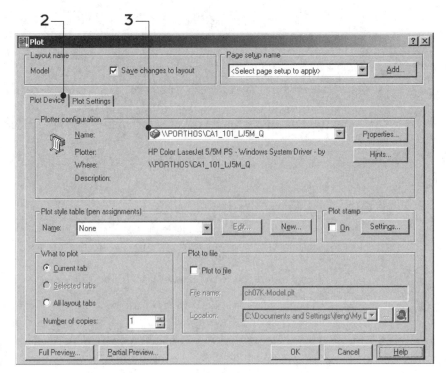

On the Plot Device page, the first group, Plotter configuration, controls the selection of the plotter and more detailed settings for that plotter. The current plotter name is shown in the Name box. If the plotter shown in the box is not what you want to use, do the following:

3 Click the Name list and select the printer/plotter you want to use.

Step 3: Set the plot settings.

1. Set paper size.

1 Click the Plot Settings tab. The Plot Settings page opens (Figure 7.11).

2 Click the Paper Size list and select the correct size.

● In this example, you need a letter-sized sheet.

● The available paper size differs from plotter to plotter. Some plotters allow user-defined paper sizes while others do not.

● When you select a paper size, you should remember that the printable area size (shown below the Paper size drop-down list) is always smaller than the paper size. The drawing contents must all be in the printable area in order to be plotted.

2. Define plot area.

In AutoCAD plotting you don't have to plot the whole drawing. There are four methods to define a particular area to plot.

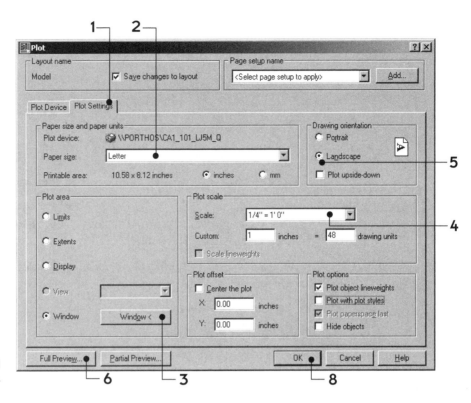

Figure 7.11
The Plot Settings page.

1. *Display:* Plot the area displayed on the screen.

2. *Extents:* Plot all drawing entities on the drawing.

3. *Limits:* Plot all drawing entities within the drawing limits.

4. *Window:* Plot an area defined by a selection window. The last method gives you the easiest and most flexible control. It does not use a fixed proportion as does the first method; it has better control than the second method; and it does not require a premeditated limit setting as the third method does.

3 Check the [Window...] button in the Plot area section.

Specify window for printing.

Specify first corner:
Pick a point.

Specify opposite corner:
**Pick a second point to include
all the drawing contents.**

- The lower-left corner of the selection window will be placed at the lower-left corner of the paper. If you want to have some space below the drawing, you may include some empty space when you pick points for the selection window. This is an easy and intuitive way of manipulating the placement of the drawing on a plot.

3. Set scale.

4   Click the Scale drop-down list and select 1/4″=1′-0″.

4. Rotate your drawing (optional)

If the orientation of the drawing is different from the orientation of the plotting sheet, your drawing may be cut off by half. To solve this problem, switch from the portrait format to the landscape format, or vise versa.

5   Check the button in front of Landscape in the Drawing Orientation section. The Paper icon changes accordingly.

6   Click [Full Preview...]. AutoCAD shows you the image on the plotting sheet, which is represented by a rectangle.

● If you need to adjust the placement of the drawing on the plot sheet, you may redefine the drawing area using the Window option.

7   Press [Esc] to exit the preview.

8   Click [OK] to print the drawing.

Step 4: Control lineweight and color.

When you look at the printout of the drawing, you may see some major lineweight and color problems. All the lines have the same thickness. If you have a color printer, the lines are printed in the same color as you set in the AutoCAD drawing, and they do not look good. If you have a black and white printer, some of the lines are printed with different shades of gray and they create a hierarchy that contradicts the drafting conventions.

AutoCAD allows you to control lineweight and color through plot styles. The most commonly used method is to assign plotting pens of different size and color, either real or virtual, to particular colors used in a drawing. In other words, colors used in a drawing can be used to control line weight. For example, all the wall lines in the floor plan are red. You can then assign a large-sized pen to the color red so that all the wall lines are plotted with a heavy lineweight. Therefore, you should be very careful to set object colors when you create them, because they may eventually be used to control the lineweight.

The control of plot styles is managed through Plot Style Tables (or more specifically, Color-Dependent Plot Style Tables). Such tables are files with a .CTB file name extension and are stored by default in the Acad2002\Plot Styles directory. A Plot Style Table is linked to a drawing through the Plot Device page of the Plot dialog box.

In this next step, you will create a Plot Style Table to assign a large-sized plotting pen to the color red to create heavy wall lines, and to assign a black plotting color to all AutoCAD object colors so that all the drawing entities will print in the same black color.

1. Create a Plot Style Table file.

1 Start a PLOT command.

2 Click the Plot Device tab. The page appears (Figure 7.12).

3 Click the Name list in the Plot Style Table section, and select Acad.ctb from the drop-down list. A Question dialog box pops up.

● Acad.ctb is the default AutoCAD Plot Style Table. You will create your own table based on it.

4 Click [Yes].

5 Click [Edit] to view the plot style settings. The Plot Style Table Editor pops up (Figure 7.13).

● From this dialog box, we can see that each plot style is named by a color, and each plot style controls a long list of properties such as color and lineweight.

6 Click Color 1 to highlight it.

● This is the color of the wall lines. You want to assign a heavy lineweight to it.

7 Click the Lineweight list and select 0.5 (mm).

● The lineweight of the wall lines is set. Follow the same procedure to set the lineweight for other lines of different colors, if you need to.

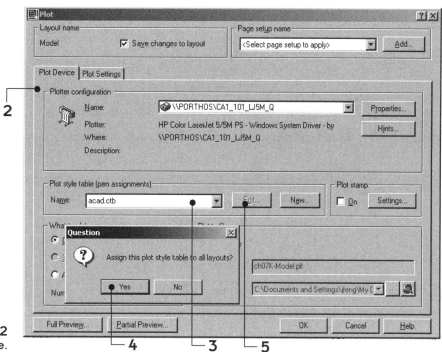

Figure 7.12
Work with Plot Style Table.

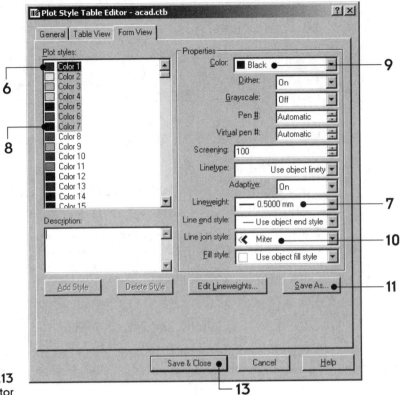

Figure 7.13
Plot Style Table Editor

8 **Click Color 1 and hold the [Shift] key and click Color 7 to highlight Colors 1 through 7.**

● These are all the colors we have used in the floor plan. Assign black ink to them so that all the objects are plotted in black.

9 **Click the Color list in the Properties section, and select Black.**

● The multiple selection allows you to change properties of a group of layers at once.

10 **Click the Line join style list and select Miter to ensure a solid-looking corner connection.**

11 **Click [Save As] to save the setting as a .ctb file.**   The Save As dialog pops up.

12 **Name the file ch07 and click [Save].**

● The Plot Style Table ch07.ctb file is created and stored in the Plot Styles directory for future use.

13 **Click [Save & Close].**

2. Link the Plot Style Table file and plot.

1 **Click the Name list in the Plot Style Table section and select ch07.** A warning message pops up.

2 Click [Yes].

3 Click [Full Preview] to see the result.

- All the drawing elements should be black. The heavy lineweight of the wall, however, is not obviously shown. Zoom in to see the lineweight effect. To zoom in into the print preview window, hold down the left mouse button and move the cursor up.

4 Press [Esc] to exit the preview.

5 Click [OK] to plot.

Plotting to a File

When a plotter is located in another computer lab in your school, or when you use other printing services, you can plot your drawing to a plot file then take the plot file to the plotter.

1 In the Plot Devices page of the Plot dialog box, check the Plot To File box in the Plot to file group.

2 Enter a file name in the File Name list. The .plt file type extension will be automatically added to the plot file name.

3 If the file directory shown in the Location: list is not where you want the plot file to go, **change the directory by clicking the list and choose the directory you want.**

4 Click [OK] to plot. A plot with the specified file name is created in the specified directory.

- The procedure to plot from a plot file (xxx.plt) may vary greatly depending on the hardware and software configurations of the plotter you use. Consult the administrator of the plotter or the plotting services to find out what to do.

Plotting from a Paper Space Layout

In the following tutorial you will set up a paper space layout to present the floor plan you created in previous chapters.

Step 1: Start a paper space layout.

In the default setting of a new AutoCAD drawing, there is a tab leading to a paper space layout named "Layout1." To start setting up a paper space layout, simply click the tab to switch to it.

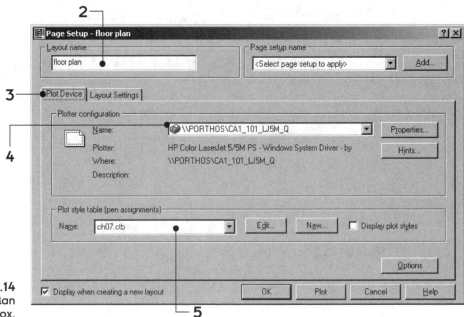

Figure 7.14
Page Setup – floor plan
dialog box.

1 **Click the Layout1 tab.** The Page Setup dialog box pops up (Figure 7.14).

● This dialog box pops up only the first time you click the layout tab. If you accidentally clicked the tab before, this dialog box will not show. You will need to call it up from the File > Page Setup menu.

● Before displaying the paper space, AutoCAD needs to know what plotter and what paper size you want to use.

2 **Change Layout name from Layout 1 to Floor plan.**

3 **Click the Plot Devices tab if it is not already open.**

4 **Make sure the right plotter is selected.**

● For this tutorial, a letter-sized laser or inkjet printer is assumed.

5 **Make sure ch07.ctb is in the Name list window in the Plot Style Table section.**

6 **Click the Layout Settings tab.** The Layout Settings page opens (Figure 7.15).

7 **Make sure letter-sized paper is selected.**

8 **Make sure Drawing orientation is Landscape.**

9 **Make sure the Plot scale is set to 1:1.**

● The plot scale for paper space layout plotting should ALWAYS be 1:1.

10 **Click [OK].** The dialog box closes and the paper space layout is displayed (Figure 7.16).

● The white-colored rectangle (against the gray background) represents the paper; the dotted rectangle inside the paper boundary represents the printable area; the

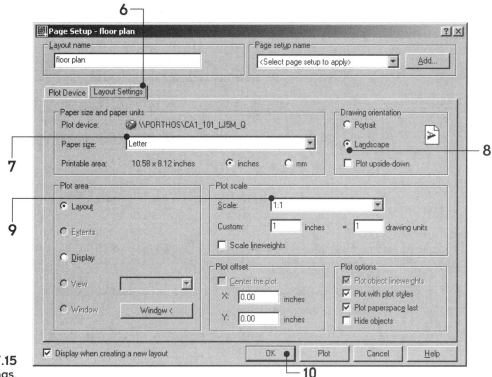

Figure 7.15
Set layout settings.

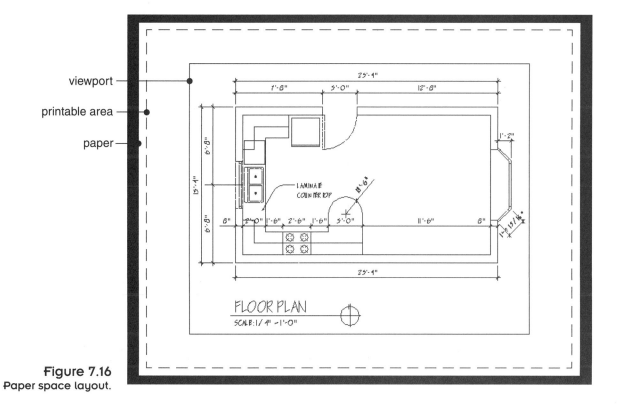

Figure 7.16
Paper space layout.

rectangle inside the printable area is a viewport automatically created by Auto-CAD during the page setup process; and the content of the model space drawing is shown inside the viewport.

Step 2: Set the drawing scale for the viewport.

When a viewport is created, the drawing elements in the model space are scaled to fit the viewport. You need to reset the scale of a viewport to what you want. In this case, you want to set the scale to 1/4"=1'-0."

1   Click the View menu and choose Toolbars. The Toolbars dialog box pops up.

2   Scroll down the list and check Viewports. The Viewports toolbar pops up.

3   Click [Close].

4   Click the viewport.   The grips appear at the corners of the viewport (Figure 7.17).

5   Click the Scale list in the toolbar and choose 1/4"=1'-0." The floor plan is slightly reduced.

6   Drag the Viewports toolbar to embed it in the window frame below the AutoCAD window.

● If you have more than one viewport in a paper space layout, you can set scales for each viewport individually by following this procedure.

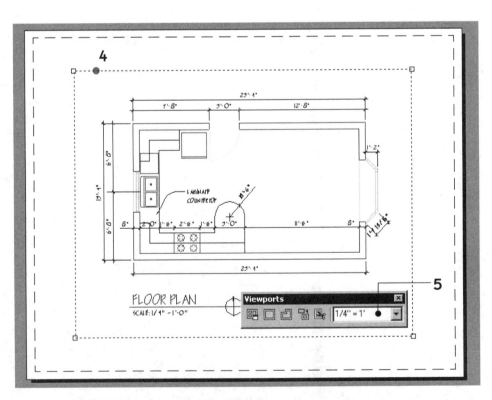

Figure 7.17
Set the viewport scale.

Step 3: Resize the viewport.

After setting the scale for the viewport, the size of the floor plan is reduced. You need to resize the viewport to match the content.

1 Turn ORTHO off (use the [F8] key).

● When ORTHO is off you can pull the grip diagonally to change the width and length of the viewport at the same time. When ORTHO is on, you can only pull the viewport in one direction, either *x* or *y*.

2 Click the grip at the lower-right corner of the viewport. The grip become hot.

3 Move the mouse to relocate the bottom and right boundaries of the viewport closer to the floor plan, and click to set their locations. (Figure 7.18)

4 Click the grip at the upper-left corner of the viewport.

5 Relocate the upper and left boundaries closer to the floor plan.

Step 4: Move the viewport in paper space

In paper space, the viewport that contains your drawing is similar to a picture. Use the MOVE command to move the viewport to the upper-left corner of the sheet.

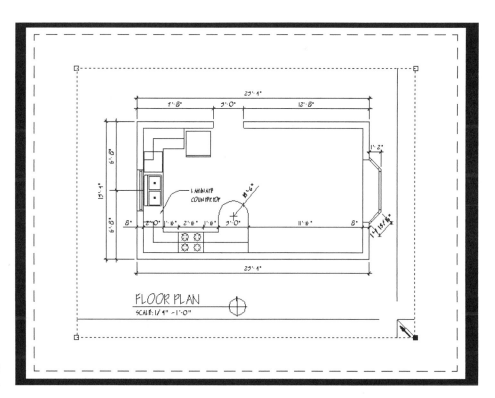

Figure 7-18
Resize the viewport.

Step 5: Reset the linetype scale.

In the plan shown in the paper space viewport the dashed linetypes all look solid. You need to reset the LTSCALE value for paper space. Since paper space is ALWAYS full-scale in the sense that the paper size is defined with its real measurements, the LTSCALE value (24) you set (in Chapter 5) in the model space is too big. Set it back to 1 or 0.5.

Command: **LTSCALE** ↵

Enter new linetype scale factor
<24.0000>: **0.5** ↵

Regenerating layout.

Regenerating model.   Dashed lines show.

- If you feel that the dashes are too big or too small, you can adjust the LTSCALE value to make them look better.

- In the AutoCAD linetype library, you'll notice a group of linetypes whose names start with ISO. These linetypes are much larger in unit size than other linetypes, which means they require a much smaller (about ten to twenty times smaller) linetype scale factor to be shown appropriately in paper space. To avoid dealing with linetype scales individually, do not use the ISO linetypes with other line-types.

Step 6: Set a second viewport.

In a paper space layout you can set up more than one viewport. Now, we want to add a second viewport to show the furniture plan of the space at 1/8″=1′-0″ scale.

1 Click the Single Viewport Creation icon.

Command: _-vports

Specify corner of viewport
or [ON/OFF/Fit/Hideplot/Lock/
Object/Polygonal/Restore/2/3/4]
<Fit>: **Pick point (1).**   (Figure 7.19)

Specify opposite corner:
Pick point (2).

Regenerating model.   The floor plan appears in the new viewport.

2 Click the new viewport.

3 Set the viewport scale at 1/8″=1′0″ (use the Viewport toolbar).

4 Adjust the shape of the viewport by its grips to better fit the drawing, and exclude the drawing title.

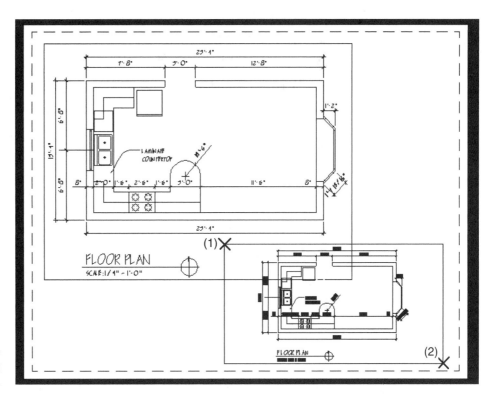

Figure 7.19
Create the second
viewport.

5 Move the second viewport to a better location to make a good composition.

Step 7: Create a polygonal viewport.

Although you may have tried to keep the two viewports apart by relocating the second viewport, the paper is too small to make it possible. In this step, you will create a polygonal viewport to avoid the overlap.

1 Turn ORTHO on.

2 Click the Polygonal Viewport icon.

Command: _-vports

Specify corner of viewport
or [ON/OFF/Fit/Hideplot/Lock/Object/
Polygonal/Restore/2/3/4] <Fit>: _p

Specify start point: **Pick point (1)**   (Figure 7.20)

Specify next point or [Arc/Length/Undo]:
Pick point (2)

Specify next point
or [Arc/Close/Length/Undo]: **Pick point (3)**

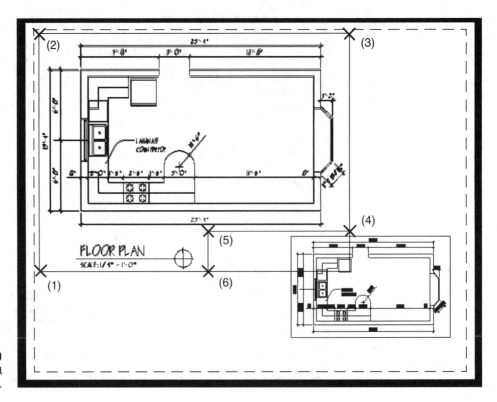

Figure 7.20
Create a polygonal viewport.

Specify next point
or [Arc/Close/Length/Undo]: **Pick point (4)**

Specify next point
or [Arc/Close/Length/Undo]: **Pick point (5)**

Specify next point
or [Arc/Close/Length/Undo]: **Pick point (6)**

Specify next point
or [Arc/Close/Length/Undo]: **C**   For Close.

Regenerating model.   The newly created polygonal viewport overlaps the rectangular one.

3 ERASE the rectangular viewport.

4 Set the scale of the new polygonal viewport to 1/4″ = 1′-0″.

Step 8: Copy the drawing title from model space to paper space.

In this step, you will create a new drawing title for the smaller scale plan by copying the drawing title from model space to paper space, using the standard Cut and Paste tools (as you do when using a word processor).

1 Click the Model tab to turn to the model space.

2 Select the drawing title by using an implied window.

Figure 7.21
Select the drawing title.

Command: **Pick point (1)**
Other corner: **Pick point (2).**   (Figure 7.21)

Grips appear around the selected drawing title.

3 **Click the Copy icon in the standard toolbar.**

Command: '_copyclip 6 found   AutoCAD puts the selected objects onto the clipboard.

4 **Click the Floorplan tab to go back to the paper space layout.**

5 **Click the Edit menu and choose Paste as block.**

_pasteblock Duplicate definition
of block _ArchTick ignored.

Specify insertion point:
**Pick a point below the floor plan
in the first viewport.**

● Tremendously huge texts appear, because in paper space the letters are shown in their real size, which was defined as 12″ when you created them in Chapter 5. Don't be scared! You just need to scale them down.

6 **Scale down the inserted drawing title.**

Command: **SCALE** ↵   The alias is SC and its icon is

Select objects: **L** ↵   The L means the Last created object.

1 found

Select objects: ↵

Specify base point: **Pick a point
below the floor plan
in the first viewport.**

Specify scale factor or [Reference]: **1/48** ↵

● The scale factor 1/48 (inverse of scale factor 48) changes the scale of the object from 1″=48″ (model space scale) to 1″=1″ (paper space scale).

Command:

7 **EXPLODE the copied drawing title.**

● Since the second viewport has a different scale from that of the first, you have to change the scale note in the drawing title from 1/4″ to 1/8″. Because the drawing title is a block, you have to EXPLODE it before you can edit it. The EXPLODE command disassembles a block into individual pieces.

Command: **EXPLODE** ↵   The alias is X and its icon is shown on the left.

Select objects:
Pick the pasted drawing title
1 found

Select objects: ↵

Command: The drawing title is exploded.

8 Change the text by using DDEDIT.

● DDEDIT is an editing tool for texts in an AutoCAD drawing.

Command: **DDEDIT** ↵   The alias is ED.

Select an annotation object
or [Undo]: **Pick the text (SCALE: 1/4″=1′-0″).**   The Edit Text dialog box pops up
                                         (Figure 7.22).

**Change the text from 1/4″ to 1/8″
and click [OK].**

Command:

9 Use the MOVE command to move the drawing title under the small floor plan.

Step 9: Differentiate the contents of the two viewports by using layer control.

Although the contents of both viewports are from the same drawing, you can make them look different by using layer controls.

1 Thaw the I-FURN and I-FLOR-PATT layers. The floor tile and furniture appear in both viewports.

2 Click the [PAPER] button in the status bar. The button changes to [MODEL]. One of the viewports is highlighted with thick boundary lines.

● In paper space layout, there are two modes: paper space and model space. The status button [PAPER] and [MODEL] status button allows you to switch between these two modes. The model space mode in paper space layout allows you to access the drawing elements in the model space through one active viewport. You can make any viewport active by clicking inside the viewport. In this step, we want to make one viewport active in order to manipulate the layer visibility of that viewport.

Figure 7.22
Edit Text dialog box.

3 Make sure the smaller viewport is active.

 4 Click the Layers icon to call up the Layer Properties Manager dialog box.

5 Click the Freeze/Thaw in current viewport icon in the I-ANON-DIMS and I-ANON-CTLN layers to freeze the dimensions in the small viewport (Figure 7.23).

- When a layer is frozen, the shining sun icon turns into a snowflake icon.

6 Click [OK].

7 Click the other viewport to make it active.

8 Freeze the I-FLOR-PATT and I-FURN layers in the current viewport.

- The floor plans in the two viewports now look different, yet they actually came from the same drawing in model space.

9 Click [MODEL] to return to paper space layout.

Step 10: Set the viewport layer as "non-plot."

Since the viewport frame should not be shown in your final presentation, you need to set the layer as a Non-plot layer.

1 Create layer I-ANON-NPLT (interior, annotation, non-plot) and click the plot icon to set it as a Non-plot layer.

The Plot icon turns into a Non-plot icon.

- When a layer is set as a Non-plot layer, it will not plot although you can see it on the screen.

2 Put both viewports onto the I-ANON-NPLT layer.

Step 11: Plot.

Now, you are ready to plot the drawing from the paper space layout. Before you start the following procedure, make sure the drawing is in the paper space mode (the status button shows [PAPER]). If you are still in the model space mode, you cannot plot the whole paper space layout.

1 Click the Plot icon in the standard toolbar. The Plot dialog box pops up.

- The plot settings for the paper space layout is very similar to model space plotting. The only significant difference is that for paper space plotting the scale should ALWAYS be (1″= 1″).

Figure 7.23
Freeze a layer in the current viewport.

Name	On	Freeze...	L.	Color	Linetype	Lineweight	Plot Style	Plot	Current...	New...
0				■ White	Continuous	—— Default	Color_7			
Defpoints				■ White	Continuous	—— Default	Color_7			
I-ANON-CTLN				White	CENTER2	—— Default	Color_7			
I-ANON-DIMS				White	Continuous	—— Default				
I-ANON-NOTE				■ White	Continuous	—— Default	Color_7			
I-DOOR				□ Yellow	Continuous	—— Default	Color_2			
I-FLOR CASE				■ Blue	Continuous	0.25 mm	Color_5			

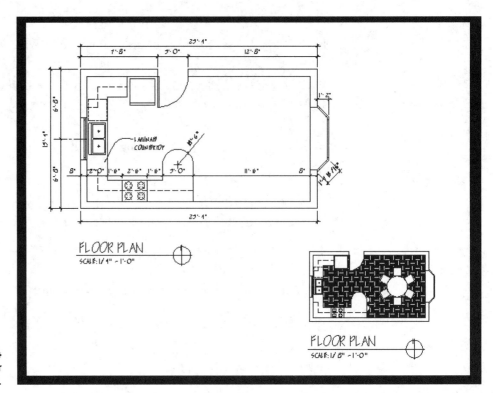

Figure 7.24
Full preview of the paper space layout plot.

2 Click the [Full Preview] button to check the plot setting.(Figure 7.24)

● The viewport boundaries disappear as a result of the non-plot layer setting.

3 Press [Esc] to exit the preview.

4 Click [OK] to plot the drawing.

5 Save drawing and exit AutoCAD.

Summary

In this chapter, you have learned the following concepts, procedures, and commands:

Knowledge/Concepts

● Model tab and paper space layouts

● Model space mode in paper space layouts

● Paper space mode in paper space layouts

● Plot Style Table

Procedures

- Plotter configuration
- Control lineweight
- Plot from model space layout
- Plot from paper space layout
- Set up viewports in paper space layout
- Move drawing entities from model space to paper space layout
- Edit texts
- Scale objects
- Control visibility in different viewports

Commands

- PLOT

- COPYCLIP (Copy to clipboard)

- PASTEBLOCK

- SCALE (SC)

- Single viewport (creation) tool

- EXPLODE (a block) (X)

Drawing an Elevation

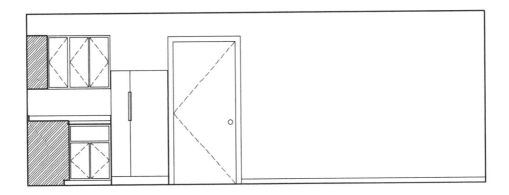

- Set up a new drawing using MVSETUP
- Attach an external reference file
- Draw an elevation
- Detach the external reference file

This chapter will show you the process of creating an interior elevation based on a floor plan. This approach is similar to that in manual drafting: projecting vertical lines from a floor plan. Although elevations can be generated from 3D models, this simple and straightforward approach is still the most widely used in the design profession. This chapter also serves as a review session that allows you to apply some of the most commonly used commands you learned in previous chapters, so that you can internalize them.

Setting Up a New Drawing Using MVSETUP

In Chapter 2, you learned a basic procedure to set up a new drawing. In that procedure, you used the real size of the space as a clue to figure out the limits of the drawing area. This is only one of the possible situations. When you start a new drawing, you may have a sheet size and a drawing scale in mind (e.g., 1/2″ scale on a 24″ × 18″ sheet). In this situation, you can use the MVSETUP (meaning Multiple View SETUP) command to let AutoCAD convert the sheet size to the site size according to the print scale.

1 **Start AutoCAD.** The AutoCAD Today window pops up.

2 **Click the minimize button to hide the AutoCAD Today window.** The Auto-CAD Today window closes and turns into a taskbar button at the bottom of the screen.

3 **Use MVSETUP to set up a new drawing (1/2″ scale on a 24″ × 18″sheet).**

Command: **MVSETUP** ↵	Start the MVSETUP command to set up a drawing sheet.
Initializing...	
Enable paper space? [No/Yes] <Y>: **N** ↵	**DON'T** say Yes.
Enter units type [Scientific/Decimal/ Engineering/Architectural/Metric]: **A** ↵	A for Architectural.
	The AutoCAD text window pops up with a list of scale factors.

Architectural Scales

(480)	1/40″	=	1′
(240)	1/20″	=	1′
(192)	1/16″	=	1′
(96)	1/8″	=	1′
(48)	1/4″	=	1′
(24)	1/2″	=	1′
(16)	3/4″	=	1′
(12)	1″	=	1′
(4)	3″	=	1′
(2)	6″	=	1′
(1)		FULL	

Enter the scale factor: **24** ↵   For 1/2″ scale.

Enter the paper width: **24** ↵

Enter the paper height: **18** ↵

Units type (Scientific/Decimal/
Engineering/Architectural/Metric):

Command: A rectangle paper boundary appears in drawing area.

● In this step, AutoCAD sets the drawing limits (48′ × 36′) for you.

4 SAVE the blank drawing as ch08.dwg.

5 Set SNAP spacing 1″ and turn it on.

6 Set the Object Snap toolbar.

7 Turn ORTHO on, if needed.

Attaching an External Reference File

In the design process, elevations are usually drawn based on floor plans. In manual drafting, you can put a sheet of vellum or tracing paper over a floor plan, and then project lines for the elevations. When drafting with AutoCAD, you can do the same by making the floor plan an "External Reference." External Reference is a very important function that allows you to display other drawings in a drawing you are working on and to use them as reference information. In this tutorial, we want to "borrow" (attach as external reference) the floor plan and use it to generate an elevation. After we finish the elevation, we will "return" the borrowed drawing by detaching it. One of the advantages of using External Reference is that it does not increase the file size of the current drawing file, while obtaining information from other drawings. Other External Reference applications will be discussed in later chapters.

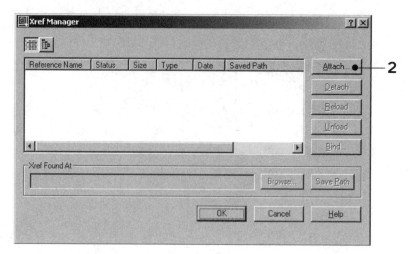

Figure 8.1
Xref Manager dialog box.

1 **Enter the XREF command.** The Reference Manager dialog box pops up (Figure 8.1).

2 Click [**Attach...**]. The Select Reference File dialog box pops up (Figure 8.2).

3 Click the **Look in list** to open the directory in which your drawings are stored.

4 **Select ch05 from the list.** Your floor plan shows in the Preview window.

5 Click [**Open**] to attach the selected file as an external reference. The External Reference dialog box pops up (Figure 8.3).

6 Click [**OK**]. AutoCAD prompts you for the insertion point.

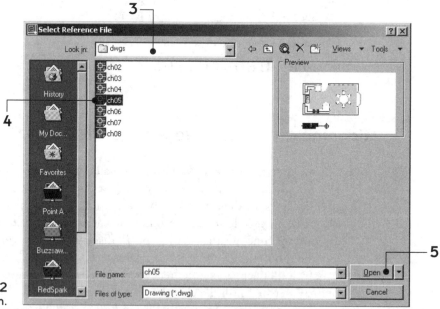

Figure 8.2
Select file to attach.

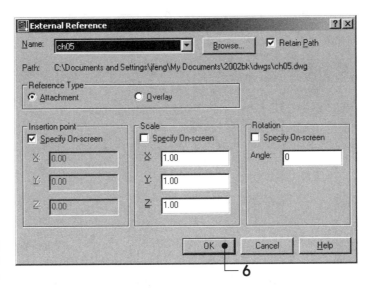

Figure 8.3
The External Reference
dialog box.

7 **Click anywhere in the drawing area** to land the floor plan. Leave some space above the floor plan for the elevation.

● This attached Xref is very much like an inserted block.

Drawing the Elevation

Step 1: Freeze unwanted layers.

When the floor plan is attached, all its layers can be controlled through the Layer Control window in the Property toolbar.

1 **Click the Layer list window.** The Layer list falls out.

● You may notice that the drawing name "ch05" is added to the layer names of the attached file. The layer names are all grayed to indicate that you cannot make changes to them except by freezing or thawing.

2 **Freeze the layers for the floor tile (Ch05|I-FLOR-PATT) and furniture (Ch05|I-FURN)** to simplify the floor plan.

Step 2: Define the floor and ceiling.

Let's assume that the ceiling height is 8′.

1 **Create a new layer, I-ELEV, and set it as current.**

2 **Draw a horizontal line above the floor plan as the floor line.**

3 **Use OFFSET to create a ceiling line 8′ above the floor line** (Figure 8.4).

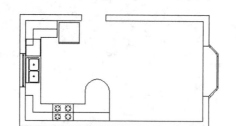

Figure 8.4
Define the floor and
ceiling.

Step 3: Draw vertical lines from the floor plan.

1 ZOOM in to look at the floor plan and the floor and ceiling lines as close as you can.

2 Use the LINE command to draw vertical lines from the floor plan (Figure 8.5).

● The running Endpoint object snap can be very handy in this process. But you have to be very careful to avoid unwanted snapping. If you choose to use the running object snap, don't forget to turn it off when you finish this process.

Step 4: Enclose the room elevation boundary.

1 Use the FILLET command to enclose the room elevation boundary (set r=0).

2 Use the TRIM command to trim off the unwanted portion of lines (Figure 8.6).

Step 5: Draw the door and casing.

1 Use OFFSET to define the top of the door (6'8″ above floor).

2 Use OFFSET to create the lines for a 3″ trim around the door.

3 Use FILLET to fix the corners (Figure 8.7).

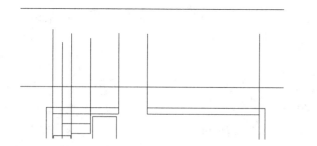

Figure 8.5
Draw vertical lines.

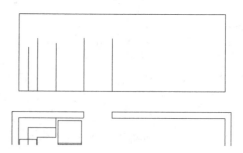

Figure 8.6
Enclose the room boundary.

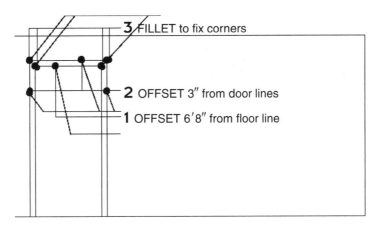

3 FILLET to fix corners

2 OFFSET 3″ from door lines

1 OFFSET 6′8″ from floor line

Figure 8.7
Draw the door and trim.

Step 6: Draw the door swing.

In elevations, you may need to indicate the swing direction of doors and windows.

1 Create a new layer and name it I-ELEV-DASH. Assign linetype HIDDEN2 for the layer. Make it current.

2 Turn on running Endpoint and Midpoint object snap.

3 Draw diagonal lines on the doors to indicate their swing (Figure 8.8).

4 Reset LTSCALE to show dash properly (if necessary).

5 Turn off running and point and Midpoint object snap.

6 Set I-ELEV layer as current (to draw more elevation lines).

Step 7: Draw the counter profile.

1 ZOOM in to look at the lower left corner of the elevation (Figure 8.9).

2 OFFSET to create a line 3′ above floor (as the countertop line).

3 OFFSET to create a line 1.5″ below the countertop line.

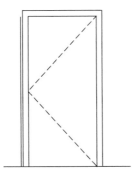

Figure 8.8
Draw the door swing.

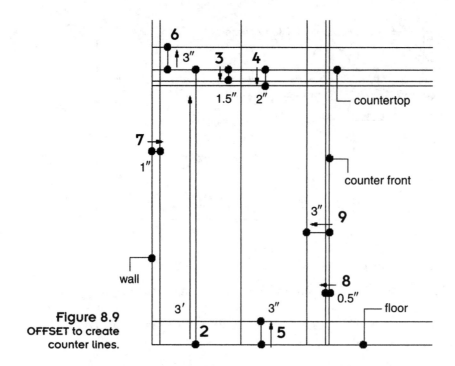

Figure 8.9
OFFSET to create
counter lines.

4 OFFSET to create a line 2″ below the countertop line.

5 OFFSET to create a line 3″ above the floor (as the toe-kick line).

6 OFFSET to create a line 3″ above the countertop line (as the top of back-splash).

7 OFFSET to create a line 1″ from the left wall (as the front of the back-splash).

8 OFFSET to create a line 0.5″ from the counter front (as the recess below the countertop).

9 OFFSET to create a line 3″ from the counter front (as the toe-kick recess).

● Since you created lines measured in some .5″ increments from each other, some of these lines fall in between the current 1″ SNAP grid. Therefore, you have to change the SNAP spacing to 0.5″ in order to snap to those lines.

Command: **SNAP** ↵

Specify snap spacing
or [ON/OFF/Aspect/Rotate/Style/Type]
<0′-1″>: **0.5** ↵

10 TRIM the backsplash (Figure 8.10).

11 ZOOM in to look at the front edge of the countertop.

12 Press [F9] to turn SNAP off.

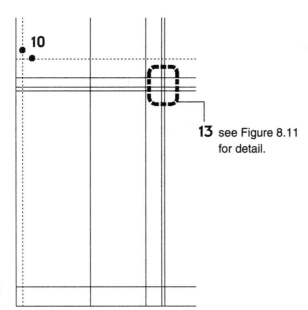

Figure 8.10
TRIM the backsplash.

13 see Figure 8.11 for detail.

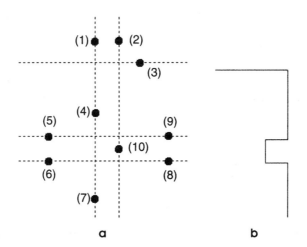

Figure 8.11
TRIM the front edge.

● Since you are not picking points, you can turn SNAP off to have a smooth cursor movement, making it easier to pick objects in the TRIM command.

13 TRIM the front edge and the recess following the order marked in Figure 8.11a. For result, see Figure 8.11b.

14 ZOOM out to see the elevation.

15 ZOOM in to look at the counter profile.

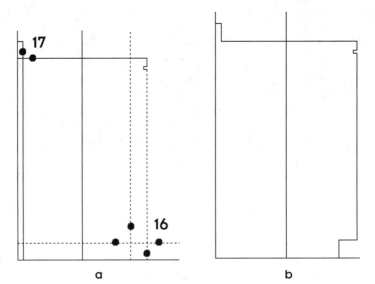

Figure 8.12
Finish the counter outline.

a   b

16 TRIM to finish the toe-kick (Figures 8.12a and 8.12b).

17 Use FILLET to connect the backsplash to the countertop.

Step 8: Draw the counter elevation.

1 Press [F9] to turn SNAP on.

2 Set running object snap mode to Endpoint and Perpendicular only.

3 Use LINE to draw lines from counter profile to the vertical counter end line (Figure 8.13).

4 Turn off running object snap (use [F3]).

Step 9: Draw the drawers and doors.

The drawers and doors of the counter are rectangles. In this step, the OFFSET and FIL-LET combination will be used to create the rectangles as we did in previous chapters. In addition, the BREAK command will be used to help make corner connections.

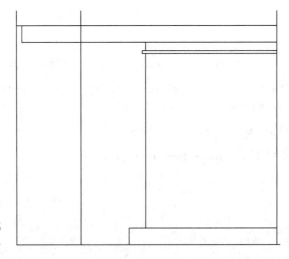

Figure 8.13
Counter elevation.

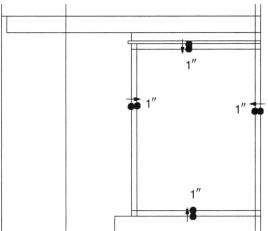

Figure 8.14
Create boundary for drawer and doors.

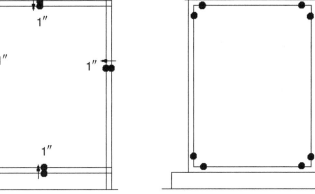

Figure 8.15
Connect the corners.

1 Use OFFSET to create boundary lines for the drawers and doors 1″ from the edges (Figure 8.14).

2 Use FILLET to connect the four corners (Figure 8.15).

3 Use OFFSET to define the upper boundary of the doors 20″ from the bottom (Figure 8.16).

4 Use OFFSET to define the lower boundary of the drawer 1″ above the door (Figure 8.16).

5 Use BREAK to break the side lines (Figure 8.17).

Command: **BREAK** ↵   The alias for BREAK is BR and its icon is.

Select object: **Pick point (1).**

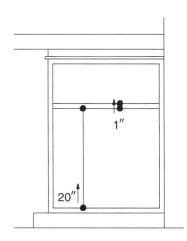

Figure 8.16
Define the drawer
and the doors.

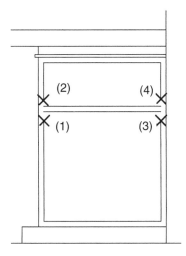

Figure 8.17
Break the side lines.

Specify second break point
or [First point]:
Pick point (2).

Command:

BREAK Select object:
Pick point (3).

Specify second break point
or [First point]: **Pick point (4).**

Command:

● The BREAK and FILLET combination is used here because the space between the drawer and the door may be too narrow for TRIM. By using this combination, you avoid a ZOOM command. Moreover, neither BREAK nor FILLET requires precise point picking. Therefore, it is a low-stress operation.

6 Use FILLET to connect the corners (Figure 8.18).

7 Use MIDpoint object snap to divide the door (Figure 8.18).

8 Use OFFSET to define a half-inch gap between the doors (OFFSET 0.25 from the center) (Figure 8.19).

9 BREAK the top and bottom lines of the door (to make corner connections) (Figure 8.19).

10 Use FILLET to connect the corners and ERASE the line at the middle (Figure 8.20).

11 Set running object snap mode to Endpoint and Midpoint only and turn it on.

12 Draw door swing lines (Figure 8.20).

13 Turn off running object snap (use [F3]).

14 Use the Match Properties tool to change the layer of the door swing lines.

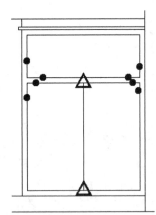

Figure 8.18
Divide the door.

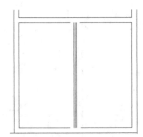

Figure 8.19
Create the doors.

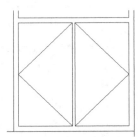

Figure 8.20
Create the doors and
door swing lines.

● Instead of using the Properties toolbar, you can use the Match Properties tool that allows you to change the properties of a drawing entity to match those of a "source object." In this case, the swing of the entrance door has been correctly set, and you can use it as a "source object" to let the swing of the base cabinet doors match it.

**ZOOM out to look at the counter
and the entrance door.**   (Figure 8.21)

 **Click the Match Properties icon
on the standard toolbar.**

Command: '_matchprop

Select source object: **Pick line [A].**

Current active settings: Color Layer
Ltype Ltscale Lineweight Thickness

PlotStyle Text Dim Hatch

Select destination object(s) or [Settings]:
Pick line [B].

Select destination object(s) or [Settings]:
Pick line [C].

Select destination object(s) or [Settings]:
Pick line [D].

Select destination object(s) or [Settings]:
Pick line [E].

Select destination object(s) or [Settings]: ↵   The lines change into dashed
                                                  lines (Figure 8.22).

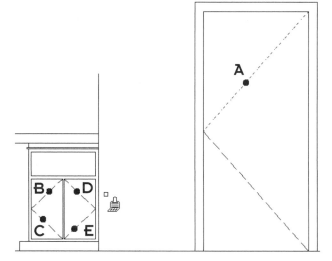

Figure 8.21
Change the layer of the door swing lines.

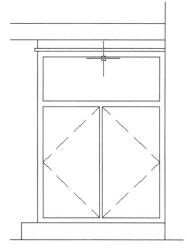

Figure 8.22
The layer changed.

- This is a very handy tool to have to change object properties when you need a "source object" to match.

Step 10: Draw the wall cabinet.

Draw the outline of the wall cabinet

1 ZOOM out to see the left half of the elevation.

2 OFFSET to create the bottom line of the wall cabinet (18″ above countertop) (Figure 8.23a).

3 OFFSET to create the top line of the wall cabinet (30″ above the bottom line).

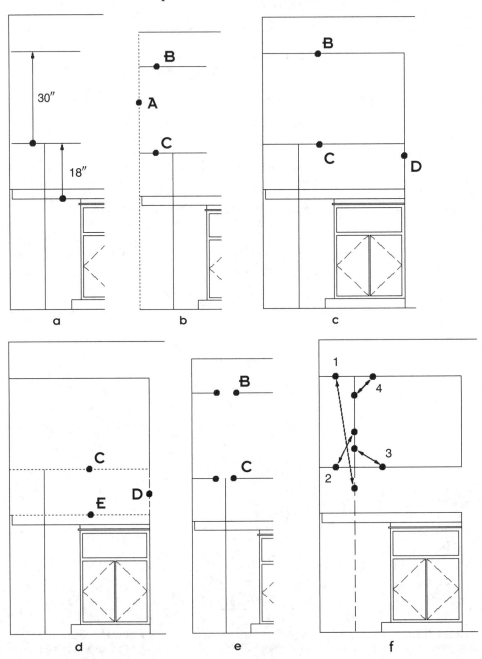

Figure 8.23
Draw the outline of the wall cabinet.

4 EXTEND the lines [B] and [C] to wall line [A] (Figure 8.23b).

5 Use FILLET to link bottom line [C] to side line [D] (Figure 8.23c).

6 Use FILLET to link top line [B] to side line [D] (Figure 8.23c).

7 TRIM side line [D] with line [C] and line [E] (Figure 8.23d).

8 BREAK continuous top and bottom lines [B] and [C] (Figure 8.23e).

9 Use FILLET to connect corners following the order from (1) to (4) (Figure 8.23f).

● This is another example of using the BREAK and FILLET combination.

Draw the wall cabinet doors

In AutoCAD drafting, you should make the best use of the duplication functions to reduce repetitive labor. In this step, you will use the COPY command to create the wall cabinet doors, even when the heights of the doors are different. You will use the STRETCH command to resize the copied doors.

1 COPY the base cabinet doors to the wall cabinet. Use Endpoint object snap to ensure the accurate location of the copied cabinet doors (Figure 8.24).

2 STRETCH the top of the cabinet doors up 8″ (Figure 8.25a).

3 STRETCH the hinge point of the door swing lines up 4″ (to make it to the midpoint of the cabinet doors) (Figure 8.25b).

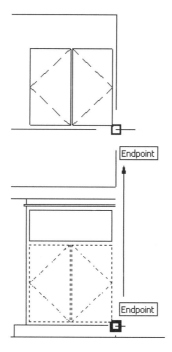

Figure 8.24
Create the wall cabinet doors.

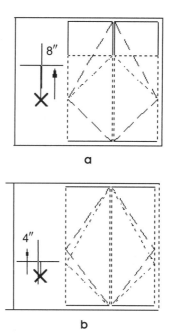

Figure 8.25
Stretch the wall cabinet doors.

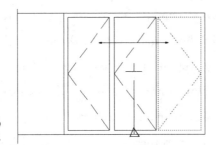

Figure 8.26
Create the third door.

4 Use MIRROR to create the third wall cabinet door. Use the midpoint of the wall cabinet outline to define the mirror line (Figure 8.26).

Step 11: HATCH the cabinet sections.

According to the architectural drawing convention, you need to hatch the sections of the wall cabinet and the counter with 45° lines. Use the BHATCH command to do this.

1 Create a new layer and name it I-ELEV-PATT. Set it as current.

2 Use BHATCH to fill the profile of the counter. (Use User-defined hatch pattern: Angle = 45, Spacing = 1″.)

3 Use BHATCH to fill the wall cabinet section (Figure 8.27).

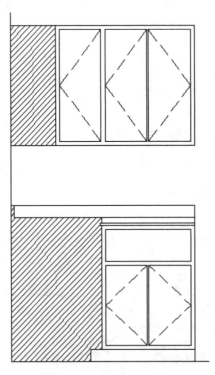

Figure 8.27
Hatch the section.

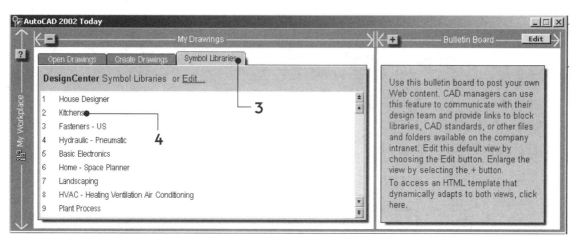

Figure 8.28
Access the Symbol Libraries.

Step 12: Create the refrigerator using the AutoCAD symbol library.

In this step, you will use the AutoCAD symbol library to create the refrigerator elevation, and then adjust the scale of the inserted block to make it fit.

1 Set the I-ELEV layer current.

 2 Click the **AutoCAD 2002 Today** button on the standard toolbar to bring up the AutoCAD Today window (Figure 8.28).

3 Click the **Symbol Libraries tab.** The library page turns up.

4 Click **Kitchen.** A side panel opens with symbols in it (Figure 8.29).

5 Find the refrigerator elevation, **DRAG** it into the drawing window, and release the mouse button to **DROP** it between the counter and the door (Figure 8.29).

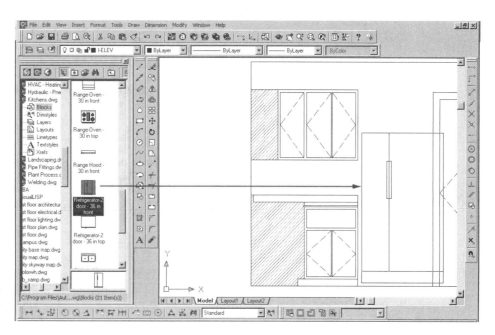

Figure 8.29
Drag-and-drop the
refrigerator symbol.

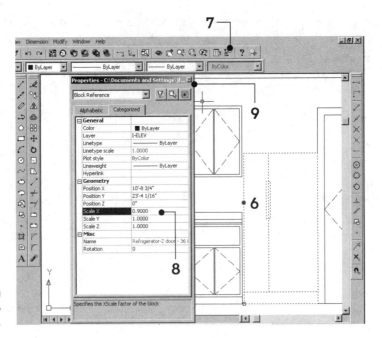

Figure 8.30
Change the width of the
refrigerator.

6 Click the refrigerator. The grips appear.

7 Click the Properties icon on the standard toolbar.

8 Change the x-scale factor value of the refrigerator block from 1 to 0.9 to reduce the width of the refrigerator and to make it fit (Figure 8.30).

9 Click the Close button to close the Properties tool window.

10 Click the Close button to close the symbol library.

11 Use MOVE command to refine the final location of the refrigerator.

Step 13: Draw the baseboard.

1 ZOOM out to see the whole room elevation.

2 OFFSET to create the baseboard line (3″ from floor).

3 TRIM off unwanted portion of the baseboard line (Figure 8.31).

Step 14: Draw the doorknob.

Use CIRCLE command to draw a doorknob ($R=1″$) approximately 3′ above floor. (Use the height of the counter top as a reference.)

Step 15: Layer and lineweight control.

Up to this point, you have finished all the lines. Since in the drawing process lines are created by duplication, it is difficult to keep everything in its appropriate layers. Now, it is time to get organized and to make your drawing look more beautiful by using good layer and lineweight control. According to architectural drawing conven-

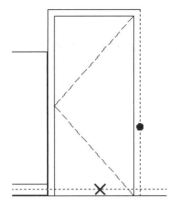

Figure 8.31
TRIM baseboard lines.

tions, you may have two different lineweights: (1) the outline of the space and section profiles, and (2) visible lines. You can make a layer list as follows:

Drawing Object	Layer Name	Color
Visible lines	I-ELEV	7 (white)
Space outline	I-ELEV-OTLN	1 (red)
Door swing	I-ELEV-DASH	4 (cyan)
Hatch patterns	I-ELEV-PATT	6 (magenta)

Control layers

1 Create layer I-ELEV-OTLN.

2 Freeze the I-ELEV-DASH and I-ELEV-PATT layers.

3 Use the Properties toolbar to change the layer of all the room profile lines and the cabinet profile lines to I-ELEV-OTLN.

4 Change colors of layers according to the list (if needed).

5 Thaw all layers.

Change lineweight

In Chapter 7 you learned how to use Plot Style Table to plot the floor plan with different lineweights. You can use the same approach in this case, but one problem of that approach is that the lineweight is not visible until you plot the drawing out. AutoCAD actually allows you to assign lineweights to layers and objects. In the following tutorial, we will assign a heavier lineweight to the I-ELEV-OTLN layer.

1 **Click the Layer icon in the Properties toolbar.** The Layer Properties Manager dialog box pops up (Figure 8.32).

Figure 8.32
Change lineweight for
I-ELEV-OTLN layer.

2 **Click the I-ELEV-OTLN layer at the Lineweight section.** The Lineweight dialog box pops up (Figure 8.33).

3 Select 0.50 mm.

4 Click [OK].

5 **Click [OK] to close the Layer Properties Manager dialog box.**

6 **Click the [LWT] button in the status line.**

● The [LWT] button toggles the display of assigned lineweight. The display of the assigned lineweight may look thicker than what it should be because it is simulated using a fixed number of pixels. You may adjust the setting to make it look better. This visual on-screen distortion of the lineweight, however, will not affect that of the plotted drawing.

7 **Click the Tools menu, and select Options.** The Options dialog box pops up.

8 **Click the User Preferences tab.**

9 **Click [Lineweight Settings...].** The Lineweight Settings dialog box pops up (Figure 8.34).

10 **Drag the Adjust Display Scale slider one mark beyond Min.**

11 **Click [Apply & Close].**

12 **Click [OK] to close the Options dialog box.** The outlines look thinner (Figure 8.35).

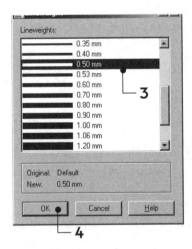

Figure 8.33
Select lineweight

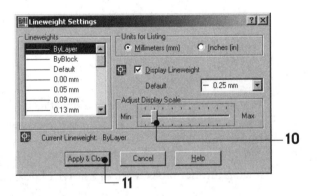

Figure 8.34
Adjust lineweight display scale.

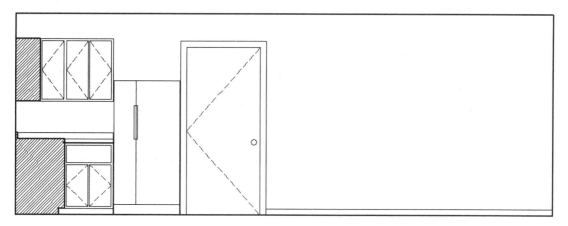

Figure 8.35
Display of lineweight.

Detaching the External Reference File

Since you have finished the elevation, you may detach the external reference file.

1 ZOOM out to see the whole drawing.

2 Use XREF to bring up the External Reference dialog box (Figure 8.36).

3 Click ch05 to highlight it.

4 Click [Detach]. The file information disappears.

5 Click [OK]. The attached floor plan disappears.

6 Save your drawing and exit AutoCAD.

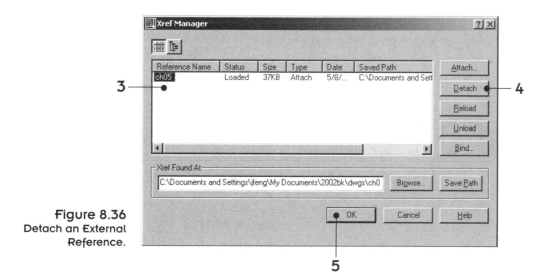

Figure 8.36
Detach an External
Reference.

Summary

In this chapter, you learned how to create an interior elevation based on a floor plan. Most of the drawing tools used in this process are familiar ones you already learned in the previous chapters. The general approach is the same as the one used in creating the floor plan: LINE-OFFSET-FILLET-TRIM. These reused drawing processes in this new application may help you to become familiar with them and use them more creatively in future applications.

In this chapter, you have learned the following concepts, procedures, and commands:

Knowledge/Concepts

- External reference
- Assigned on-screen lineweight

Procedures

- Set up a new drawing with MVSETUP
- Attach an external reference file
- Detach an external reference file
- Break a line
- Modify block insertion settings
- Match properties
- Set layer lineweight

Commands

- MVSETUP

- XREF

- BREAK (BR)

- Match Properties tool

Draw a Detail

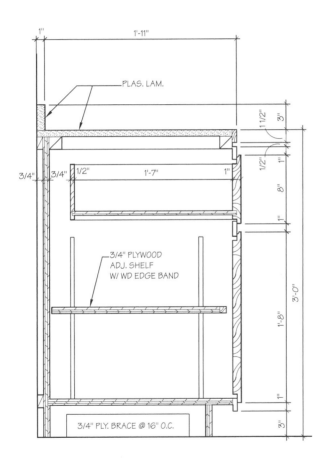

- Prepare to draw a detail
- Draw the detail lines
- Draw material symbols
- Create dimensions and notes

In this chapter, you will create a section detail of a kitchen counter. In the process, you will use a portion of the elevation you created in the previous chapter and fill in more details with some basic drawing and editing commands.

Preparations

Step 1: Set up a new drawing using Wizard.

In this step, we want to set up a new drawing using the Create Drawings wizard.

1 **Start AutoCAD.** The AutoCAD Today window pops up (Figure 9.1).

2 **Click the Create Drawings tab.**

3 **Select Wizards from the Select how to begin drop-down list.**

4 **Click Quick Setup.** The Quick Setup dialog box pops up with the Units page displayed (Figure 9.2).

5 **Check Architectural.**

6 **Click [Next].** The Quick Setup dialog box shows the page area (Figure 9.3).

7 **Enter 8′ in the Width field.**

8 **Enter 6′ in the Length field.**

● Since the size of the counter profile is 2′ wide × 3′ high, a drawing area of 8′ × 6′ will be enough to hold the drawing with margins. Steps 7 and 8 actually set the drawing limits, as did the command LIMITS in Chapter 2.

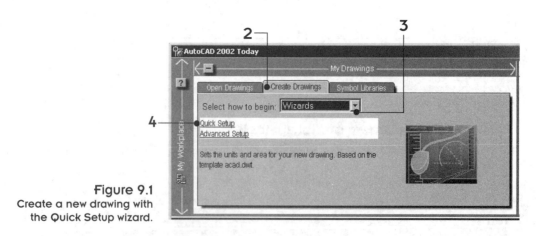

Figure 9.1
Create a new drawing with the Quick Setup wizard.

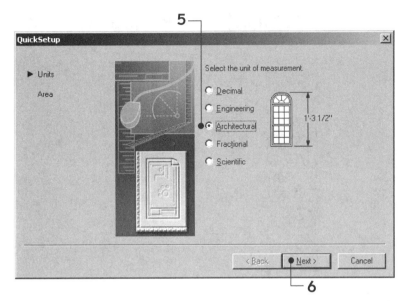

Figure 9.2
Set up unit format.

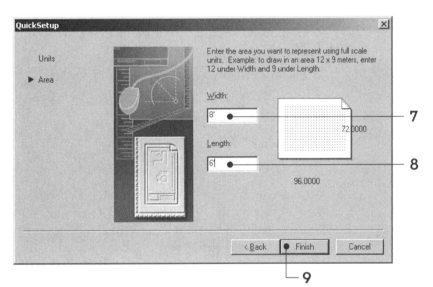

Figure 9.3
Set up drawing area.

9 Click [Finish]. The Quick Setup dialog box closes.

10 Save the drawing as ch09.

Step 2: Load the usable from the elevation drawing.

When you open a drawing, you can choose to open a certain part of that drawing in order to reduce the loaded file size and to simplify your task. When you work with large-sized files, the effect of this function will become more significant. In this tutorial we want to use the outline of the kitchen counter. Therefore, we will use the partial opening to load only the I-ELEV-OTLN layer.

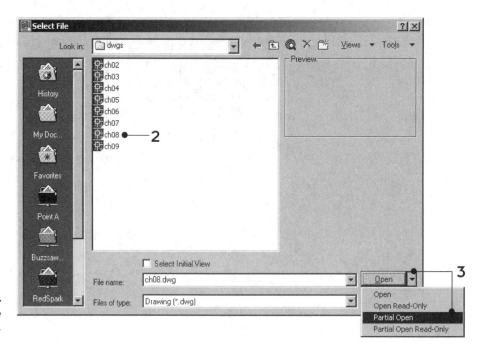

Figure 9.4
The Select File
dialog box.

1 **Click the Open icon on the standard toolbar.** The Select File dialog box pops up (Figure 9.4).

2 **Find file ch08.dwg and select it.**

3 **Click the drop-down button next to [Open] and select Partial Open.** The Partial Open dialog box pops up (Figure 9.5).

4 **Check the box next to the I-ELEV-OTLN layer name.**

5 **Click [Open].** The drawing opens (Figure 9.6).

● You may have observed that the hatch patterns are loaded in spite of the fact that you did not select the I-ELEV-PATT layer. This is because the hatch patterns are associated with the outline as their boundaries. You can freeze the I-ELEV-PATT layer to hide the hatch patterns from view.

6 **Freeze the I-ELEV-PATT layer.**

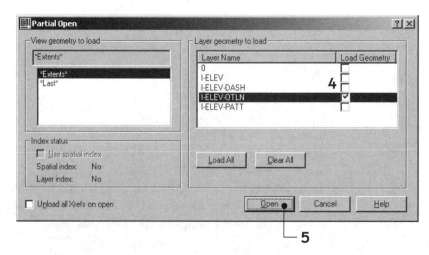

Figure 9.5
The Partial Open
dialog box.

Figure 9.6
Partially loaded
ch08.dwg.

Step 3: Set up tiled windows.

After you set up the new drawing, you have two drawings that are open simultaneously. You can grab a selection of drawing elements in one drawing and drop them into the other. Setting up two drawing windows side by side allows you to see both drawings and thus make the drag-and-drop operation easy and intuitive.

1 Click the Window menu and select Tile vertically. Two windows are set side by side (Figure 9.7).

2 Click the window showing the elevation to make it active.

● Only one window can be active at one time. The active status of the window is indicated by the color of the title bar. If the color of the title bar turns gray, it is not active.

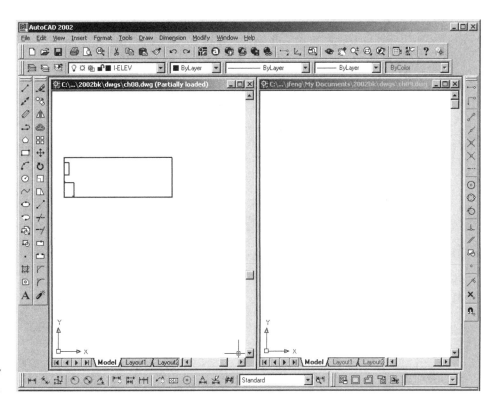

Figure 9.7
Multiple drawing windows.

Step 4: Copy the counter profile from ch08.dwg to ch09.dwg.

1 ZOOM to see the whole image of the elevation profile lines.

2 Select (with a crossing window) the counter outline, the floor line, and the wall next to the counter. Grips appear.

3 Click one of the selected lines (not at a grip) and hold down the left mouse button to drag the selected elements into the other drawing window and release the button to drop them.

- "Drag" means to move the mouse while holding the left mouse button.

- After copying the usable drawing elements from ch08.dwg to ch09.dwg, ch08.dwg is no longer useful. You want to close it to make space for ch09.

4 Click the Close button at the upper-right corner of the drawing window. An AutoCAD warning dialog box pops up asking if you want to save the drawing.

5 Click [No]. The drawing window closes.

6 Click the Maximize button of the remaining window. The window expands to fill the AutoCAD window.

7 ZOOM out to see all the drawing elements.

8 Using grips to shorten the wall line and the floor line.

Step 5: Put the drawing elements back on the snap grid.

In the process of dragging and dropping, the copied drawing elements usually fall out of the snap grid even when the snap is on. It is important to put them back on the grid to ensure accuracy.

1 MOVE the drawing elements.

Command: **M** ↵

MOVE

Select objects: **Pick point**
Specify opposite corner:
Pick point 12 found

Use an implied window to select all drawing elements.

Select objects: ↵

Specify base point or displacement:
END ↵

of **pick the lower left corner**

Specify second point of displacement
or <use first point as displacement>: **12,12** ↵

- The second point (12,12) is simply a conveniently picked point on the snap grid that is 1′ from the corner of the defined drawing area.

2 ZOOM to look at the counter profile closely.

Drawing the Detail Lines

Step 1: Draw the lines.

1 Set SNAP spacing to 1/4″.

● In a detail drawing, you need to deal in fraction-of-an-inch measurements.

2 Use EXTEND, OFFSET, TRIM, FILLET, LINE, and CIRCLE to draw lines of the detail section according to dimensions given in Figure 9.8. (Don't draw the dimension.)

3 Create layer I-DETL (Interior, Detail). Make sure the lineweight is set at Default.

4 Change the layer of all the lines of the detail section to I-DETL.

Step 2: Create a profile line set.

In a detail section of the cabinetry, the profile lines (the boundaries of the materials being cut) need to be enhanced with a lineweight heavier than that of visible lines. Whatever approach you take (printer pen assignment or layer lineweight), the separation of the profile lines and the visible lines is essential.

In this step, let's try to create a profile line set based on the lines you just finished.

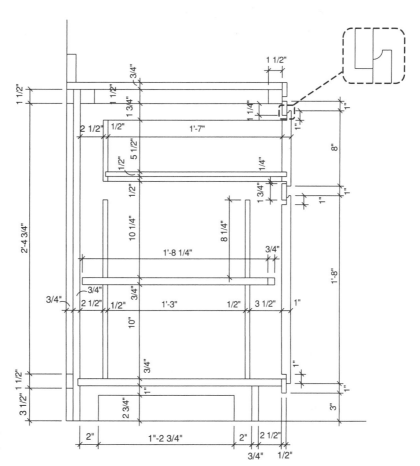

Figure 9.8
Lines of the detail section.

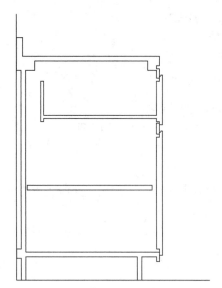

Figure 9.9
The profile line set.

1 Create layer I-DETL-MCUT (Interior, Detail, Material being cut). Set color red for the layer and set the lineweight to 0.5 mm.

2 Make a COPY of the detail drawing and place it in an empty space.

3 Use TRIM, FILLET, and ERASE to create the profiles as shown in Figure 9.9.

4 Change the layer of the profiles to I-DETL-MCUT.

5 MOVE the profile line set on top of the original line set.

● This move must be precise. Use Endpoint object snap to catch movement defining points as in Figure 9.10.

6 Click the [LWT] button to turn on the lineweight display. The lineweight effect shows (Figure 9.11).

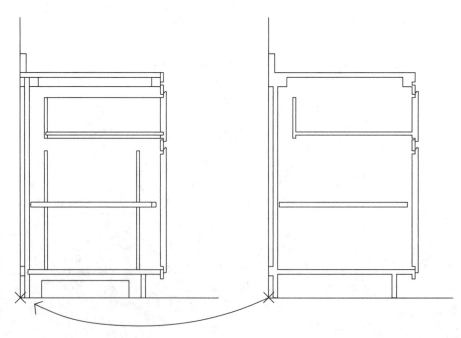

Figure 9.10
Move the profile line set
on to the original set.

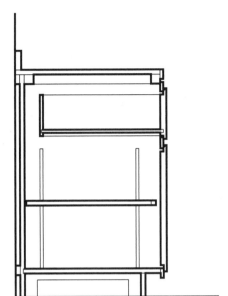

Figure 9.11
Completed heavy profile
lines.

Drawing Material Symbols

Step 1: Draw the lumber material symbol.

1 Create layer I-DETL-PATT (Interior, Detail, Pattern) and set it as the current layer.

2 Draw the diagonals to represent unfinished lumber as shown in Figure 9.12. (Use LINE command with object snap.)

Step 2: Draw the particleboard material symbol.

To draw material symbols, it is best to use the BHATCH command, especially when you can find a hatch pattern to meet your need.

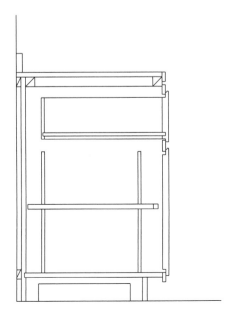

Figure 9.12
Draw diagonal lines on
lumber parts.

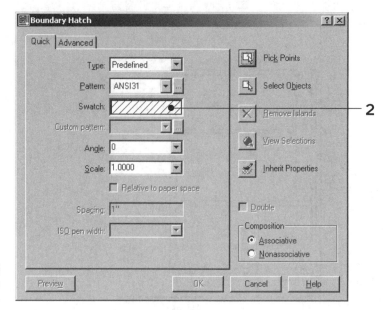

Figure 9.13
The Boundary Hatch
dialog box.

1 Enter BHATCH to hatch the particleboard. The Boundary Hatch dialog box pops up (Figure 9.13).

2 Click the Swatch window. The Hatch Pattern Palette dialog box pops up (Figure 9.14).

3 Click the Other Predefined tab. The dialog box flips a page.

4 Click on the sand pattern (AR-SAND).

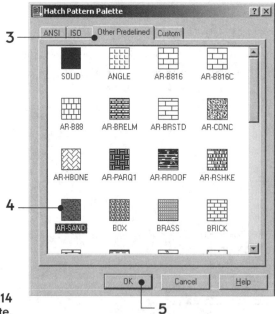

Figure 9.14
Hatch pattern palette.

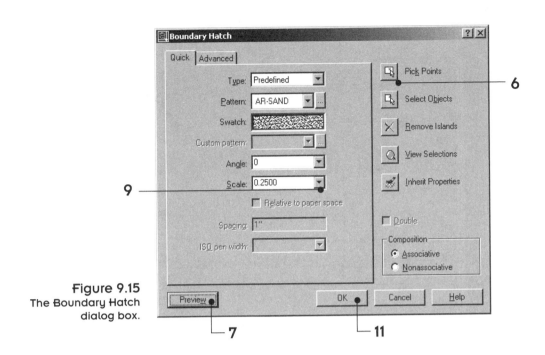

Figure 9.15
The Boundary Hatch
dialog box.

5 Click [OK]. The Boundary Hatch dialog box reappears (Figure 9.15). AR-SAND pattern appears in the Pattern window.

6 Click [Pick Points] and click inside the spaces to be hatched (the backsplash board, the countertop board, and the front board). Press [Enter] when you finish. The Boundary Hatch dialog box reappears.

● AutoCAD will detect the hatch boundary only if the entire boundary is shown on screen. Temporarily turning off snap may help when picking the small areas.

7 Click [Preview]. Hatch pattern shown as currently set. You may feel that the density of the dots is too low, especially in small areas.

8 Right-click to go back to the previous dialog box.

9 Click the Scale list and select 0.25 to increase the density.

● The value of the scale factor is decided based on visual observations of the preview.

10 Repeat 7 and 8 to re-examine the appearance of the pattern.

11 Click [OK] to end the command (Figure 9.16).

Step 3: Draw the plywood symbol.

The Hatch Pattern Palette does not have a ready-made (predefined) pattern for the plywood symbol. You need to draw it yourself by combining two simple hatch patterns.

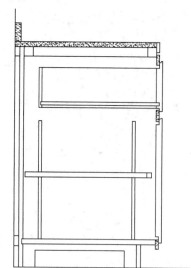

Figure 9.16
Hatch pattern for
particleboard.

1 ZOOM in to look at the shelf as closely as possible (Figure 9.17a).

2 Use BHATCH to fill the core of the shelf with the User-Defined parallel line pattern (**spacing = 0.25″, angle = 0**). The space is divided into three layers (Figure 9.17b).

3 EXPLODE the hatch pattern.

● Only when a hatch pattern is exploded can the components be used as boundaries of other hatch patterns.

4 Turn SNAP off (use the [F9] key).

5 Use BHATCH to fill the first and third layers with the User Defined parallel line pattern (**spacing = 1″, angle = 45**) (Figure 9.17c).

6 Use BHATCH to fill the second layer with the User Defined parallel line pattern (**spacing =1″, angle = 135**) (Figure 9.17d).

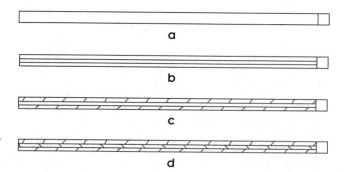

Figure 9.17
Hatch the plywood shelf.

Step 4: Draw the wood grain.

Since the wood grain is not included in the standard hatch pattern palette, you have to draw it. A simple way of drawing it is to use the ARC command.

1 ZOOM in to look at the edge band of the shelf.

2 Turn ORTHO off.

3 Set running object snap mode to Nearest only.

 ● The Nearest object snap allows you to snap to the nearest object. You will use it to ensure the arc starts and ends from points on the edge of the shape. For the one-time-only application of this object snap mode, you can either key in NEAR or click the icon.

4 Start the ARC (A) command.

Command: **A** ↵

ARC Specify start point of arc
or [CEnter]: **Pick point (1).**

Use Nearest object snap to catch the edge (Figure 9.18).

Specify second point of arc
or [CEnter/ENd]: **Pick point (2).**

Specify end point of arc:
Pick point (3).

An arc is defined by three points.

Command: ↵

Restart the ARC command.

ARC Specify start point of arc
or [CEnter]: **Pick point (4).**

Specify second point of arc
or [CEnter/ENd]: **Pick point (5).**

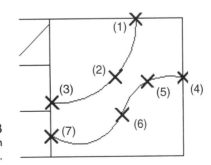

Figure 9.18
Draw the wood grain with ARC.

Specify end point of arc: **Pick point (6).**

Command: ↵   Restart the ARC command.

ARC Specify start point of arc or [CEnter]: ↵   Continue from the endpoint of
                                                 the last arc.

Specify end point of arc: **Pick point (7).**

Command:

- This combination of two smoothly connected arcs creates a natural-looking curve. You may combine the simple arc and combined arc to create unlimited variety.

Step 5: Draw more material symbols.

1 Draw the wood grain pattern in the front and back of the drawer and in the door.

2 Hatch the bottom of the drawer and the counter with the plywood symbol.

3 Hatch the back and the baseboard of the counter with the plywood symbol.

- The User-Defined hatch pattern for the layer of the plywood needs to be turned 90° for the vertical plywood.

- See Figure 9.19 for completed material symbols.

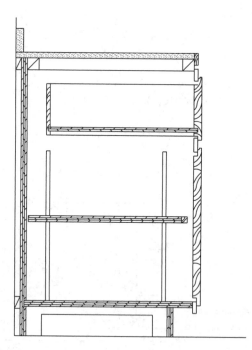

Figure 9.19
Material symbols.

Creating Dimensions and Notes

As you learned in Chapter 6, you need dimension styles and text styles to create dimensions and notes. Instead of repeating the steps as you did before to set the styles in this drawing, you can load them from ch06.dwg by using the AutoCAD DesignCenter.

Step 1: Load a dimension style.

AutoCAD DesignCenter allows you to load many drawing settings, in addition to symbol blocks, into a drawing from other drawings. Dimension style is one of the settings you can load. Since you need to dimension this counter detail, you can load the dimension style from ch06.dwg instead of redefining it from scratch.

1 **Click the AutoCAD DesignCenter icon in the standard toolbar.** The AutoCAD DesignCenter appears as a tiled window (Figure 9.20).

2 **Click the Load icon.** The Load DesignCenter Palette dialog box pops up (Figure 9.20).

3 **Click the Look in list and choose the directory where you saved the Chapter 6 drawing.** The list of .dwg files appears.

4 **Click the Chapter 6 drawing to highlight it.**

5 **Click [Open].** The Load DesignCenter Palette dialog box closes. The categories of usable entities appear in the DesignCenter panel (Figure 9.21).

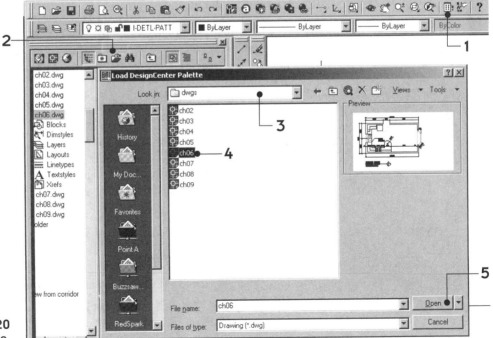

Figure 9.20
Select the file.

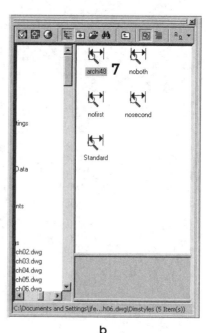

a   b

Figure 9.21
DesignCenter categories.

6 **Double-click Dimstyles.** All dimension styles stored in the Chapter 6 drawing show on the panel.

7 **Click archi48 to highlight it.**

8 **Drag it into the drawing window and release the held mouse button to drop it into the drawing.** AutoCAD says in the prompt area: Dimstyle(s) added. Duplicate definitions will be ignored.

● From the Look for list in the Find dialog box, you can see that through the Auto-CAD DesignCenter you can load blocks, dimension styles, drawings, layers, layouts, linetypes, text styles, and external references. The procedure is similar: find it, drag it, and drop it.

Step 2: Load a text style.

Loading a text style is basically the same as loading a dimension style.

1 **Click the Up icon in the AutoCAD DesignCenter to go back to the category level.** The categories show in the panel.

2 **Double-click Textstyles.**

3 **Double-click Notes.** AutoCAD says in the prompt area: Textstyle(s) added. Duplicate definitions will be ignored.

● Double-clicking an item in the DesignCenter panel equals dragging and dropping.

4 **Click the Close button to close AutoCAD DesignCenter.**

Step 3: Create a new dimension style for a different scale.

Since archi48 was originally set for dimensioning the floor plan at 1/4″ scale, the geometric features will be too big for the detail drawing. After loading archi48 from ch06.dwg, you need to create a new dimension style based on Archi48 for 1 1/2″ scale drawings.

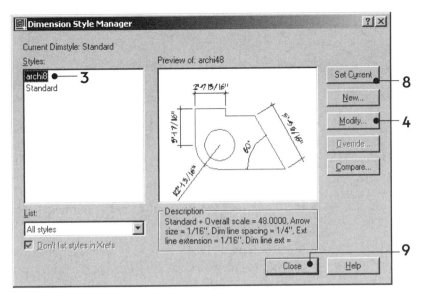

Figure 9.22
Dimension Style Manager
dialog box.

1 Set the Dimension toolbar.

2 Click the Dimension Style icon in the Dimension toolbar. The Dimension Style Manager dialog box pops up (Figure 9.22).

3 Click the archi48 style name in Styles and rename it archi8. The number 8 in the name represents the scale factor for 1 1/2″ scale.

4 Click [Modify]. The Modify Dimension Style dialog box pops up.

5 Click the Fit tab. The dialog turns to the Fit page (Figure 9.23).

6 Change the Use Overall Scale of value from 48 to 8.

7 Click [OK]. The Dimension Styles Manager dialog box comes back.

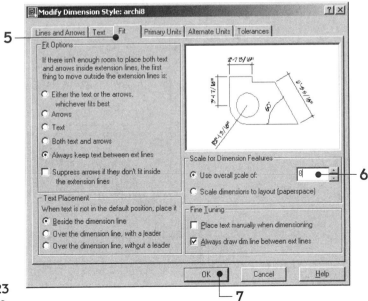

Figure 9.23
Set overall scale.

8 Click [Set Current] to make the archi8 style the current dimension style (Figure 9.22).

9 Click [Close].

Step 4: Add dimension and notes.

1 ZOOM to look at the entire detail section allowing some space around it (for dimension).

2 Create a new layer I-DETL-DIMS (Interior, Detail, Dimension) and set it as current.

3 Use dimension tools from the toolbar to draw dimensions and leaders as shown in Figure 9.24.

● When you use DTEXT to type in note texts, the text height should be 1″ to match the dimension text. The text height = dimension text height (1/8″) × overall dimension scale (8).

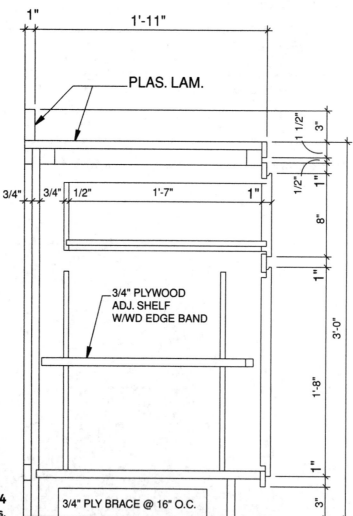

Figure 9.24
Dimensions and notes.

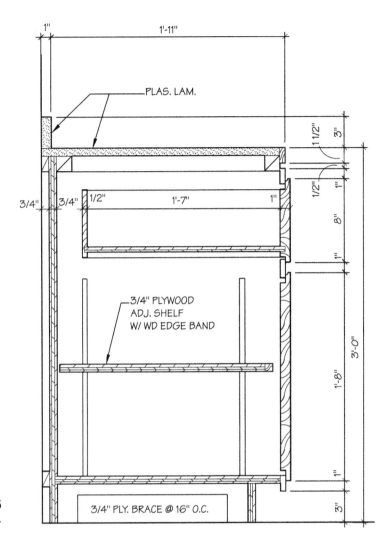

Figure 9.25
Completed detail drawing.

4 Thaw the **I-DETL-PATT** and **I-DETL-MCUT** layers to see the completed detail section (Figure 9.25).

5 Save your drawing and exit.

Summary

In this tutorial, you created a section detail of a kitchen counter. Although the drawing is simplified, it contains the major components of a detail drawing-visible lines, section profile lines, material symbols, dimension, and notes. The general procedure includes the following steps:

1. Borrow the profile from elevation drawings.

2. Construct visible lines with OFFSET, EXTEND, TRIM, and FILLET.

3. Enhance the section profile lines with lineweight setting.

4. Load dimension and text styles from another drawing.

5. Create new dimension style for a different scale.

6. Draw material symbols.

7. Draw dimensions and place notes.

In this chapter, you have learned the following new concepts, procedures, and commands:

Knowledge/concept

- Partial open of a drawing
- Tiled drawing windows

Procedures

- Use wizard to start a new drawing
- Import drawing elements into the current drawing from other drawings
- Import dimension and text styles by using the AutoCAD DesignCenter
- Drag-and-drop copy of drawing element
- Move objects back to snap grid
- Use predefined hatch patterns with a scale
- Explode hatch patterns
- Draw continuous arcs
- Use Nearest object snap

Command

 ● Nearest (NEAR)

Chapter 10

Assembling the Finished Drawing

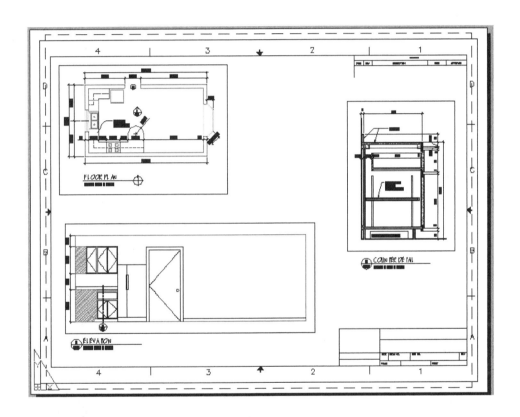

- Set up the sheet file
- Create reference symbols
- Create drawing titles
- Create annotation markers
- Create dimensions in paper space layout
- Create a drawing template

Up to this point, you have finished the floor plan, the elevation, and the counter detail. In this tutorial, you will put these components together to make a finished drawing, that is, the drawing file ready for plotting. This drawing file is also called a sheet file, as suggested in the *CAD Layer Guidelines* compiled by The American Institute of Architects. In these files, the component drawings are linked as external reference files and shown in viewports in a paper space layout with a title block.

Setting Up the Sheet File

Step 1: Create a new drawing using a template.

AutoCAD has many standard drawing templates that you can use to start a new drawing.

1 **Start AutoCAD.** The AutoCAD 2002 Today window pops up (Figure 10.1a).

2 **Click the Create Drawing tab.**

3 **Click the Select how to begin list, then select Template.** An alphabetical index list appears.

4 **Click the "A" template group.** The "A" template list appears (Figure 10.1b).

5 Select ANSI_c -color dependent plot style.dwt from the list. A layout with title block and border appears (Figure 10.2).

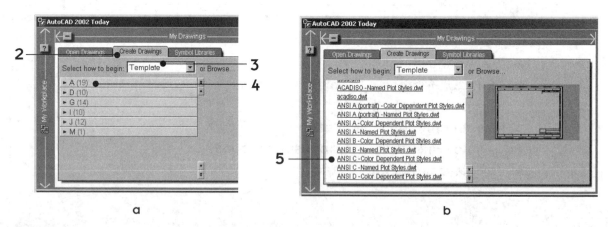

a   b

Figure 10.1
Startup - Use a Template dialog boxes.

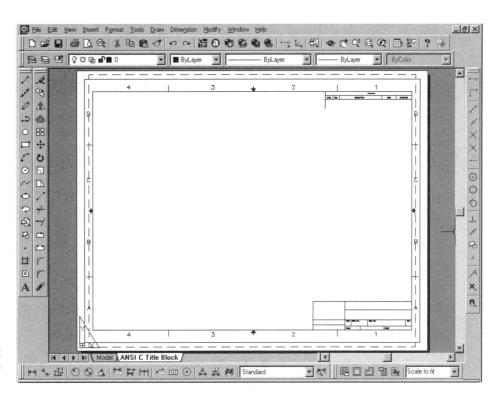

Figure 10.2
Create a new drawing with
a template.

● ANSI stands for American National Standard Institute, and "c" is the C drawing size. The ANSI_c.dwt template file is stored in the Template directory under Acad.

6 Set UNITS to Architectural.

7 Save the drawing as Ch10.dwg.

● The ansi_c.dwt drawing template is a generic drawing sheet that may be used for many disciplines. It has only standard text and dimension styles and three layers: 0, Title Block, and Viewport. A large polygon viewport fills the drawing area.

● There are two .dwt files for each sheet size: one for color dependent plot styles and the other for named plot styles. Since the former is the commonly used method, you should choose the one with color dependent plot styles when you select a template.

Step 2: Use XREF to attach drawing files.

In today's design practice, a drawing for final printing is usually made of a few interconnected files through external referencing. The file for final printing (or the sheet file) may have only the connections to other drawing files (called model files). In this step, you will assemble a drawing using XREF and organize the components in paper space layout.

1 Click the Model tab. An empty drawing appears.

2 Set drawing LIMITS to 60′ × 60′.

● The default limit size of the model space is 12″ × 9″. It needs to be enlarged to hold the drawing components.

3 Use GRID to set a 12″ grid.

4 ZOOM-All.

5 Enter XREF. The Xref Manager dialog box pops up (Figure 10.3).

6 Click [**Attach...**]. The Select Reference File dialog box pops up (Figure 10.4).

7 Click the Look in list to open the directory where Ch06.dwg is located.

8 Click to select Ch06.dwg.

9 Click [**Open**]. The External Reference dialog box pops up (Figure 10.5).

10 Click [**OK**]. AutoCAD prompts you to pick an insertion point.

11 Pick a point (anywhere). The command ends.

12 Use XREF to attach Ch08.dwg (elevation).

13 Use XREF to attach Ch09.dwg (detail).

● As long as you can keep the XREFs from overlapping, you can place them wherever you want. Your drawing may look like what is shown in Figure 10.6.

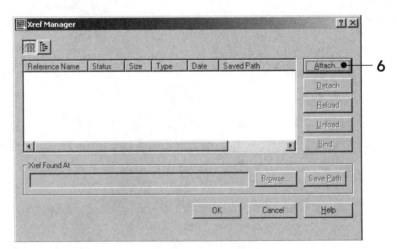

Figure 10.3
Xref Manager dialog box.

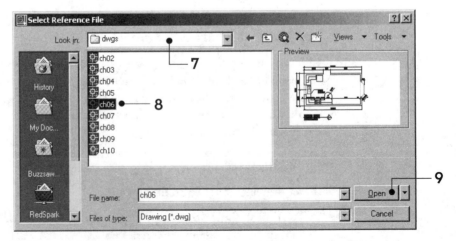

Figure 10.4
Select Reference File dialog box.

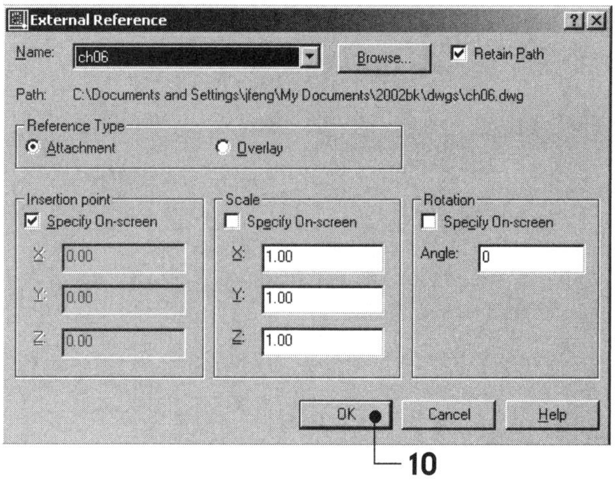

Figure 10.5
External Reference dialog box.

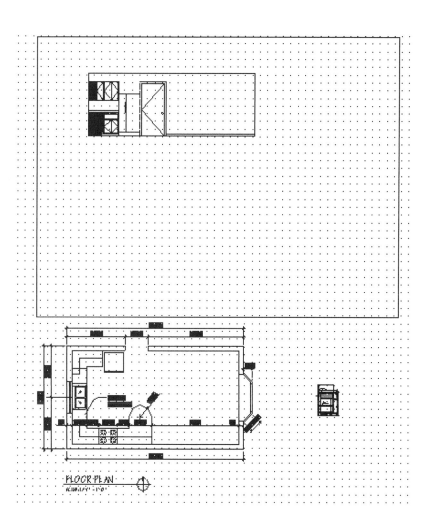

Figure 10.6
Attached drawings in model space.

Step 3: Use viewport to organize the drawings.

1 Click the ANSI c Title Block tab.

2 Set the Viewport layer current.

3 Freeze the Title Block layer. A large viewport is now visible.

4 Set the Viewport toolbar (View (menu) >Toolbar).

5 Use the Single viewport icon three times to set three viewports for the three drawings. For the shape, size, and location of viewports, see Figure 10.7.

6 Click [PAPER] in the status bar to switch to viewport model space mode.

7 Click the upper-left viewport to make it active.

8 Use ZOOM to set the floor plan at 1/4″ scale.

Command: **ZOOM** ↵

Specify corner of window, enter
a scale factor (nX or nXP), or

[All/Center/Dynamic/Extents/Previous/
Scale/Window] <real time>: **C** ↵   For Center.

Specify center point: **Pick near the center
of the floor plan (approximately).**

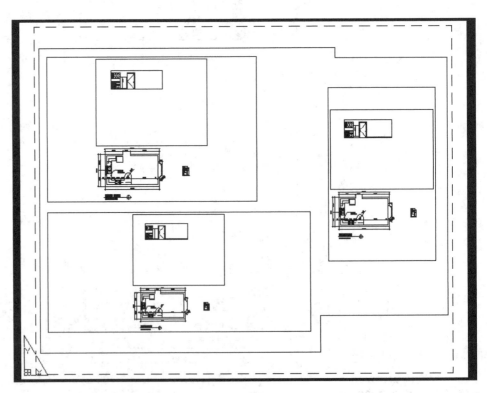

Figure 10.7
Set three viewports.

Enter magnification or height <58′-1 5/16″>:
1/48XP ↵

● Different from the procedure you learned in Chapter 7, this method is good for large drawings because you will never lose the portion of the drawing you want to show in the viewport. The magnification factor, 1/48, is the inverse of the drawing scale factor. XP qualifies the factor as the scale for paper space. If you forget the "XP," the drawing will be reduced to a small dot.

9 Click the lower-left viewport and use the ZOOM command to set the elevation at 1/2″ scale (ZOOM - C - 1/24XP).

10 Click the viewport on the right and use the ZOOM command to set the detail at 1 1/2″ scale (ZOOM - C - 1/8XP).

● If you need to move the drawing inside the viewport, you may use the PAN tool while the viewport is active.

11 Switch to paper space mode by clicking [MODEL] on the status bar.

12 Adjust the viewport size to make it fit the drawings.

13 Set LTSCALE=0.5 (to make the linetypes look appropriate).

14 ERASE the large viewport.

15 Thaw the Title Block layer (Figure 10.8).

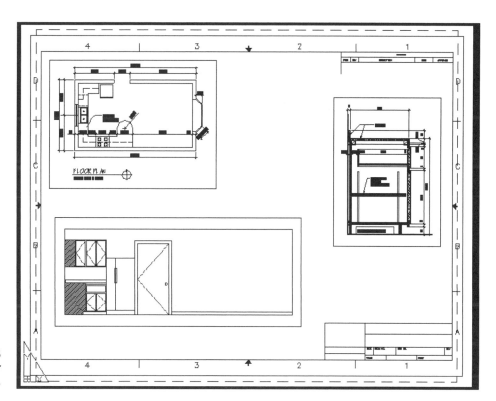

Figure 10.8
Paper space layout after
scale setting.

Creating Reference Symbols

According to design drawing conventions, related drawings are symbolically linked by reference symbols such as elevation symbols and bubbles. Elevation symbols in floor plans indicate the viewing orientation and point to the sheet number and drawing numbers of the elevations. In the drawing title of an elevation, a bubble, corresponding to the elevation bubble in the floor plan, identifies the elevation with the drawing number and sheet number. Bubbles are also used for sections and details. Paper space is a good place for these bubbles, since you can easily avoid dealing with the different scales associated with each individual drawing.

Step 1: Draw an elevation symbol.

1 Set layer 0 current. For making blocks.

2 Set snap spacing 1/16″ and turn SNAP and ORTHO on.

3 ZOOM in to look at the floor plan.

4 Draw a circle in an empty space (R=3/16).

5 ZOOM in to look at the circle closely.

6 Use LINE to draw the pointer. Use Quadrant object snap if you like (Figure 10.9a).

7 ROTATE the pointer −45° (Figure 10.9b).

Command: **ROTATE** ↵

Current positive angle in UCS:
ANGDIR=counterclockwise ANGBASE=0

Select objects: **Pick point**
Specify opposite corner:
Pick point 3 found

> Use implied selection window to select the circle and the pointer.

Select objects: ↵

Specify base point: **CEN** ↵

Of **pick the circle**

Specify rotation angle or [Reference]: **−45** ↵

Command:

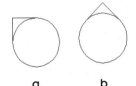

Figure 10.9
Draw the pointer.   a   b

Figure 10.10
Finished elevation
symbol.

8 Start the BHATCH command to hatch the pointer with solid pattern. The Boundary Hatch dialog box pops up.

9 Click the Swatch window.

10 Click the Other Predefined tab and click the Solid pattern to select it.

11 Click [OK].

12 Click [Pick point] and pick a point inside the pointer.

13 Press [Enter].

14 Click [Preview] to see if it looks correct.

15 Press [Enter] to exit from the preview.

16 Click [OK] to apply the pattern and end the command. (Figure 10.10)

17 Make the elevation symbol a block and name it ELVSYMB. When picking the insertion point, use the Center object snap to catch the center of the circle.

18 ZOOM to the previous view.

Step 2: Fill in the text.

The next step is to fill in the text in the elevation symbol. Before putting in text, you need to set a text style. Since we want to use the NOTES style that you defined in Chapter 5, you need to use the AutoCAD DesignCenter to load that style.

1 Use the AutoCAD DesignCenter to load NOTES text style, and set it as the current style.

2 ZOOM to look at the floor plan.

3 Create layer I-ANON-SYMB and set it as the current layer.

4 INSERT the ELVSYMB block inside the floor plan and make it point to the door.

5 ZOOM in to look at it closely.

● If you see the circle turn into a polygon, don't worry about it. It is only AutoCAD's way to display a circle quickly. If you want to see a smoother circle, you can use the REGEN command to make AutoCAD do a better job.

6 Draw a horizontal line in the bubble to divide the circle into two equal parts (using object snap).

7 Use DTEXT to fill in the E1 elevation drawing number above the line and the A02 sheet number below the line. Text height = 3/32″. Use center justification.

Command: **DTEXT** ↵

Current text style: "Standard"
Text height: 0'-0 3/16"

Specify start point of text
or [Justify/Style]: **J** ↵

Enter an option [Align/Fit/Center/Middle/
Right/TL/TC/TR/ML/MC/MR/BL/BC/BR]: **C** ↵

Specify center point of text:
**Pick a point above the midpoint
of the line.**

Specify height <0'-0 3/16">: **3/32** ↵

Specify rotation angle of text <0>: ↵

Enter text: **E1** ↵

Enter text: **A02** ↵

Enter text: ↵

Command:

- The center justification allows you to reuse this bubble in the future (by changing the text with DDEDIT command) without affecting the text alignment. E1 is an arbitrary designation to identify the elevation, and the A02 sheet number is also arbitrarily made as an example.

7 MOVE the texts to adjust their vertical locations to make them fit well inside the bubble. (Temporarily turn SNAP [F9] off if needed, and turn it back on after the MOVE command.) (Figure 10.11)

Step 3: Create a detail bubble.

1 ZOOM out to see the whole drawing.

2 Make a copy of the elevation symbol and place it below the elevation.

3 Zoom in to look at the copied elevation symbol.

4 EXPLODE (X) the elevation symbol.

5 ERASE (E) the pointer.

6 Use SCALE to enlarge the bubble by 1.33 (4/3) times.

Figure 10.11
The finished elevation
bubble.

Figure 10.12
The finished detail
bubble.

Command: **SCALE** ↵

Select objects: **Pick point**
Specify opposite corner:
Pick point 4 found

Pull out a selection window to
catch the circle and the texts in it.

Select objects: ↵

End selection.

Specify base point:
Pick a point inside the circle.

Specify scale factor or [Reference]: **4/3** ↵

Command:

The bubble is enlarged 1.33
times (Figure 10.12).

● A detail bubble looks like an elevation symbol without a pointer. To be visually
comparable with the elevation bubble, it needs to be slightly larger than the elevation bubble; therefore, it is enlarged 1.33 times, based on aesthetic judgment.

Step 4: Create the detail section (cutting plane) symbol.

1 ZOOM to look at the whole drawing.

2 Copy the elevation symbol in the floor plan drawing to the elevation drawing.

3 ZOOM in to look at the elevation.

4 EXPLODE (X) the copied elevation symbol block.

5 ERASE (E) the pointer.

6 Use DDEDIT to change the drawing number from E1 to 12.

● The number 12 is an arbitrary number used to identify the section detail.

7 MOVE the symbol slightly below the counter elevation.

8 Use PLINE to draw a polyline (width = 1/32″) as the cutting plane from the
top of the circle up slightly beyond the countertop.

● Using Polyline to control lineweights is another approach—in addition to the
ones you have learned in previous chapters. When a polyline is created, you have
an option to define its width and the lineweight shows accurately on the screen.
The lineweight of a polyline will also be plotted by default. Since the heavy
lineweight is required for only one object, using this approach saves you from setting color, layer, lineweight, and plot style.

Command: **PL** ↵   Use the PL alias to start the PLINE command.

PLINE

Specify start point:
Pick the top of the circle.

Current line-width is 0'-0"

Specify next point or [Arc/Close/
Halfwidth/Length/Undo/Width]:
W ↵   Start setting line width.

Specify starting width <0'-0">:
1/32 ↵

Specify ending width <0'-1/32">: ↵   Accept the default value.

Specify next point or [Arc/Close/
Halfwidth/Length/Undo/Width]:

**Pick a point above
the countertop.**

Specify next point or [Arc/Close/
Halfwidth/Length/Undo/Width]: ↵   No more points.

Command:

9 Click the Linetype window in the Properties toolbar and select Other to load the Phantom2 linetype (Figure 10.13). The Linetype Manager dialog box pops up.

10 Click [**Load**]. The Load or Reload Linetypes dialog box pops up.

11 Select Phantom2 and click [OK]. The linetype Phantom2 appears on the list.

12 Click [OK]. Closes the Linetype Manager dialog box.

13 Click the polyline to change its linetype. Grips appear.

14 Click the linetype window in the Properties toolbar and select the Phantom2 linetype. The linetype of the polyline changes (Figure 10.14).

15 Press [Esc] to cancel the grips.

● The procedure of changing the linetype of an object is very similar to that of changing the layer of an object.

16 ZOOM-All.

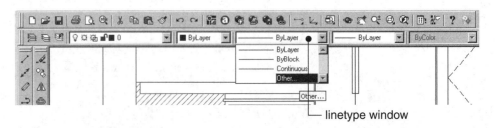

Figure 10.13
The linetype window.

linetype window

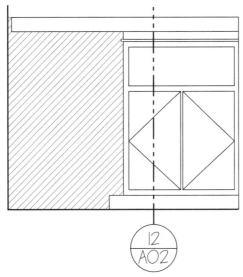

Figure 10.14
The Finished Section
symbol.

Creating Drawing Titles

Since you already created the ch07.dwg drawing title for the floor plan in the paper space layout, you can simply Copy and Paste it into the current drawing. In addition to using it for the floor plan, you can also use it as a model for the other two drawings.

Step 1: Transport the drawing title from ch07.dwg.

1 Open ch07.dwg.

2 Click the paper space layout floorplan tab.

3 Select the drawing title below the small floor plan with a selection window.

 4 Click the Copy icon in the standard toolbar.

5 Click the Close button to close the drawing without saving. The Chapter 10 drawing returns.

 6 Click the Paste icon in the standard toolbar. The drawing title floats with the cursor.

7 Insert the drawing title below the elevation.

Step 2: Create the drawing title for the elevation.

1 ZOOM in to look at the drawing title.

2 ERASE (E) the north arrow.

3 Use DDEDIT (ED) to change the drawing title text to ELEVATION.

4 Use DDEDIT (ED) to change the scale text to 1/2″=1′-0″.

Figure 10.15
Finished elevation drawing title.

Figure 10.16
Drawing title for counter detail.

5 MOVE the detail bubble to connect to the horizontal line under the drawing title text.

6 Use grips to adjust the length of the line under the drawing title (Figure 10.15).

7 ZOOM-All to see the whole drawing.

8 Adjust the location of the drawing title (if needed).

Step 3: Create the drawing title for the counter detail.

1 COPY the elevation drawing title and place it below the counter detail.

2 ZOOM in to look at the copied drawing title closely.

3 Use DDEDIT (ED) to change the texts.

4 Adjust the length of the line below the drawing title (Figure 10.16).

5 ZOOM-All.

Creating Annotation Markers

Annotation markers are used in drawings at specific reference points to refer to notes and schedule items (e.g., door numbers). They are composed of a textual identification, numbers or letters, and a graphic boundary of simple shapes. Although they are small in size, making them look good and consistent throughout your drawings can be a tedious and challenging task. Therefore, making a reusable collection of them will make your life much easier in the future.

Step 1: Define an Attribute.

Since the identification in the annotation marker is a variable, making it a simple block will not work. Instead, you need to use a special type of block associated with "attributes." You will have a better understanding of how an attribute works after making and using it.

1 Enter DDATTDEF (Attribute definition) to define an attribute. The Attribute Definition dialog box pops up (Figure 10.17).

2 Type ID (identification) in the Tag text box.

3 Type MARKER ID in the Prompt text box.

4 Type ? in Value text box.

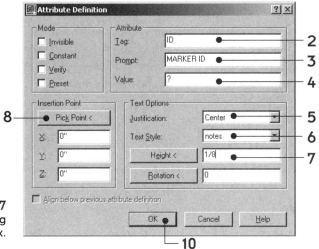

Figure 10.17
Attribute Definition dialog
box.

- Now, the value of the attribute (the number or the letter of the marker) is still a question. You will fill it in when you insert a block with this attribute.

5 Click the Justification list and choose Center.

6 Make sure NOTES is the text style.

7 Change text height to 1/8″.

- The Text Options settings control the appearance of the text.

8 Click [Pick Point <].

9 Pick a point in an empty area.

10 Click [OK]. You will see the ID text on the drawing.

Step 2: Make a block with attribute.

1 ZOOM in to look at the created attribute closely.

2 Draw a circle (*R*=1/8) to enclose the ID text.

3 Use MOVE to adjust the position of the attribute in the circle (if needed) (Figure 10.18).

4 Change the layer of the circle and the ID attribute text to 0.

5 Make a block including both the tag and the circle and name it MARK. (Pick the center of the circle as the insertion point.)

6 ZOOM out to look at the floor plan.

Figure 10.18
Adjust location of
attribute text in the circle.

Step 3: Insert the MARK block.

Inserting a block with attribute is the best way to understand the concept. Let us assume that we need a marker to identify the door. First, insert the MARK block. In the INSERT command, you will be prompted to enter the MARKER ID value. After a value is entered, a door type marker is created.

1 Insert the MARK block.

Command: **INSERT** ↵   The Insert dialog box pops up.

**Select the MARK block name
from the Name list.**

Click [OK].

Specify insertion point or [Scale/X/Y/Z/
Rotate/PScale/PX/PY/PZ/PRotate]:

**Pick a point at the door opening
in the floor plan.**

Enter attribute values   AutoCAD asks you (with the
                                                              prompt) to enter the value.

MARKER ID <?>: **A** ↵   Assume the door type is A.

Command: The letter "A" appears in the
                                                              circle (Figure 10.19).

2 ZOOM **in to look at the inserted marker.**

Step 4: Change the attribute value.

The value of an attribute can be changed by using the DDATTE command. Let us assume that you need to change the door type from A to D.

1 Start the DDATTE (Edit Attributes dialog box) command.

Command: **DDATTE** ↵

Select block: **Select the door
number marker.**   The Edit Attributes dialog box
                                                              pops up (Figure 10.20).

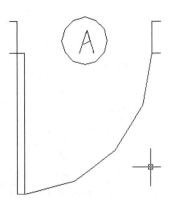

Figure 10.19
The circular annotation
marker.

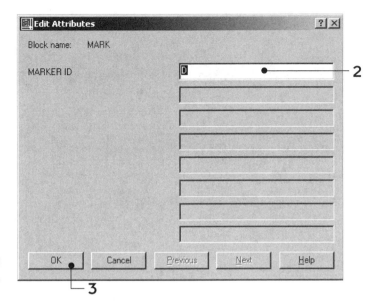

Figure 10.20
Edit Attributes dialog box.

2 Type D to replace A.

3 Click [OK]. The door type marker changes from A to D.

● This is a simple example of using an attribute. In this example, you enjoy both the consistency of block and flexibility of editable texts. There are many other applications of attributes to attach textual information to graphic entities for the purpose of management. You can associate more than one attribute to a block for more complex applications.

Creating Dimension in Paper Space Layout

In the design profession, some people prefer to create dimensions in paper space; therefore, you need to know how to set your dimension style to do that.

Step 1: Load archi48 through DesignCenter.

Although the three drawing files have been attached to this drawing, what you really have are their images, and you have no access to their dimension styles; therefore, you need to load the dimension style from the Chapter 6 drawing file using the DesignCenter.

Step 2: Set a dimension style for the elevation drawing in paper space.

In order to add dimensions to the 1/2″ scale elevation in paper space, you need to readjust the dimension style.

1 **Enter command alias D.** The Dimension Style Manager dialog pops up (Figure 10.21).

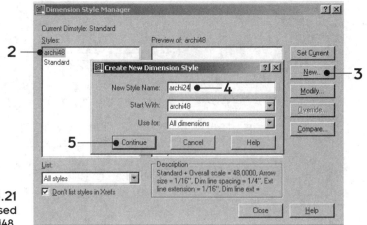

Figure 10.21
Create a new style based
on archi48.

2 Click archi48 to highlight it.

3 Click [**New**]. The Create New Dimension Style dialog box pops up.

4 Name the new style as archi24.

5 Click [**Continue**]. The New Dimension Style dialog box pops up (Figure 10.22).

6 Click the **Fit tab.** The Fit page opens (Figure 10.22).

7 Change the scale factor from 48 to 24.

● 24 is the scale factor of 1/2″ =1′-0″ scale drawings.

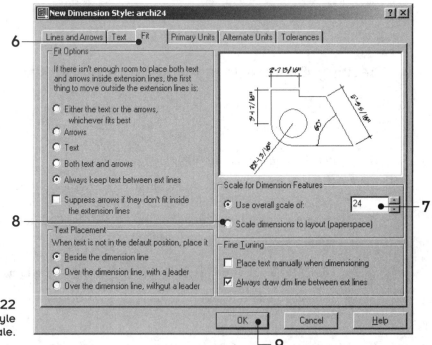

Figure 10.22
Set the dimension style
scale.

8 Click the circular button in front of Scale dimensions to layout.

● This makes the dimension style work in paper space.

9 Click [OK]. The New Dimension Style dialog box closes.

10 Click [Set Current] to set the style as the current dimension style.

11 Click [Close] to exit the dialog box.

Step 3: Dimension the elevation (in paper space).

1 ZOOM to look at the left half of the elevation drawing.

2 Freeze the Ch08|I-ELEV-PATT layer to avoid picking unwanted points.

3 Create the I-ANON-DIMS layer and set it current.

4 Turn running Endpoint object snap mode on (if you like).

5 Set Dimension toolbar (if needed).

  6 Use the Linear Dimension tool and the Continue Dimension tool to draw dimensions as shown in Figure 10.23.

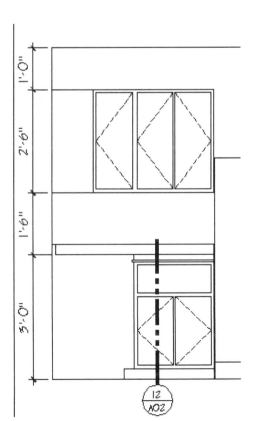

Figure 10.23
Dimension in paper space.

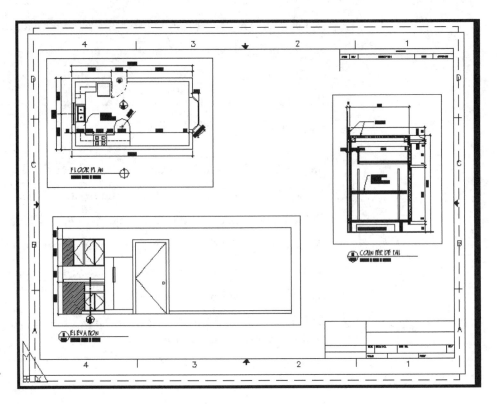

Figure 10.24
Finished sheet.

7 Turn running object snap off. (If you turned it on.)

8 Thaw the Ch08li-elev-patt layer.

9 ZOOM-All to see the whole drawing (Figure 10.24).

10 Set the Viewport layer to Not-to-plot.

11 Save the drawing.

Creating a Drawing Template

In the assembled drawing you have many reusable things, such as text styles, symbols, bubbles, and the title block. These elements will very likely be used in your next drawing. You can save the drawing as a template that carries all these reusable elements. The next time you use them to create a new drawing, you won't have to redefine these elements, or reload them from other drawings.

Step 1: Clean up the drawing.

Before you save the drawing as a template, you need to clean up your drawing. Except for the reusable elements, all drawing entities should be erased and all attached Xrefs should be detached.

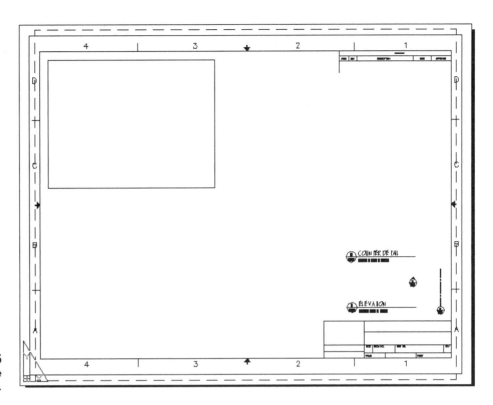

Figure 10.25
Organize the paper space items.

1 Detach the attached Xrefs.

2 Erase two of the three viewports and the dimensions.

3 Erase the door type marker.

● Since the marker has been preserved in the form of a block (MARK), there is no need to keep it on the drawing, because blocks will be saved with the drawing.

4 MOVE all drawing titles and symbols close to the title block (Figure 10.25).

Step 2: Create the template file.

1 Set 0 layer current.

2 Enter the SAVE command. The Save Drawing As dialog box pops up (Figure 10.26).

3 Click the Files of type drop-down list and choose AutoCAD Drawing Template File [*.dwt].

4 Type MY_C (my C size template) in the File name text box.

● AutoCAD automatically shows its Templates folder. In a network setting, however, you may not be able to save your file to it. In this situation, you need to find your own working directory in which to save your template file, or you may save it to your floppy disk (A:\).

5 Find the directory in which you want to save your template file.

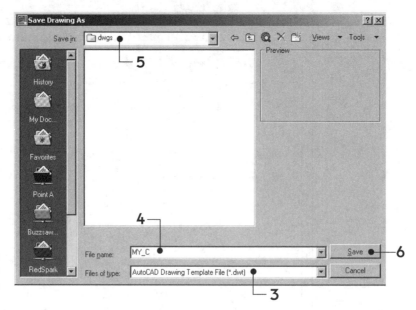

Figure 10.26
The Save Drawing As
dialog box.

6 Click [Save]. The 'Template Description dialog box pops up with a description inherited from the ANSI C template (Figure 10.27).

7 Click [OK].

 8 Click the Close button to close the ch10.dwg drawing. (Do NOT save it.)

Step 3: Test the new template.

1 Click the New file icon in the standard toolbar. The Create New Drawing dialog box pops up (Figure 10.28).

2 Click and select Template from the Select how to begin list.

3 Click [Browse...]. The Select File dialog box pops up (Figure 10.29).

4 Click the Look in list to locate the directory where the file is saved.

5 Select MY_C.dwt.

6 Click [Open]. You should have a drawing similar to Figure 10.25.

● The paper space viewport can be changed in the future after you finish your basic drawings in model space. The drawing titles can be changed according to your need. The north arrow can be rotated. The section symbols and bubbles can be copied or moved for new drawings.

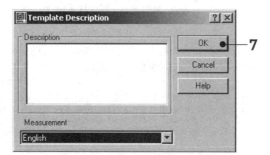

Figure 10.27
The Template Description
dialog box.

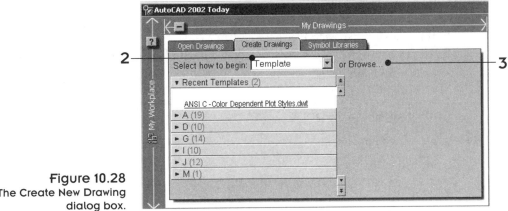

Figure 10.28
The Create New Drawing
dialog box.

7 Click Insert in the menu bar and choose Block.

8 Click the Name list to see the available blocks. A list of blocks appears. They are ready for you to insert into your new drawing.

9 Press [Esc] to cancel the INSERT command.

10 Click Format in the menu bar and choose Text Style to see the available text styles. Notes is the current style.

11 Press [Esc] to cancel the text style command.

● Now you are certain that the settings and some frequently used drawing elements that you created are all saved in this template. They are ready to use. If you want to design your own title block, you can simply create it to replace the existing ANSI standard one and save it as a template to update the template file. You may also create more templates of different sizes.

12 Click the Close button to edit the test drawing. (Do NOT save it.)

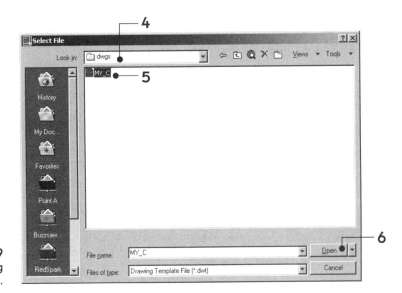

Figure 10.29
The Select File dialog
box.

Summary

In this chapter, you assembled a typical AutoCAD drawing with external references. Based on that drawing, you created a drawing template for future use. In the process, you learned the following new concepts, procedures, and commands:

Knowledge/concepts

- Drawing template
- .dwt file
- Sheet file
- Model file
- Attribute

Procedures

- Use a Template file to set up a new drawing
- Set dimension style for paper space
- Enter text with justification
- Draw a polyline with width
- Load a linetype through the linetype window
- Change the linetype of an object
- Define an attribute
- Make a block with attribute
- Insert a block with attribute
- Change the attribute value
- Create a drawing template

Commands

- NEW

- PLINE (PL)

- DDATTDEF

- DDATTE

Building a 3D Model

- Build the walls
- Create the window and door openings
- Create the bay window
- Create the door, trim, and baseboard
- Create the table
- Create the chair
- Create the floor and ceiling
- Create a picture
- Set perspective views

Computer 3D modeling is usually perceived as an extremely sophisticated process. This may be true in the creation of animated dinosaurs; however, if the task is to create interior space composed primarily of simple planes, it is actually quite simple. In this chapter you will use a simplified approach to build a 3D model of the dining space you have been drawing in previous chapters.

Building the Walls

Step 1: Prepare the floor plan.

1 Start AutoCAD.

2 Set a new drawing with architectural units and define a working area of 40′ × 40′.

3 Set SNAP spacing to 1″ and turn it on.

4 Set GRID spacing to 12″ and turn it on.

5 ZOOM-All to see the entire drawing area.

6 Attach ch05.dwg as an external reference and save the drawing as ch11.dwg.

7 Freeze all layers except the Wall layer (ch05|I-WALL).

8 Create a new layer, name it "wall," and set it as the current layer. (Set blue as the layer color.)

● The naming of layers in this chapter is simplified, yet descriptive. The naming convention introduced in Chapter 4 is not followed because 3D modeling does not belong to shared design documentations.

Step 2: Set an axonometric view.

An axonometric view can be most easily set by using the View toolbar.

1 Click View in the menu bar and select Toolbars. The Toolbars dialog box pops up.

2 Find View and check the box. The View toolbar appears (Figure 11.1).

Figure 11.1
The View toolbar.

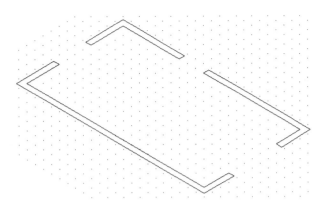

Figure 11.2
An axonometric view of
the plan.

3 Click [Close] to close the dialog box.

4 Embed the toolbar into the frame of the AutoCAD drawing window.

5 Click the Southeast View icon on the View toolbar. The view changes (Figure 11.2).

Step 3: Set up the Solid Model toolbar.

There are three groups of modeling toolbars: Solids, Solids Editing, and Surfaces. In this tutorial, you will use mainly the solid modeling tools. Therefore, you need to set up the Solid Modeling toolbar for convenience.

1 Click View in the menu bar and select Toolbars.

2 Check the box before Solids. (If you still have the Dimension toolbar checked, you may clear the box to close the toolbar to make space for the 3D modeling tools.) The Solids toolbar appears (Figure 11.3).

3 Click [Close].

4 Embed the new toolbar into the frame of your AutoCAD drawing window.

Step 4: Create the massing boxes.

In this step, you will create two boxes: one has the same size as the exterior of the space and the other has the same size as the interior space. They are both solid boxes, and we will call them massing solids. You will subtract the smaller one from the larger one to create the walls and the space within.

1 Turn Endpoint running object snap on.

2 Click the Box icon.

Figure 11.3
The Solids toolbar.

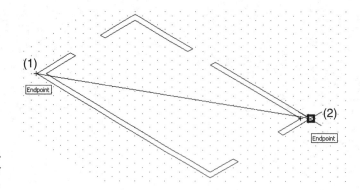

Figure 11.4
Create the exterior
massing solid.

Command: _box

Specify corner of box or [CEnter] <0,0,0>:
Pick point (1). (Figure 11.4)

Specify corner or [Cube/Length]:
Pick point (2).

Specify height: **8′** ↵

Command: The box is created (Figure 11.5).

  3 Click the Box icon.

Command: _box

Specify corner of box or [CEnter] <0,0,0>:
Pick point (3).   (Figure 11.5)

Specify corner or [Cube/Length]:
Pick point (4).

Specify height: 8′ ↵

Command: The box is created.

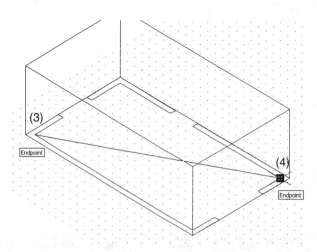

Figure 11.5
Create the interior
massing solid.

Step 5: Subtract the interior solid from the exterior solid.

In this step, you will use the SUBTRACT command to "carve out" the interior space by subtracting the inside box from the outside box. The result will be solid walls surrounding the hollow space in the middle.

Command: **SUBTRACT** ↵

Select solids and regions
to subtract from...

Select objects:
Pick the outside solid 1 found

Select objects: ↵

● It is important to remember that the object you pick first will remain.

Select solids and regions
to subtract...

Select objects:
Pick the inside solid 1 found

Select objects: ↵

● The interior space is carved out, but there is no visible change in the view.

Step 6: Examine the wall in a hideline view.

There are a few different shading modes in AutoCAD that include wireframe, hideline, and shaded. Up to this point, you have been using the wireframe mode that shows a 3D model as if the model is made of wires. Although the wireframe model allows you to see all the edges of the model, it is confusing when you try to determine the spatial relationship between wireframe lines. A hideline view shows the solid surfaces as solid blank areas that block all the lines that are behind them. In a shaded view, the surfaces of solid objects will be filled with different shades of the object color assuming a generic light shining on the model from a point above your left shoulder. The shading mode can be easily controlled through the Shade toolbar. Let's create a hideline view to examine your model.

1 Click View in the menu bar and select Toolbars. The Customize dialog box pops up.

2 Find Shade and check the box. The Shade toolbar appears (Figure 11.6).

3 Click [Close] to exit the dialog box.

4 Embed the toolbar into the AutoCAD window frame.

Figure 11.6
The Shade toolbar.

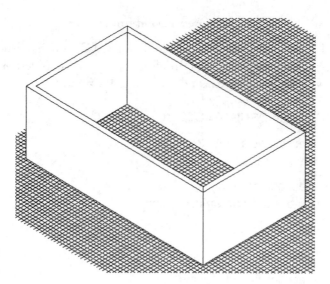

Figure 11.7
Hideline view.

5 **Click the Hide icon.** Lines behind solid surfaces become hidden (Figure 11.7).

6 Click the 2D wireframe icon to go back to a wireframe view.

Creating the Window and Door Openings

Similar to creating the interior space, you will create massing solids the same sizes as the door and window openings, and then subtract them from the wall.

Step 1: Create the door opening massing solid.

1 ZOOM in to look at the door opening (on the floor).

2 Click the Solid Box icon from the Solids toolbar.

Command: _box

Specify corner of box
or [CEnter] <0,0,0>:
**Pick the inside corner
of the door opening.**   (Figure 11.8)

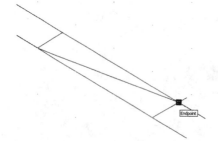

Figure 11.8
Create the door massing
solid.

Specify corner or [Cube/Length]:

**Pick the outside corner
of the door opening
on the opposite side.**

Specify height: **80** ⏎

3 ZOOM to previous view to see the door opening massing solid.

Step 2: Subtract the door opening massing solid from the wall solid.

Command: **SU** ⏎   Use the alias SU to start the
                                               SUBTRACT command.

Select solids and regions
to subtract from...

Select objects:
Pick the wall 1 found

Select objects: ⏎

Select solids and regions
to subtract...

Select objects:
 Pick the door opening massing solid
1 found

Select objects: ⏎

Step 3: Examine the door opening in a shaded view.

 1 Click the Flat shaded icon. The model is shaded (Figure 11.9).

 2 Click the 2D wireframe icon to go back to a wireframe view.

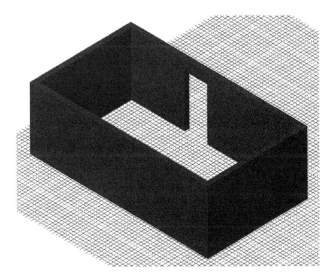

Figure 11.9
Shaded view.

Step 4: Create window opening massing solids.

This step is similar to step 1. The difference is that the window opening massing solids need to be moved 30″ above the floor. You can use the MOVE command to move them in the direction of the z axis by entering the 3D displacement coordinates (0,0,30). To differentiate the move in the z direction from the 2D move, we will call it "lift."

1 ZOOM in to look at the opening of the bay window.

2 Use the Solid Box tool to create the opening massing solid based on the floor plan. (height = 50″).

3 Lift the massing solids up 30″.

Command: **M** ↵

MOVE

Select objects:
Pick the massing solid 1 found

Select objects: ↵

Specify base point or displacement:
0,0,30 ↵

Specify second point of displacement
or <use first point as displacement>: ↵

4 ZOOM out to the previous view.

Step 5: Subtract window opening massing solids from the wall solid.

Command: **SU** ↵

Select solids and regions
to subtract from…

Select objects:
 Pick the wall 1 found

Select objects: ↵

Select solids and regions
to subtract…

Select objects:
Pick the window opening massing solid
1 found

Select objects: ↵

Step 6: Examine the window openings in a shaded view.

1 Click the Flat shaded icon. The model is shaded (Figure 11.10).

2 Click the 2D wireframe icon to go back to a wireframe view.

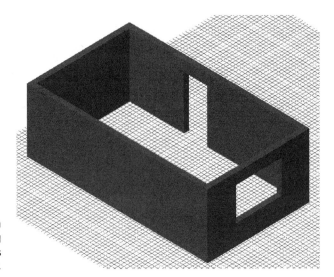

Figure 11.10
Finished door and window openings in a shaded view.

Creating the Bay Window

The bay window is a little different from the walls, because it has angled lines; therefore, the Box tool does not work. You will take a different approach to create 3D solids. First, start by creating enclosed polyline boundaries and then extrude the boundaries into 3D solids. You can then subtract the massing solids to create the window frame. The glass will be made from lines with a "thickness" value.

Step 1: Preparation.

1 Create a layer called Window and set it as the current layer. (Set layer color red.)

2 Freeze the wall layers.

3 Thaw the ch05|I-GLAZ layer.

Step 2: Create a window frame exterior massing solid.

Similar to creating the wall, you will create a large exterior massing solid and a small interior massing solid for the subtraction in the next step.

1 ZOOM in to look at the window lines (on the floor).

2 Trace the bay window along the exterior lines with a polyline.

Command: **PL** ↵

PLINE

Specify start point: **Pick point (1).**

Current line-width is 0'-0"

Specify next point or [Arc/Halfwidth/
Length/Undo/Width]: **Pick point (2).**

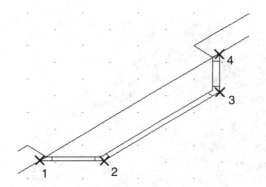

Figure 11.11
Solid boxes for window
frames.

Specify next point or [Arc/Close/Halfwidth/
Length/Undo/Width]: **Pick point (3).**

Specify next point or [Arc/Close/Halfwidth/
Length/Undo/Width]: **Pick point (4).**

Specify next point or [Arc/Close/Halfwidth/
Length/Undo/Width]: **C ↵**   (Figure 11.11)

Command:

3 Use the EXTRUDE tool to create the exterior massing solid.

 Click the EXTRUDE icon.

Command: _extrude

Current wire frame density: ISOLINES=4

Select objects: **L ↵**   L for last created.

1 found

Select objects: ↵

Specify height of extrusion or [Path]: **54**   The dimension includes a 2″ top
                                                 and a 2″ bottom in addition to
                                                 the 50″ window frame.

Specify angle of taper for extrusion <0>: ↵

Command: The massing solid is extruded
                                                  from the polyline boundary.

Creating a 3D solid by extruding a polyline boundary is a very useful procedure in
3D modeling of interior spaces. When the base shape of a space is not as simple as a
rectangle, you need to use this procedure.

Step 3: Create a window frame interior massing solid.

In this step, you will use the BOUNDARY command to generate the polyline
boundary by clicking a point inside an area enclosed by many objects, which means
you do not need to trace the boundary point by point.

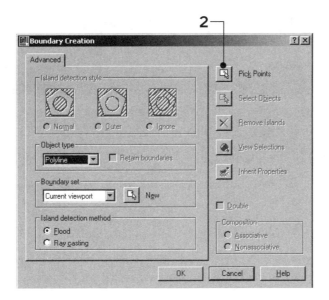

Figure 11.12
Boundary Creation
dialog box.

1 Use BOUNDARY to create a polyline boundary for the interior massing solid.

Command: **BOUNDARY** ↵   The Boundary Creating dialog
                                            box pops up (Figure 11.12).

2 Click the Pick Points button.

Select internal point:
Pick point (5) Selecting everything…   (Figure 11.13)

Selecting everything visible…

Analyzing the selected data…

Analyzing internal islands…

Select internal point: ↵

BOUNDARY created 1 polyline   AutoCAD reports that the
                                            boundary is created.

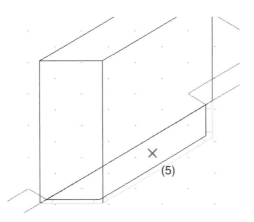

Figure 11.13
Use **BOUNDARY**
command.

Boundary entity on locked or frozen layer.
Associative hatch not updated.

Command:

2 Use the EXTRUDE tool to create the interior massing solid (height=50″).

Step 4: Subtract the interior solid from the exterior solid.

1 Lift the interior solid up 2″.

2 SUBTRACT the interior solid from the exterior solid. (Select the exterior solid first.)

Step 5: Create a void between window frames.

1 Use BOUNDARY to create a polyline boundary for the space between the window frames on the slanting side of the bay window.

2 EXTRUDE the boundary into 3D solid (46″ high).

3 Lift the 3D solid 4″ up.

4 Use MIRROR to create a copy of the solid on the opposite side of the bay window. (Use Midpoint object snap to define the mirror line.)

5 Use the BOX tool to create the massing solid for the middle pane (46″ high).

6 Lift the massing solid 4″ up.

7 SUBTRACT the massing solids from the window solid.

8 View the window frame in Hideline view (Figure 11.14).

9 Return to wireframe view.

Figure 11.14
Finished window frame.

Step 6: Create the glass panes.

1 Create a layer called Glass and set it as the current layer. (Set layer color maginta.)

2 Freeze the Window layer.

3 ZOOM in to look at the window lines (on the floor).

4 Use LINE to add a glass line (to each window pane). Use MIDpoint object snap (Figure 11.15).

5 Use the CHPROP command to assign a thickness value to the glass lines.

- The term *thickness* in AutoCAD is a property of drawing entities and is the measurement of an object in the third dimension. It is somewhat misleading because we have used the term in 2D drawings to mean the weight (or the width) of lines. By default, the initial value of the thickness of drawing entities such as lines is 0. When a different value is assigned, a line pops up as a vertical surface. The property thickness of a drawing entity can be easily changed by the Properties tool, or the equivalent CHPROP (meaning CHange PROPerty) command.

Command: **CHPROP** ↵

Select objects:
Pick the first glass line 1 found

Select objects:
Pick the second glass line 1 found, 2 total

Select objects:
Pick the third glass line 1 found, 3 total

Select objects: ↵

Enter property to change [Color/LAyer/LType/ltScale/LWeight/Thickness]: **T** ↵

Specify new thickness <0'-0">: **46** ↵

Enter property to change [Color/LAyer/LType/ltScale/LWeight/Thickness]: ↵

The lines pop up into vertical planes (Figure 11.16).

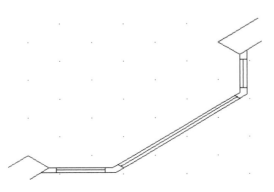

Figure 11.15
Add glass lines.

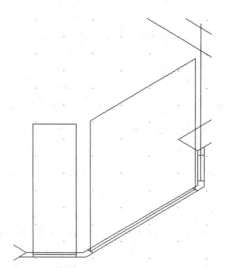

Figure 11.16
Lines with a thickness value.

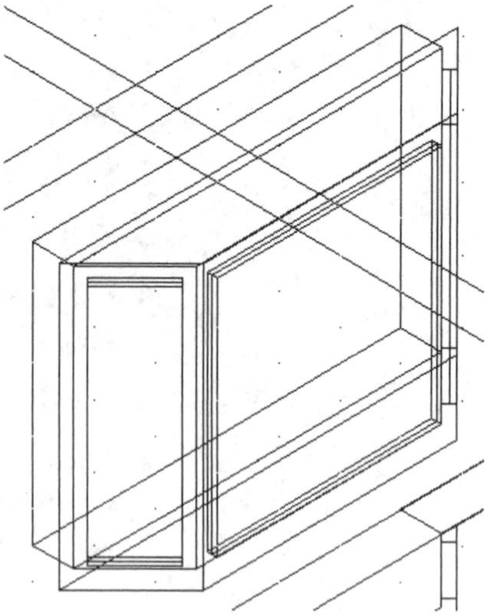

Figure 11.17
Lift the window into position.

Step 7: Lift the window up into position.

1 Lift the glass panes up 4″.

2 Thaw the Window layer.

3 Lift the window (frames + class panes) up 28″.

4 Thaw the Wall layer.

5 ZOOM out (Figure 11.17).

Creating the Door, Trim, and Baseboard

The door is simply a solid box. To create the baseboard, you will use the subtracting solid boxes approach. In the creation of the door casing, the Interfere solid modeling tool will be used.

Step 1: Preparation.

1 Create a layer named Door and set it as the current layer. Set layer color brown (22).

2 ZOOM in to look at the door opening.

Step 2: Create the door casing and the door.

1 Use the Solid Box tool to create a box from the corner of the door opening. Define the opposite corner @42,1 (height = 83″).

Command: _box

Specify corner of box or [CEnter] <0,0,0>:
**Pick the inside-left corner
of the door opening.**

Specify corner or [Cube/Length]: **@42,1** ↵

Specify height: **83** ↵   83=door height 6′-8″ + trim width 3″ (Figure 11.18a).

2 **Move the massing solid 3″ to the left** (Figure 11.18b).

3 **Click the Interfere icon to create the door casing.**

● When two solid objects run into each other, they create a volume of interference (that is, the space shared by both objects). The Interfere tool detects the form of this shared space and creates a new solid object in the same form. When you moved the massing solid in [2], you actually created an interfered space around the door opening; thus, use the Interfere tool to create the casing.

Command: _interfere Select first set of solids:

Select objects: **Pick the massing solid** 1 found

Select objects: ↵

Select second set of solids:

Select objects: **Pick the wall** 1 found

Select objects: ↵

Comparing 1 solid against 1 solid.

Interfering solids (first set): 1
                    (second set): 1

Interfering pairs: 1

Create interference solids? [Yes/No] <N>: **Y** ↵   (Figure 11.18c)

● The casing solid is created. But it is still in the wall. You need to move it out.

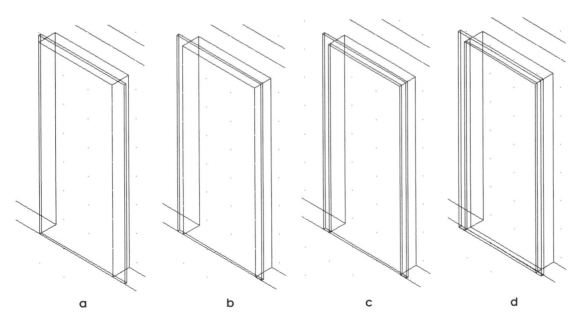

a   b   c   d

Figure 11.18
Create the door casing and the door.

4 Move the newly created casing and the door casing massing solid out of the wall (1″ toward the interior).

5 Use the Solid Box tool to create the door (starting from the corner of the door opening). Define the opposite corner @36,2 (height = 80″) (Figure 11.18d).

● The first massing solid should not be erased because you will use it later to create the baseboard.

Step 3: Create the doorknob.

1 ZOOM in to look at the bottom of the door.

2 Create a solid box (1″ wide × 2″ long, height = 1″) near the right-bottom corner of the door (Figure 11.19).

3 Click the Solid Sphere icon.

Command: _sphere

Current wire frame
density: ISOLINES=4

Specify center of sphere <0,0,0>:
Pick a point near the end of the box.

Specify radius of sphere or [Diameter]: **1** ↵

4 Lift the sphere 0.5″ up.

5 Use the PLAN command to switch to plan view.

● Aligning objects in an axonometric view is very difficult, especially when the objects are at different elevations. Therefore, you should NEVER try to align object in an axonometric view, unless you know that the objects are at the same elevation.

● You may also go back to the plan view by clicking the Top View icon.

6 ZOOM in to look at the box and the sphere.

7 Turn running object snap off.

8 Use MOVE to align and connect the box and the sphere (Figure 11.20). (Set SNAP to 0.5″ if necessary.)

9 MOVE the box and the sphere against the front surface of the door (Figure 11.21).

Figure 11.19
Create a doorknob.

Figure 11.20
Align the sphere with the box.

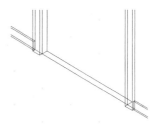

Figure 11.21
Locate the door knob

Figure 11.22
Finished baseboard at
the door.

10 Lift the sphere and the box up 3′.

11 Create a layer called Doorknob.

12 Change the layer of the box and the sphere to Doorknob.

13 Switch back to the axonometric view.

Step 4: Create the baseboard.

1 Freeze the Wall layer.

2 Use PLINE or RECTANGLE to create a polyline boundary along the interior wall line. Use Endpoint object snap to catch the corners of the walls.

3 Freeze the ch05|I-WALL layer.

4 Use OFFSET to create an offset of the boundary 1/2″ inside the first boundary.

5 ZOOM in to look at the boundary lines at the door opening.

6 Use EXTRUDE to extrude the two polyline boundaries into 3D solids (height = 3″).

7 Use SUBTRACT to subtract the inside solid from the outside one.

8 Use SUBTRACT to subtract the door casing massing solid from the baseboard solid (Figure 11.22).

Creating the Table

Let us now assume that the table is made of a wood tabletop and a metal base. These components can all be seen as cylinders of different sizes and elevations.

Step 1: Build the tabletop.

1 Create a layer called Tabletop and set it as the current layer.

2 Thaw the ch05|I-FURN layer and freeze the Door, Window, and Glass layers.

3 ZOOM to look at the table.

 4 Click the Cylinder icon in the Solid Modeling toolbar.

Command: _cylinder

Current wire frame density:
ISOLINES=4

Specify center point for base of cylinder
or [Elliptical] <0,0,0>: **CEN** ↵

Of **pick the circle**

Specify radius for base of cylinder
or [Diameter]: **24** ↵

Specify height of cylinder
or [Center of other end]: **2** ↵   (Figure 11.23)

5 Lift (MOVE) the tabletop up 28″ (Figure 11.24).

Step 2: **Build the table base and support.**

1 Create a layer called Tablebase and set it as the current layer.

2 Click the Cylinder icon in the Solid Modeling toolbar.

Command: _cylinder

Current wire frame density:
ISOLINES=4

Specify center point for base of cylinder
or [Elliptical] <0,0,0>: **CEN** ↵

Of **pick the circle (on the floor)**

Specify radius for base
of cylinder or [Diameter]: **2** ↵

Specify height of cylinder
or [Center of other end]: **28** ↵

3 Click the Cylinder icon in the Solid Modeling toolbar.

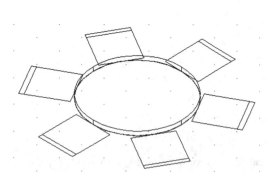

Figure 11.23
Create the tabletop.

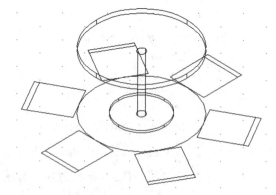

Figure 11.24
Finished dining table.

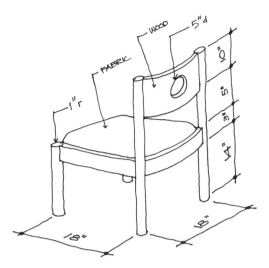

Figure 11.25
The sketch of the chair.

Command: _cylinder

Current wire frame density:
ISOLINES=4

Specify center point for base
of cylinder or [Elliptical] <0,0,0>: **CEN** ↵

Of **pick the circle (on the floor)**

Specify radius for base of cylinder
or [Diameter]: **12** ↵

Specify height of cylinder
or [Center of other end]: **1** ↵

Creating the Chair

Before you begin to construct a complex 3D model, you should draw a sketch of the object and work out the dimensions as shown in Figure 11.25.

Step 1: Draw a plan of the chair.

1 Use the PLAN command to go back to the plan view.

2 Create a few layers for building the chair: CHAIRLEG, CHAIRSEAT, CHAIR-BACK, and CHAIRFRAME.

3 Draw a plan of the chair on the floor (anywhere) (Figure 11.26).

● This plan will help you to create the parts of the chair and to align them. In the plan, the corners of the chair are not trimmed by the circular legs to preserve the entirety of the shapes of the seat and back that will be used to generate the forms. The back of the chair is drawn with the ARC command. The distance between the arcs is 0.5″ and the seat cushion is 1″ from the edge of the chair.

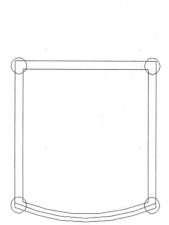

Figure 11.26
The plan of the chair.

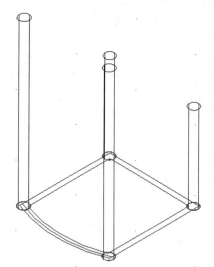

Figure 11.27
Create the legs.

Step 2: Create the legs.

1 Click the Southeast View icon to return to the axonometric view.

2 ZOOM to look at the plan of the chair (lying on the floor).

3 Set the CHAIRLEG layer as the current layer.

4 Use the Solid Cylinder icon to create the legs according to the sketch. Front legs: (r=1″, h=17″); rear legs: (r=1″, h=32″) (Figure 11.27).

5 Set the CHAIRBACK layer as the current layer and freeze the CHAIRLEG layer.

6 ERASE the circles that represent the legs in the plan of the chair.

Step 3: Create the back.

There is a round hole in the back. It can be imagined as resulted from subtracting a cylinder from a curved solid.

1 ZOOM in to look at the curved chairback in the plan.

2 Enter BOUNDARY and create a polyline boundary of the back.

Command: **BOUNDARY** ↵   The Boundary Creation dialog box pops up.

Click the Pick Point button.

Select internal point:
Pick a point in between the two arcs.

Selecting everything...

Selecting everything visible...

Analyzing the selected data...

Analyzing internal islands...

Select internal point: ↵

BOUNDARY created 1 polyline

3 Click the Extrude icon in the Solid Model toolbar.

Command: _extrude

Current wire frame density:
ISOLINES=4

Select objects: **L** ↵   Select the last created object.

1 found

Select objects: ↵

Specify height of extrusion
or [Path]: **10** ↵

Specify angle of taper
for extrusion <0>: ↵

Command: (Figure 11.28)

- This example shows that the combination of the EXTRUDE tool and the BOUND-ARY command allows you to make more complex forms than rectangles.

4 Click the cylinder icon in the Solid Model toolbar to create a cylinder (R=2.5, Height=10) at the midpoint of the arc (Figure 11.29).

5 Make sure ORTHO is on.

6 Use ROTATE3D to rotate the cylinder 90°.

Command: **ROTATE3D** ↵

Current positive angle:
ANGDIR=counterclockwise
ANGBASE=0

Select objects:
Pick the cylinder 1 found

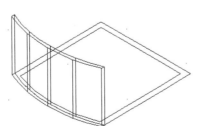

Figure 11.28
Extruded chairback piece.

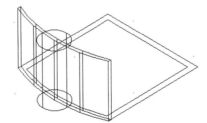

Figure 11.29
Create the cylinder massing solid.

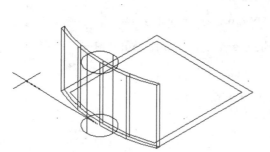

Figure 11.30
The direction of the rotation axis.

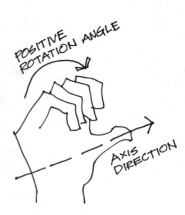

Figure 11.31
The right-hand rule of rotation.

Select objects: ↵

Specify first point on axis
or define axis by

[Object/Last/View/Xaxis/
Yaxis/Zaxis/2points]: **CEN** ↵   (Figure 11.30)

of **pick the bottom of the cylinder**
Specify second point on axis:
Pick a point to the left.

Specify rotation angle or [Reference]:
90 ↵

Command   The cylinder falls into the seat.

- The ROTATE3D command allows you to rotate drawing entities about an axis
  defined by you. The default method of defining the axis with two points is an
  easy one to use. The direction of rotation is decided by the picking order of the
  two points. You may use the right-hand rule to figure out the direction of rotation: Hold out your right hand and make a hitchhike sign (Figure 11.31). When
  your thumb points to the direction from the first point to the second point, the
  object will rotate in the direction your other fingers point to.

7 Lift the cylinder up 5″.

8 Move the cylinder a little to ensure that it penetrates the back.

9 View the model in a hideline view (Figure 11.32).

10 Return to wireframe view.

11 Use SUBTRACT to subtract the cylinder from the curved back (Figure 11.33).

12 Lift the chairback up 22″.

13 Set the CHAIRSEAT layer as the current layer and freeze the CHAIRBACK
layer.

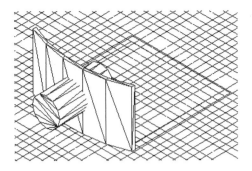

Figure 11.32
Let the cylinder penetrate the back.

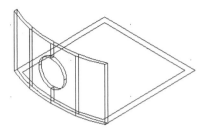

Figure 11.33
The result of subtraction.

Step 4. Create the seat (cushion).

1 Use BOUNDARY to create a polyline boundary.

2 EXTRUDE the boundary (1″ up) into a solid piece (Figure 11.34a).

3 Lift the seat (cushion) up 17″.

4 Use FILLET to round the edges.

Command: **F** ↵

Use the FILLET alias to start the command.

FILLET

Current settings:
Mode = TRIM, Radius = 0′-0″

Select first object or [Polyline/Radius/Trim]:
Pick one edge.

Enter fillet radius: **1** ↵

Select an edge or [Chain/Radius]:
Pick the second edge.

Select an edge or [Chain/Radius]:
Pick the third edge.

Select an edge or [Chain/Radius]:
Pick the last edge.

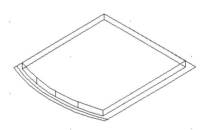
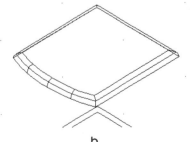

Figure 11.34
Create the seat (cushion).

a

b

Select an edge or [Chain/Radius]: ↵

4 edge(s) selected for fillet.

Command: (Figure 11.34b)

● This is another use of the FILLET command. It is a great tool for making furniture.

5 Set the CHAIRFRAME layer as the current layer and freeze the CHAIRSEAT layer.

Step 5: Create the seat frame.

For a real chair, the seat frame would be built with a few pieces of wood to save material. For this CAD model, however, you can simply make a solid piece to support the seat cushion. This not only simplifies your work now, but can also reduce calculation time for rendering it in the future.

1 ERASE the outline of the seat cushion and the back.

2 Use BOUNDARY to create a polyline boundary.

3 EXTRUDE the boundary (3″ up) into a solid piece.

4 Lift the piece up 14″.

5 Thaw all the chair layers: CHAIRBACK, CHAIRLEG, and CHAIRSEAT. (Figure 11.35)

6 Put the legs, the frame, and the back all in the CHAIRFRAME layer.

● Since these parts are all built with the same material, putting them together will save you time when you assign materials to them for rendering.

Step 6: Examine your model.

Use HIDE or SHADE to check your model, and return to 2D-wireframe view.

Step 7: Make the chair a block.

1 Use the BLOCK command to make the chair a block. Name the block 3dchair. Pick the midpoint of the front of the chair outline ON THE FLOOR.

2 ERASE the chair outline on the floor.

3 ZOOM out to see the table and chairs.

Step 8: Insert the chair.

1 Set the 0 layer as the current layer.

2 Use the INSERT command to insert the 3dchair block. *Hint:* Use Quadrant object snap to catch the insertion point on the circle on the floor.

3 Use the ARRAY-polar command to duplicate the chair (Figure 11.36).

4 Use XREF to detach the floor plan.

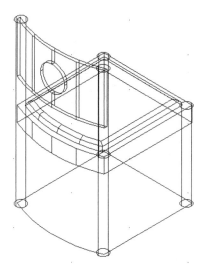

Figure 11.35
Finished chair.

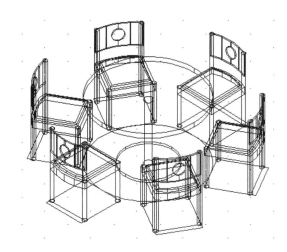

Figure 11.36
Table and chairs.

Creating the Floor and Ceiling

The floor and the ceiling are two horizontal planes. A horizontal plane can be easily made with "3D face," a special type of AutoCAD drawing entity. After creating the floor, you can simply copy it with a vertical displacement to lift it to its appropriate altitude (elevation).

Step 1: Create the floor.

1 Create the Floor layer and set it current; THAW the Wall layer.

2 Use the PLAN command to switch to plan view.

3 ZOOM-All to see the plan with space around it.

4 Make sure ORTHO is on.

5 Use the 3DFACE command to create a floor.

Command: **3DFACE** ↵

Specify first point or [Invisible]:
Pick a point near the
upper-left outside corner   (Figure 11.37)

Specify second point
or [Invisible]: **24′** ↵   Use the direct-distance entry method:

                                                Use your mouse to direct the rubber band
                                                line direction while entering the distance.

Specify third point
or [Invisible] <exit>: **14′** ↵   Use the direct-distance entry method.

Specify fourth point or [Invisible]
<create three-sided face>: **24′** ↵   Use the direct-distance entry method.

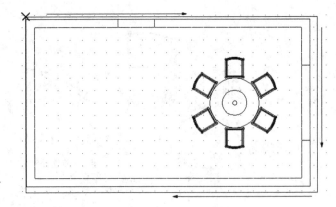

Figure 11.37.
Create a floor
with 3DFACE.

Specify third point
or [Invisible] <exit>: ↵   End command.

Command:

- The floor is made slightly larger than the footprint of the wall in order to make future selection easier.

Step 2: Create the ceiling.

1 Create the Ceiling layer.

2 Set an axonometric view.

3 Use the COPY command to copy the floor and put the copy 8′ above the floor.

Command: **COPY** ↵

Select objects: **Pick the floor** 1 found

Select objects: ↵

Specify base point or displacement,
or [Multiple]: **0,0,8′** ↵

Specify second point of displacement
or <use first point as displacement>: ↵

Command:

4 Change the layer of the ceiling to Ceiling.

Creating a Picture

To make the eventual rendering of the space look better, a picture on the wall is helpful. In this step, you will make a simple box and move it up on the wall. Later, you will "paste" a picture on it.

1 Create the Picture layer and set it as the current layer.

2 Change to the plan view.

3 Create a box (48 × .5 × 36) along the south wall (using the solid box).

4 Lift (MOVE) it up 3′.

5 MOVE to align it with the dining table.

Setting Perspective Views

Setting a perspective is similar to taking a photograph in an interior space. You hold a camera and aim at a certain point; you move back and forth or you adjust the zoom lens to change the scope of the view. In AutoCAD you need to define a target point and a camera point; you adjust the distance between the camera and the target or change the zoom value to change the scope of the view. You may also rotate the camera or the target point to change the view. When the view is set, you can save it as a named view that can be called out whenever you need it.

Step 1: Set up a one-point perspective.

1 ZOOM to look at the floor plan.

2 Use the DVIEW (dynamic view) command to set up the view.

Command: **DVIEW** ↵

Select objects
or <use DVIEWBLOCK>:
Pick a point.

Specify opposite corner:
Pick a point 13 found   Use implied cross window to
                                              select the walls and the furniture.

Select objects
or <use DVIEWBLOCK>: ↵

Enter option [CAmera/TArget/
Distance/POints/PAn/Zoom/
TWist/CLip/Hide/Off/Undo]: **PO** ↵

Specify target point
<15′-4 3/4″, 16′-6″, 3′-8 1/2″>: **.XY** ↵

of **pick point (1)** (need Z): **5′** ↵   (Figure 11.38a)

● At this point, AutoCAD wants a 3D point. You can enter the coordinates *(x,y,z)* if you know them, but you usually don't. Since picking a 3D point directly from the drawing area is very difficult, you need to use .XY (called a "point filter"), which allows you to pick the location of a point on the floor and enter how far you want

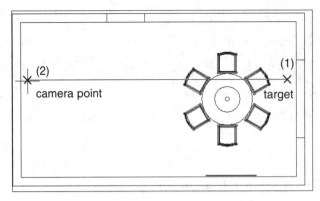

a

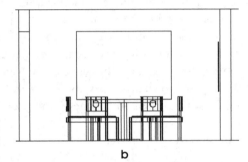

Figure 11.38
Set the target and
camera points.

b

it to be above (or below) the picked point. AutoCAD takes the *x* and *y* coordinates from the point you pick, and adds the z coordinate you enter to make it a 3D-point coordinate. The 5′ you enter is the normal eye-level.

Specify camera point
<15′-4 3/4″, 16′-6″, 3′-9 1/2″>:
Press [F8] <Ortho on> **.XY** ↵

of **pick point (2)** (need Z): **5′** ↵   An elevation view appears
                                                 (Figure 11.38b).

● Make sure that ORTHO is on to ensure the line between the target point and the camera point is horizontal. The same height for the camera point and the target point makes a straightforward view in which all vertical elements remain vertical. If your camera point has a different height from that of the target point, the vertical lines of your model will converge to a vertical vanishing point and make the view look like a 3-point perspective.

Enter option [CAmera/TArget/
Distance/POints/PAn/Zoom/TWist/
CLip/Hide/Off/Undo]: **D** ↵

Specify new camera-target
distance <20′-8 1/4″>: ↵

          Accept the default value. The view turns into a perspective (Figure 11.39).

          The default value may be different in your drawing.

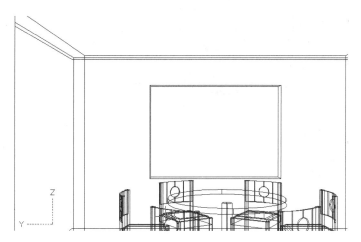

Figure 11.39
Set the viewing distance.

● At this point, you can drag your mouse to interactively set the distance. Since your camera point is already near the wall, you can easily get out of the room by using a small movement of the mouse; therefore, DO NOT drag to set the distance.

Enter option [CAmera/TArget/
Distance/POints/PAn/Zoom/
TWist/CLip/Hide/Off/Undo]: **Z** ↵

Specify lens length <50.000mm>:
24 ↵   (Figure 11.40)

● 24mm makes it a wide-angle lens that is needed for most interior views. You may try a different focal length to see different effects.

Enter option [CAmera/TArget/
Distance/POints/PAn/Zoom/
TWist/CLip/Hide/Off/Undo]: **H** ↵

Look at the hideline view to examine the view.

● The hideline view allows you to see if the camera point has moved outside the space. If that is the case, the view will turn blank because the camera is blocked by the wall. If that happens, you need to adjust the distance to move the camera a little closer to the target.

Figure 11.40
Set the Zoom
focal length.

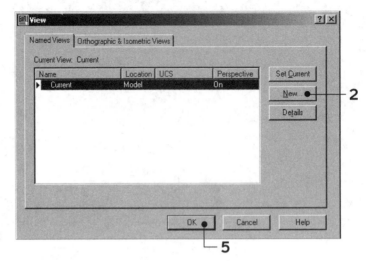

Figure 11.41
The View dialog box

Enter option [CAmera/TArget/
Distance/POints/PAn/Zoom/
TWist/CLip/Hide/Off/Undo]: ↵

Regenerating model.

Command:

● You are now in a perspective view. If you don't like it, you can repeat step 1 to reset it with different camera and target points.

Step 2: Save the view.

A view on the screen can be saved as a named view within the drawing by the VIEW command. A named view can be restored at the time you want by the same VIEW command.

1 **Enter the VIEW command or its alias V.** The View dialog box pops up (Figure 11.41).

2 **Click [New].** The New View dialog box pops up (Figure 11.42).

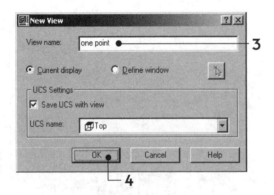

Figure 11.42
The New View dialog box.

3 Enter "one point" in the View name text box.

4 Click [OK]. The New View dialog box closes.

5 **Click [OK] in the View dialog box.** A view named "one point" is saved in the drawing.

Step 3: Set up a two-point perspective.

Setting a 2-point perspective is basically the same as setting a 1-point perspective shown in step 2. The only difference is that the direction from the camera to the target is not parallel to any walls.

1 **Follow the same procedure as in step 2 and set the target and camera points as shown in Figure 11.43.** The result is shown in Figure 11.44.

2 Save the view as two point (VIEW).

Step 4: Restore a saved view.

1 **Enter the VIEW command.** The View dialog box pops up (Figure 11.45).

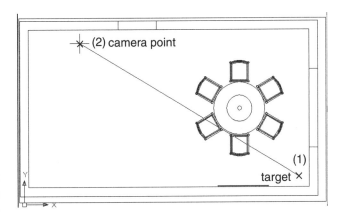

Figure 11.43
Set a 2-point perspective view.

Figure 11.44
A 2-point perspective view.

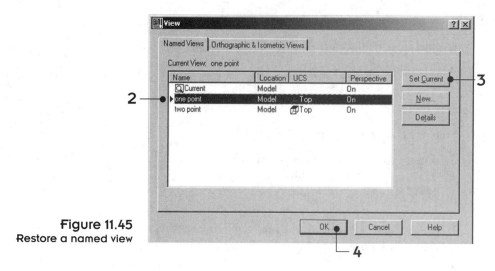

Figure 11.45
Restore a named view

2 Select "one point."

3 Click [Set current].

4 Click [OK]. The saved "one point" view is shown.

Step 5: Plot a hideline perspective view from model space.

Sometimes you may need to plot a perspective view from model space.

1 Thaw all layers.

2 Enter PLOT. The Plot dialog box pops up (Figure 11.46).

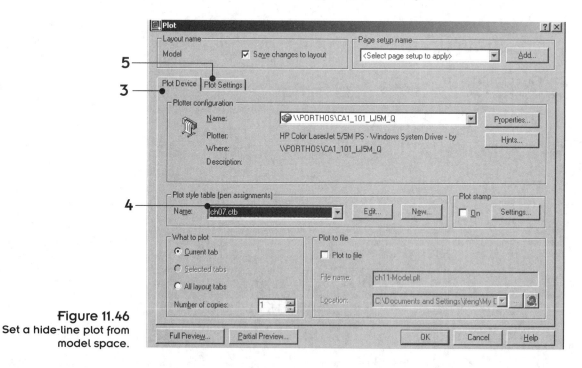

Figure 11.46
Set a hide-line plot from
model space.

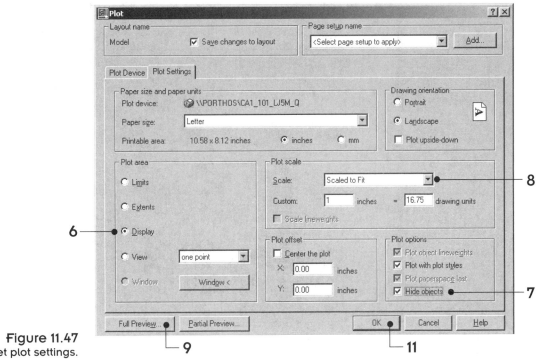

Figure 11.47
Set plot settings.

3 Click the Plot Device tab.

4 Load the ch07.ctb Plot Style Table.

● This will make all the lines plotted in the same black color.

5 Click the Plot Settings tab. (Figure 11.47)

6 Check the Display circular button if it not already checked.

7 Check the Hide-objects box.

● This function does not work in paper space.

8 Click the Scale list and select Scaled to Fit.

9 Click [Full Preview…] to preview the plot.

10 Press the [Esc] key to exit Preview.

11 Click [OK] to plot.

Step 6: Plot a hideline perspective view in paper space layout.

Plotting perspective views in paper space layout is very similar to plotting a floor plan. One more procedure, however, is needed to turn on the hideplot mode of the viewport.

1 Click the Layout1 tab. (Click [OK] if prompted with the "Page Setup" dialog.)

2 Click the Paper button in the status bar to switch to the model space mode.

Figure 11.48
Perspective views
in paper space.

3 Use the VIEW command to set the "two point" view current. The "two point" view appears (Figure 11.48).

4 Click the Model button in the status bar to switch to the paper space mode.

5 Use MVIEW to turn on the hideplot mode of the viewport.

Command: **MVIEW** ↵

Specify corner of viewport
or [ON/OFF/Fit/Hideplot/
Lock/Object/Polygonal/Restore/2/3/4]
<Fit>: **H** ↵   For Hideplot.

Hidden line removal for plotting
[ON/OFF]: **ON** ↵

Select objects:
Select the viewport 1 found

Select objects: ↵

Command: You don't see any obvious change.

- The alias for MVIEW is MV. The MVIEW command is equivalent to the Single viewport icon that you used in previous chapters.

6 Plot the paper space drawing as usual (PLOT) (Figure 11.49).

7 Save your drawing and exit AutoCAD.

Figure 11.49
Result of HIDEPLOT.

Summary

In this chapter, you have built a 3D model from the floor plan and set two perspective views. In this process, you have learned the following concepts, procedures, and commands:

Knowledge/Concepts

- Thickness
- Solid model
- Massing solid
- Right-hand rule of rotation
- Wireframe image
- Hideline image
- Shading modes
- 3Dface
- Point filter
- Views

Procedures

- Set an axonometric view
- Lift an object up (using vertical displacement to define 3D movement)
- Define thickness

- Switch to a plan view
- Set up a one-point perspective view
- Use point filter to define a 3D point
- Set up a two-point perspective view
- Save a named view
- Restore a named view
- Present a hideline view in paper space
- Plot a hideline view from model space

Commands

 - BOX

 - CYLINDER

 - SPHERE

 - EXTRUDE (EXT)

 - INTERFERE

 - SE Isometric View tool

- BOUNDARY
- CHPROP
- PLAN

 - Top View tool

- ROTATE3D
- SUBTRACT (SU)

 - HIDE (HI)

 - SHADE

 - 2D wireframe view

 - 3DFACE

- DVIEW (DV)
- VIEW (V)
- MVIEW (MV)

Rendering

- Set up lighting
- Select and apply materials
- Set a background image
- Render and fine-tune an image
- Render a final rendering
- Print out the rendered image

In this chapter, you will learn the basics of rendering in AutoCAD to generate a photo-real view of the dining area.

Setting Up Lighting

Light is essential to vision in the real world; virtual light is critical in computer visualization. Only under appropriate lighting will the materials show properly in an AutoCAD rendering; therefore, lighting must be set up before you begin to work on the materials.

Step 1: Set the Render toolbar.

1 Open drawing ch11.dwg and save it as ch12.dwg.

2 Click View on the menu bar.

3 Select Toolbars.

4 Check the box before Render.

5 Clear all other boxes.

6 Click [Close].

7 Embed the toolbar into the frame of the drawing window.

8 Click the Model tab.

9 Use the PLAN command to look at the model in a plan view.

10 Make sure ORTHO and OSNAP are off.

Step 2: Create a point light above the dining table.

A point light works like a bare bulb that emits light in all directions equally. We want to use one point light above the dining table to provide general lighting for the entire space.

1 **Click the Light icon.** The Lights dialog box pops up (Figure 12.1).

2 Click the light type list and choose Point Light.

3 Click [New]. The New Point Light dialog box pops up (Figure 12.2).

4 Name the light P1.

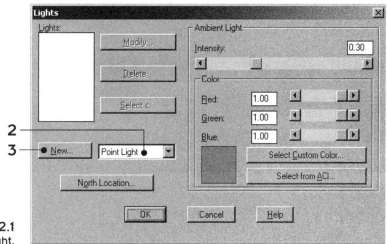

Figure 12.1
Set up a point light.

5 Adjust the intensity to 35 (approximately).

- The number 35 is chosen after much trial and error and aesthetic judgment. It is not physically based.

6 Check the box before Shadow On to make the light cast shadow.

- Casting shadow may take substantial time for large models. Turning it off can save time in the process of fine tuning. It can be turned on before the final rendering.

7 Click [Modify] to locate the light.

Enter light location <current>:
.XY ⏎   Use point filter to set a 3D point.

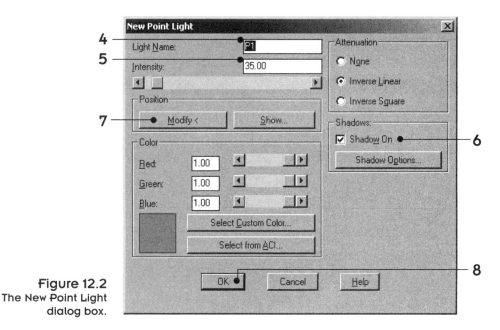

Figure 12.2
The New Point Light dialog box.

of **click at the center
of the table** (need Z): **6′** ⏎   Don't use object snap.

Command:

8 Click [OK]. The Lights dialog box returns.

9 Click [OK].

Step 3: Adjust the Light icon size.

An icon (called light icon) representing the light appears in the view. It is so small that you may barely see it. You can adjust its size. The Light icon will not be visible in rendered images.

1 **Click the Render Preferences icon on the Render toolbar.** The Render Preferences dialog box pops up (Figure 12.3).

2 **Change the value for Light Icon Scale from 1 to 10.**

3 Click [OK]. The Light icon becomes visible (Figure 12.4).

Step 4: Create a spotlight to light the picture.

A spotlight emits light within a cone. The cone has two components: hotspot and falloff. Hotspot creates a pool of light with great brightness; falloff creates a soft pool of light. The falloff can never be smaller than the hotspot (Figure 12.5). Spotlights are usually used to highlight objects of interest to create focal points in a rendered scene. We will create a spotlight to highlight the picture on the wall.

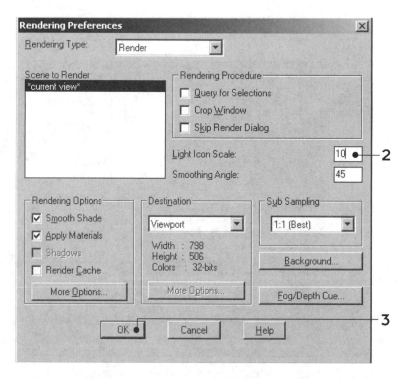

Figure 12.3
Adjust the Light
Icon Scale.

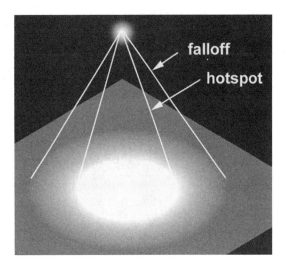

Figure 12.4
Light icon.

Figure 12.5
Hotspot and falloff.

1 Click the Lights icon, click the Type list, and choose Spotlight in the Lights dialog box.

2 Click [New]. The New Spotlight dialog box pops up (Figure 12.6).

3 Name the light SP1.

4 Change Intensity to about 30.

5 Change Hotspot to 0. To create a soft pool of light.

6 Check the box before Shadow On.

7 Click [Modify <] to locate the light and its aiming direction.

● For the spotlight, you need to define both the light position and the aiming target.

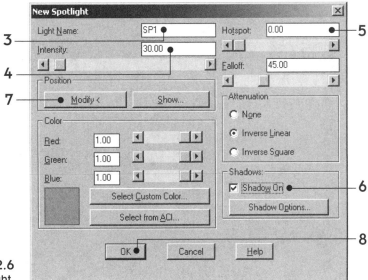

Figure 12.6
Create a spotlight.

Enter light target <current>: **.XY** ↵

of **pick the midpoint of the picture**
(in plan view) (need Z): **5'** ↵

● This defines the center point on the picture.

Enter light location <current>: **.XY** ↵

of **pick a point approximately 18"**
in front of the picture (need Z): **7'11** ↵

● The height of the light should be a little bit off the ceiling surface to avoid being blocked by the surface.

Command:

8 Click [OK]. The dialog box closes.

9 Click [OK] to close the Lights dialog box.

Selecting and Applying Materials

Step 1: Select and import materials from the material library.

AutoCAD has a material library with many ready-made materials. Similar to line-types, the materials in the material library need to be imported first from the library to your drawing before you can apply them on to your model.

1 Click the Material Library icon. The Materials Library dialog box pops up (Figure 12.7).

2 Click on BEIGE MATTE in the material list.

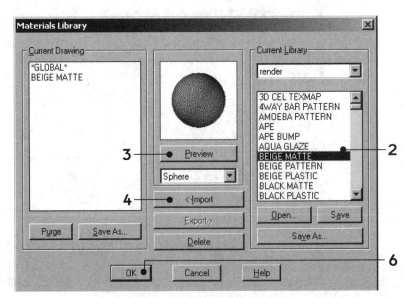

Figure 12.7
Select and import
materials.

3 Click [Preview] to examine the appearance of the material.

4 Click [<-Import] to import the material into your drawing.

5 Repeat steps 2 through 4 to import the following materials:

BLACK PLASTIC
BRASS GIFMAP
GLASS
TILE PINKGRANITE
V PATTERN
WHITE MATTE
WHITE PLASTIC
WOOD DARK RED
WOOD WHITE ASH

6 Click [OK].

Step 2: Create a new material for the picture.

In addition to the ready-made materials, you can create your own materials. In this step, you will create a material for the picture on the wall from an image file stored in AutoCAD. In the future, you can follow this procedure to create your own image files of your interior materials with a scanner and create materials to apply to your model.

1 Click the **Materials** icon. The Materials dialog box pops up (Figure 12.8).

2 Click [**New**]. The New Standard Material dialog box pops up (Figure 12.9).

3 Name the new material PICTURE.

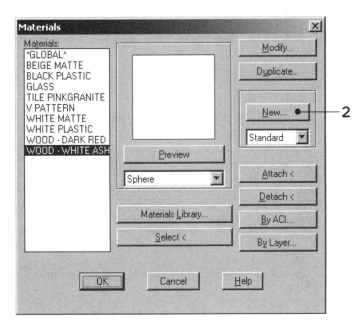

Figure 12.8
Create a new material.

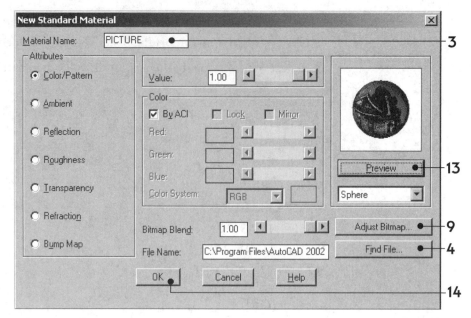

Figure 12.9
Create new materials.

4 Click [**Find File...**]. The Bitmap File dialog box pops up (Figure 12.10).

5 **In the Bitmap File dialog box find the Texture directory (folder) within the Acad 2002 directory, and double-click to open it.**

● The location of the Acad 2002 directory may differ, but the file should always be accessible. Since the .bmp default type does not match the type of the files in the directory, the file name field appears to be empty. You need to change the file type to .tga.

6 **Click the Files of type: list and choose *.tga.** File names appear.

7 **Find the house.tga file and select it.**

8 Click [**Open**]. The Bitmap File dialog box closes.

9 Click [**Adjust Bitmap**] **in the New Standard Materials dialog box** (Figure 12.9). The Adjust Material Bitmap Placement dialog box pops up (Figure 12.11).

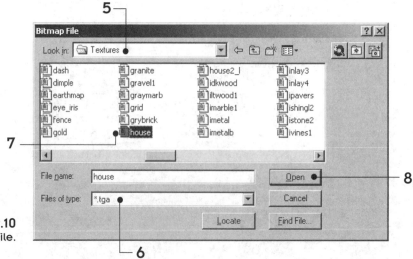

Figure 12.10
Find the bitmap file.

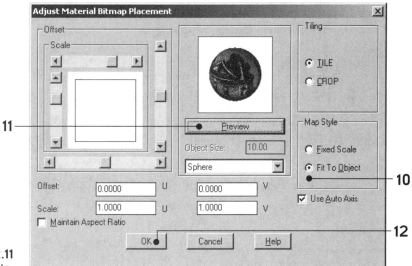

Figure 12.11
Adjust the mapping style.

10 Check the button before Fit To Object in the Map Style group.

11 Click [Preview] to examine the image. A picture of a house appears.

12 [OK] to close the dialog box.

13 Click [Preview] to examine the image (Figure 12.9).

14 Click [OK]. The new PICTURE material appears in the material list.

Step 3: Attach materials to objects by layers.

1 Click [By Layer] in the Materials dialog box. The Attach by Layer dialog box pops up (Figure 12.12).

2 Click to select the BEIGE MATTE material.

3 Click to select the Wall layer.

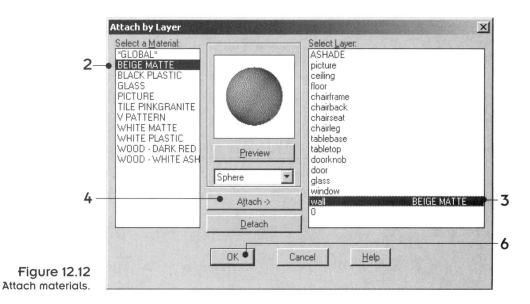

Figure 12.12
Attach materials.

4 Click [Attach ->]. The material name appears in the Layer list.

● If you don't remember the appearance of the material, you can click [Preview] to have a look.

5 Follow the same procedure as from steps 2 through 4 to attach materials to layers as shown in the following list.

Material	Layer
BLACK PLASTIC	tablebase
BRASS GIFMAP	doorknob
GLASS	glass
PICTURE	picture
TILE PINKGRANITE	floor
V PATTERN	chairseat
WHITE MATTE	ceiling
WHITE PLASTIC	window
WOOD DARK RED	tabletop
WOOD WHITE ASH	chairframe, door

6 Click [OK].

7 Click [OK] in the Materials dialog box.

Setting a Background Image

The background in AutoCAD rendering is like a backdrop on a stage. You can put up a landscape image so that you can see it through the windows.

 1 Click the Background icon. The Background dialog box pops up (Figure 12.13).

2 Check the circular button in front of Image.

3 Click [Find File...]. The Background Image dialog box pops up.

4 Find and open the vally_1.tga file from the TEXTURE directory within the Acad 2002 directory.

5 Click [Preview] to see the image.

6 Click [OK].

7 Use the VIEW command to set "one point" current.

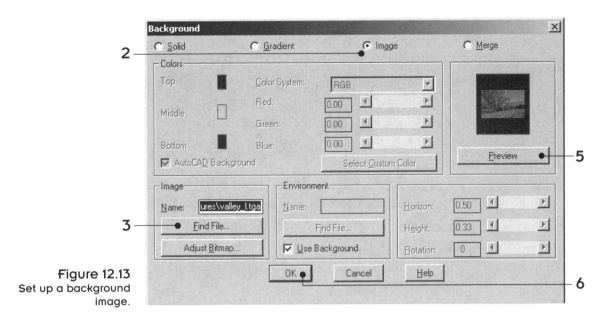

Figure 12.13
Set up a background
image.

Rendering and Fine-Tuning an Image

Step 1: Set rendering settings and render the view.

1 **Click the Render icon.** The Render dialog box pops up (Figure 12.14).

2 **Click the Rendering Type list and choose Photo Raytrace.**

● Photo Raytrace is the best among the three types.

3 **Check the Shadows box to produce shadow in the rendering.**

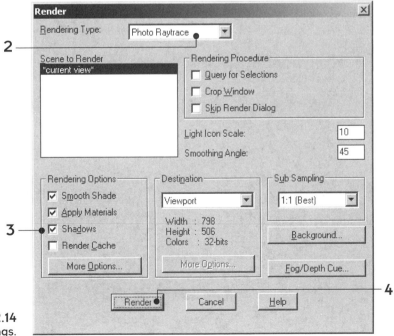

Figure 12.14
Rendering settings.

- To cast shadow in a rendering you need to check the shadow box not only in this dialog, but also in the Light Setting dialog. (You already did.) If you want to reduce the rendering time in test renderings, you can clear the box to turn it off.

- In the Rendering Options group, the Smooth Shade and Apply Materials boxes should be checked by default. If not, check them.

4 Click [Render] to start the rendering process.

- It will take some time to generate the rendered image. When you look at the rendered image (Figure 12.15), you may find some problems. The room is rather dark (especially in the shadow). The floor tile is not showing correctly. You need to make some adjustments to fix these problems. The rendering is very much a trial-and-error process. Going back and forth to adjust lighting and materials is common. It would be a miracle if you could get a perfect rendering without several rounds of fine-tuning.

Step 2: Adjust lighting.

1 Click the Light icon. The Lights dialog box pops up (Figure 12.16).

2 Adjust the Ambient light level to .70.

- The ambient light level controls the brightness of shadows. It has a great impact on your perception of the brightness of the space, since it controls the brightness ratio of the scene.

3 Click [OK]. The dialog box closes.

- If you are curious about the effect of the above adjustment, you can render it and see the result.

Step 3: Adjust material mapping scale.

The problem of the floor seen in the first test rendering is a problem of scaling. The tiling of the bitmap (by default) appears to be too small. You need to adjust the scale

Figure 12.15
First test rendering.

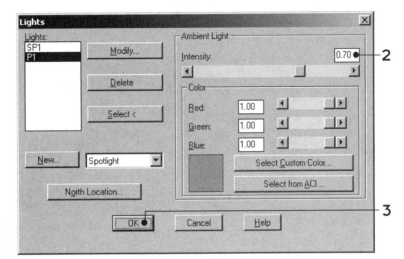

Figure 12.16
Adjust the ambient
light level.

according to the actual size of the tile and the room. The scaling of a bitmap is controlled at two different levels: the material and the object. The bitmap scaling at the material level has a global effect on all the objects the material is assigned to; the scaling at the object level affects individual objects. The scale of a bitmap mapping on an object is determined by the multiplication of the scale factors at the two levels.

Adjust the material mapping scale at the materials level.

1 **Click the Materials icon.** The Materials dialog box pops up (Figure 12.17).

2 **Click the TILE PINKGRANITE material.**

3 **Click [Modify].** The Modify Standard Material dialog box pops up (Figure 12.18).

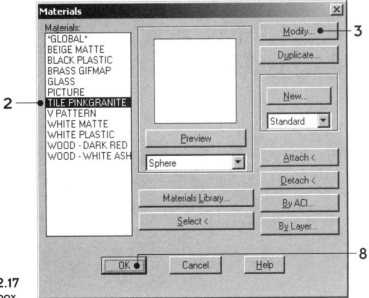

Figure 12.17
The Materials dialog box.

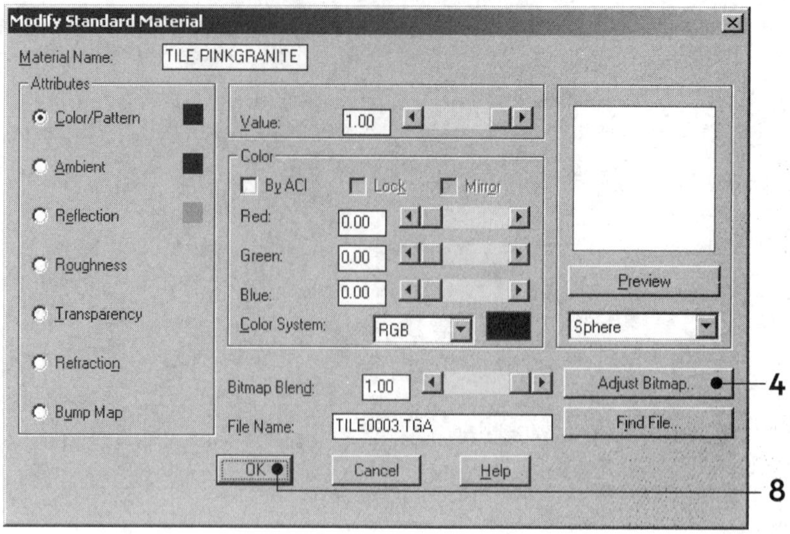

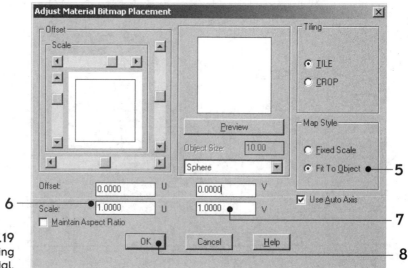

Figure 12.18
The Modify Standard
Material dialog box.

4 Click [**Adjust Bitmap...**]. The Adjust Materials Bitmap Placement dialog box pops up (Figure 12.19).

5 Check the button before Fit to Object.

6 Change U scale factor to 1.

7 Change V scale factor to 1.

● This setting allows us to figure out easily the scale factor at the object level according to the actual size of the material surface, such as the floor plane.

8 Click [OK] three times to close all dialog boxes.

Adjust the material mapping scale at the objects level.

Applying a material on an object is technically called "mapping" in AutoCAD. You need to use the mapping tool to change the way the material is applied to the objects.

Figure 12.19
Adjust the bitmap scaling
of the material.

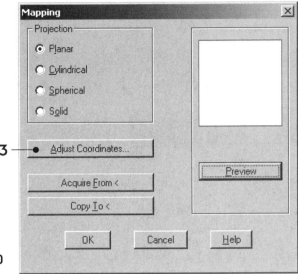

Figure 12.20
Mapping control.

1 Use the REGEN command to return to the wireframe view from the rendered view.

2 **Click the Mapping icon. Select the floor by its edge.** The Mapping dialog box pops up (Figure 12.20).

3 Click [**Adjust Coordinates...**]. The Adjust Planar Coordinates dialog box pops up (Figure 12.21).

4 Click [**Adjust Bitmap...**]. The Adjust Object Bitmap Placement dialog box pops up (Figure 12.22).

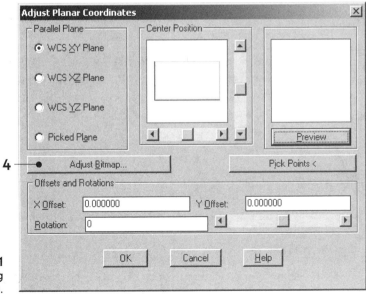

Figure 12.21
Adjust mapping
coordinates.

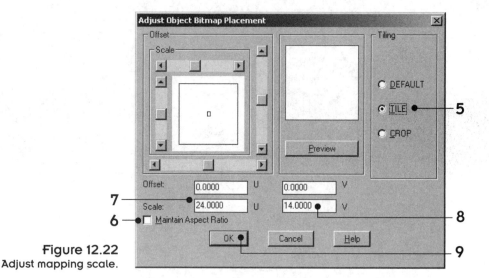

Figure 12.22
Adjust mapping scale.

5 Make sure Tile in the Tiling group is checked on.

6 Make sure Maintain Aspect Ratio is checked off (clear).

7 Change the U scale to 24. The rectangle appears in the image window.

8 Change the V scale to 14. The rectangle turns into a very small rectangle.

● The U and V (like X and Y in the drawing coordinate system) are the two dimensions in a second coordinate system for material mapping. The U or V value means the times the material image will be repeated in the dimension of U or V. Since the size of the floor is approximately 24′ × 14′, the values 24 and 14 will produce 1-ft square tiles. (If the value changes a little after you enter it, it doesn't matter.) The red-colored boxes represents the object, and the white and magenta box represent the tile size of the bitmap.

9 Click [OK] (3 times) to exit the Mapping dialogs.

Step 4: Render the scene.

Do a test render of the scene with shadow on to see if the adjustments are satisfactory. If you still see some problems, you can repeat the above described procedures to fix them. The result may look like what is shown in Figure 12.23.

Final Rendering

Now you are ready to create a high-quality image of your model.

Step 1: Set the Anti-Aliasing high.

Anti-aliasing makes jagged edges smooth. The process, however, may substantially increase the rendering time of the image; therefore, you should set the anti-aliasing on the high level only when you are ready for the final rendering.

Figure 12.23
Rendered image after
adjustments.

1 Click the Render icon to access the Render dialog box.

2 Click [More Options] in the Rendering Options group. The Photo Raytrace Render Options dialog box pops up (Figure 12.24).

3 Click the High circular button (in the Anti-Aliasing box).

4 Click [OK]. The Render dialog box appears.

Step 2: Render to a viewport and save the screen image to a file.

At this point, you can send the rendered image either to your monitor (viewport) or to a file. Since sending the rendering to viewport is the default setting, you already have been doing that in your previous test renderings. After you see the image on the screen, you can save it to a file. This approach allows you to have a look at the image before you save it. But the resolution (fineness) of the image is limited to the size of the screen.

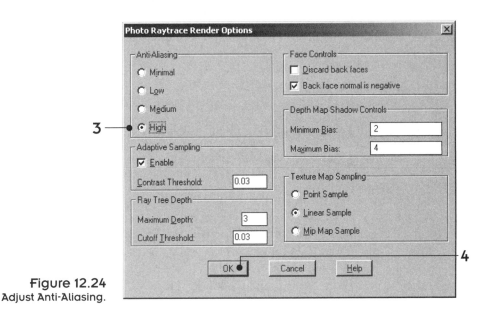

Figure 12.24
Adjust Anti-Aliasing.

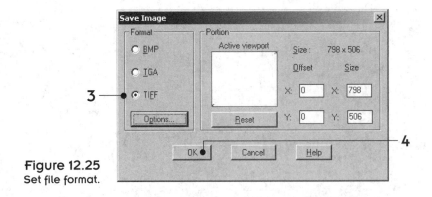

Figure 12.25
Set file format.

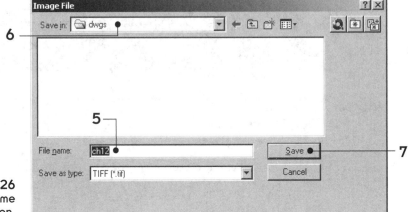

Figure 12.26
Set file name
and location.

1 **Click [OK] to start the rendering.** AutoCAD reports the progress time until the rendering is complete.

2 **Enter the SAVEIMG command.** The Save Image dialog box pops up (Figure 12.25).

3 **Click the TIFF circular button to choose the file format.**

● TIFF is a high-quality graphic file format acceptable to most graphics software.

4 **Click [OK].** The Image File dialog box pops up (Figure 12.26).

5 **Type in a file name.**

● AutoCAD will automatically put the drawing file name and the image file extension in the File name text box. You may type in another name if you like.

6 **Click the Save in: list and choose the directory you want the file to save to.**

7 **Click [Save].** AutoCAD reports "Save Image done!"

Step 3: Render to a file.

In order to have an image resolution higher than the screen resolution, you need to render the image directly to a file. This approach gives you more choices of the image resolution and file formats. If you want to make a high resolution print of your drawing, you should use this approach. Keep in mind that the higher the resolution, the larger the file size, and the longer it takes to render.

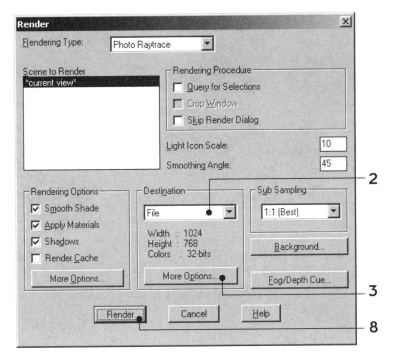

Figure 12.27
The Render dialog box.

1 Click the Render icon to access the Render dialog box (Figure 12.27).

2 Click the Destination list and choose File.

3 Click [**More Options...**]. The File Output Configuration dialog box pops up (Figure 12.28).

4 Click the File Type list and choose TIFF.

5 Click the Resolution list and choose an image resolution (1024 × 768).

6 Make sure color depth is 32 bits.

7 Click [OK].

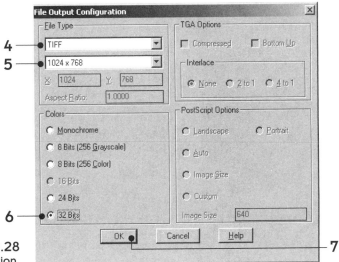

Figure 12.28
Set image resolution.

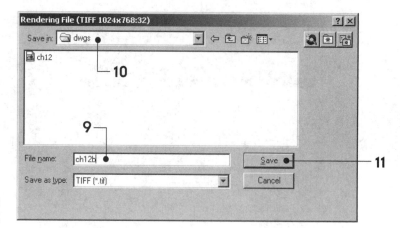

Figure 12.29
Set file name.

8 Click [Render] in the Render dialog box. The Rendering File dialog box pops up (Figure 12.29).

9 Change the file name to Ch12b.

10 Click the Save in: list and choose the directory you want the file to save to.

11 Click [Save]. AutoCAD starts to write the image file. It reports progress until it's done.

Printing Out the Rendered Image

The rendered image file (in TIFF or other graphic file formats) can work in most of the image-processing programs. You can use these programs to retouch your rendered images and print them out. You can also print out rendered images with Auto-CAD. The following are steps to print the rendered image with AutoCAD.

1 Click the Layout1 tab to go to paper space.

2 ERASE the existing viewport.

3 Click Insert in the menu bar and choose Raster Image. The Select Image File dialog box pops up (Figure 12.30).

● A raster image is also called a bitmap image that is made of colored dots.

4 Click the Look in list to locate the directory where the image file is saved.

5 Select the image file. The image appears in the preview window.

● The selected file type in the Files of type list must match or include the file type of the image file you want to select. Otherwise your image file will not be displayed. If so, you need to change the file type to either All image files or TIFF [*.tif].

6 Click [Open]. The Attach Image dialog box pops up (Figure 12.31).

7 Click [OK]. A rectangle attached to the cursor appears.

8 Move the cursor to locate the lower-left corner of the image in the paper space drawing with a click. (Figure 12.32)

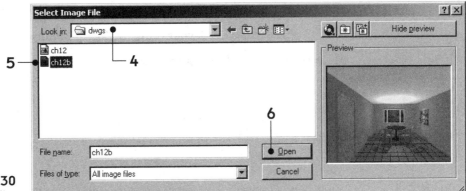

Figure 12.30
Select the image file.

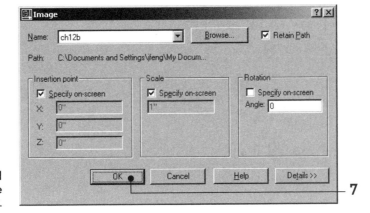

Figure 12.31
The Attach Image
dialog box.

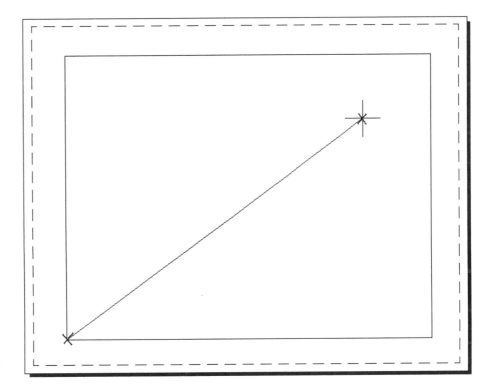

Figure 12.32
Insert a raster image.

9 Move the cursor to adjust the size of the image. Click to set.

10 Print the paper space layout using the PLOT command.

11 Save your file and exit AutoCAD.

Summary

In this chapter, you have used the rendering tools to create a rendered image of your model. In this process, you have learned the following concepts, procedures, and commands:

Knowledge/Concepts

- Point light
- Spotlight
- Hotspot
- Falloff
- Material library
- Rendering
- Photo raytrace
- Light icon scale
- Ambient light
- Mapping
- Mapping scale
- Mapping coordinates
- Anti-aliasing
- Raster image file

Procedures

- Set up a point light
- Set up a spotlight
- Select materials
- Import materials
- Create a new material
- Attach materials to objects

- Set background image
- Set rendering settings
- Adjust ambient light level
- Adjust mapping scale
- Adjust mapping coordinates
- Save a rendered image to a file
- Render to a file
- Attach an image file to a drawing

Commands

- RENDER (RR)

- Render Preference

- LIGHT

- Materials

- Materials library

- Mapping

- Background

- REGEN

- SAVEIMG

Chapter **13**

Posting the Drawings
to the Web

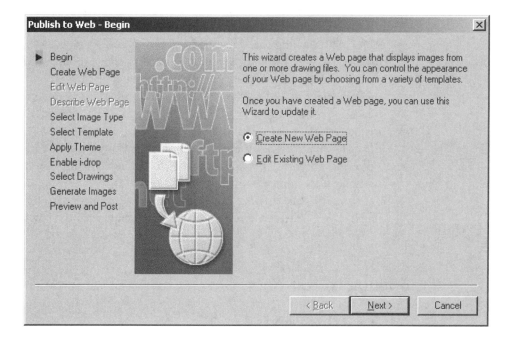

- Create a Web page
- Test your Web page

In recent years, the world-wide-web (www) has become an important place for people to exchange information and ideas. CAD drawings also can be displayed on the Web so that they are easily accessible to people involved in the design and construction process. To assist you in posting your drawings on the Web, AutoCAD r2002 provides a wizard so that you can communicate with other people about your design anywhere in the world. In the following tutorial, you will use the wizard to create a Web page for the AutoCAD drawings you have created in previous chapters.

Before you proceed, we need to discuss some basic concepts regarding how AutoCAD drawings are presented on the Web. As you may know, Web pages are usually HTML files stored on Web servers that are connected to the Internet. Graphic images on a Web page are usually image files (in the format of JPEG or GIF files) that are linked to HTML files. For AutoCAD drawings, however, a special image file format known as DWF (Drawing Web File) was developed by AutoDesk for better image quality and added viewing functions. Viewers can read the DWF file using the free Volo View Express program running inside Internet Explorer. The Volo View Express program can be downloaded from the AutoDesk Web site: www.autodesk.com.

To do this tutorial, you need to have completed the CH05.DWG and CH12.DWG files according to the previous chapters of this book.

Creating a Web Page

Step 1: Open the drawing.

1 Start AutoCAD.

2 Open drawing CH05.DWG.

Step 2: Start the wizard.

1 Click Tools on the menu bar.

2 Click Wizards and choose Publish to Web. The Publish to Web dialog box pops up (Figure 13.1).

• You can also complete this step by clicking the Toolbar icon on the standard toolbar.

3 Make sure Create New Web Page is selected.

4 Click [Next>]. The Publish to Web dialog turns to the Create Web Page (Figure 13.2).

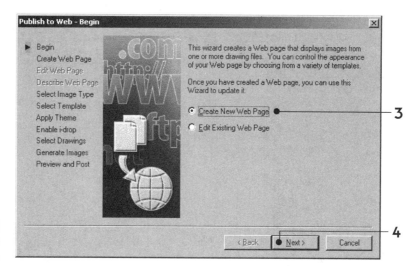

Figure 13.1
The Publish to Web
dialog begins.

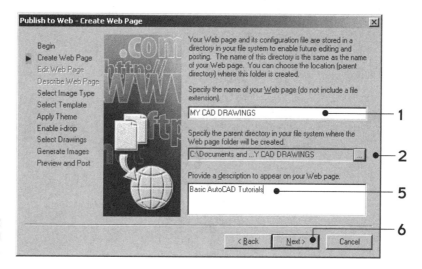

Figure 13.2
Name the file and
create titles.

Step 3: Name your Web page.

1 Enter a name for your Web page (MY CAD DRAWINGS).

● This will be the main title of your Web page.

2 Click the Browse button to select the directory where you want to store the files of your Web page. The Select Directory to Place Web Page dialog box pops up (Figure 13.3).

3 Click the Look in list and locate a directory where you want to store your files.

● A subdirectory that contains your Web page files will be created in this directory.

4 Click [Open]. The previous dialog returns (Figure 13.2).

5 Enter some description about your Web page.

● This will be the subtitle of your Web page.

6 Click [Next>]. The dialog turns to the Select Image Type page (Figure 13.4).

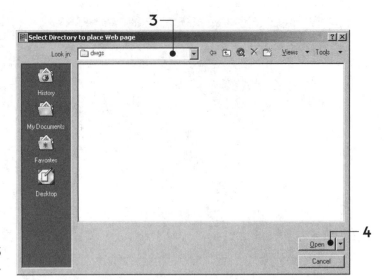

Figure 13.3
Select a template.

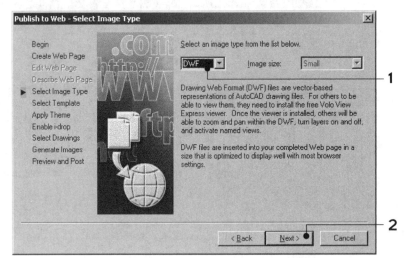

Figure 13.4
Select a file type.

Step 4: Select a file type.

In this step, you will select a file type to present your AutoCAD drawings. Since the DWF file provides a better quality image than the other two possible file types, you will use it for your Web page.

1 Make sure DWF is selected.

2 Click [Next>]. The dialog turns to the Select Template page (Figure 13.5).

Step 5: Select a template.

Templates are pre-made Web page designs that allow you to plug in your own contents. There are four templates available.

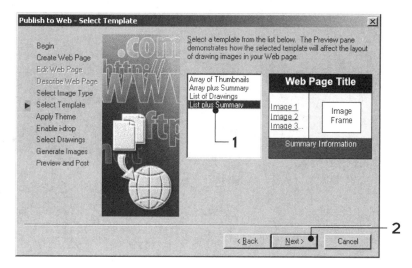

Figure 13.5
Select a template.

1 **Select List plus Summary.**

2 **Click [Next>].** The dialog turns to the Apply Theme page (Figure 13.6).

Step 6: Apply a theme.

Themes are different combinations of colors and text fonts that you can apply to a template. In this step, we will use the Classic theme.

1 **Click the Themes list and select Classic.** The colors and text style of the theme show in the preview window.

2 **Click [Next>].** The dialog turns to the Enable i-drop page (Figure 13.7).

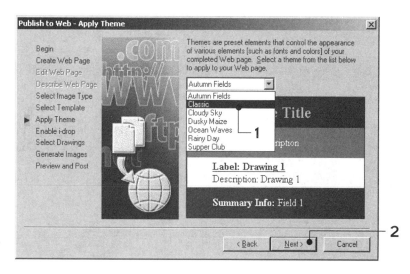

Figure 13-6
Apply a theme.

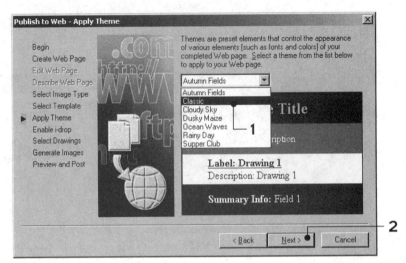

Figure 13.7
Enable i-drop.

Step 7: Enable i-drop.

I-drop is a Web function that allows the viewer of a Web page to drag-and-drop the posted AutoCAD drawings into an AutoCAD drawing. Using i-drop is an effective way to collaborate in the design process. In this step, you will choose to enable the i-drop function for the Web page you are creating.

1 Check the box in front of Enable i-drop.

2 Click [Next>]. The dialog turns to the Select Drawings page (Figure 13.8).

Step 8: Set the first drawing image.

1 Make sure the drawing you want to put on the Web page is shown in the Drawing list.

● Since ch05.dwg is the current drawing you just opened, it should appear in the Drawing list by default. If you want to have another drawing other than the current one you are working on, you may need to use the Browse button to locate it as you will do in the next step.

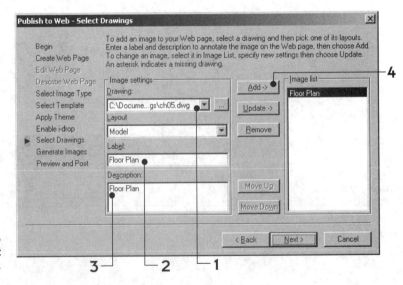

Figure 13.8
Set the first
drawing image.

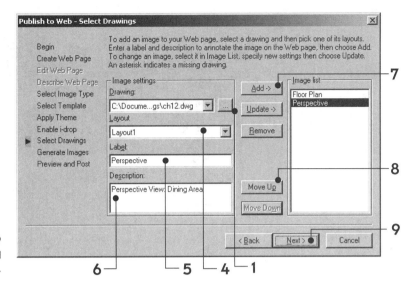

Figure 13.9
Set the second
drawing image.

2 Enter Floor Plan in the Label text field.

● This will appear on the Web page as an item in the contents list.

3 Enter Floor Plan in the Description text field.

● This will appear as the caption of the image.

4 Click [Add->]. The name of the image appears in the Image list.

Step 9: Set the second drawing image from another drawing file.

1 Click the Browse button next to the Drawing list (Figure 13.9). The Publish to Web dialog box pops up (Figure 13.10).

2 Find and select drawing file CH12. The thumbnail image of the drawing appears in the Preview window.

3 Click [Open]. The Select Drawings page returns (Figure 13.9).

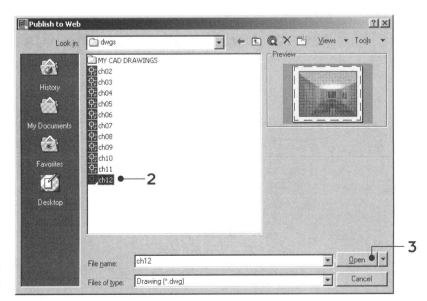

Figure 13.10
The Publish to Web
dialog box.

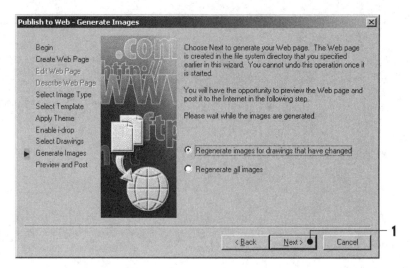

Figure 13.11
Generate Images page.

4 Make sure that Layout1 is shown in the Layout list.

5 Change the label to Perspective.

6 Enter a description for the perspective view.

7 Click [**Add ->**]. The image name is added to the list.

Step 10: Change the order of the images.

This step shows how you can change the order in which the images are shown on the Web page.

8 Click [**Move Up**]. The perspective view is moved to the top of the list.

9 Click [**Next >**]. The Generate Images page appears (Figure 13.11).

Step 11: Generate the Web page.

1 Click [**Next>**]. The Preview and Post page appears (Figure 13.12).

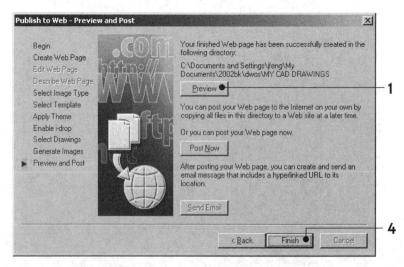

Figure 13.12
The Preview and
Post page.

- Since the administration of Web servers differs, the procedure to post your files to the Web server may be unique. You need to learn how to do that from your Web administrator.

Step 12: Preview the Web page.

1 Click [Preview]. The Web page is shown (Figure 13.13).

2 Click Floor Plan. The floor plan shows in the image frame (Figure 13.14).

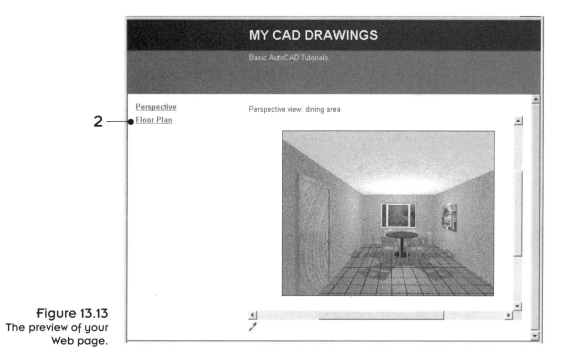

Figure 13.13
The preview of your Web page.

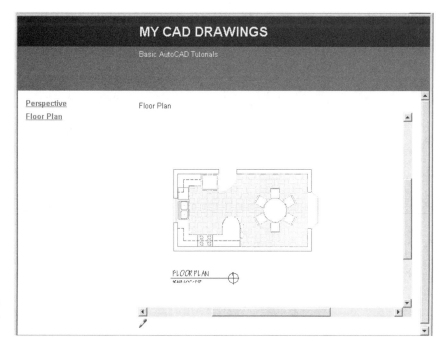

Figure 13.14
Preview of the second image.

3 Close the preview window by clicking the Close button. The Preview and Post page returns (Figure 13.12).

4 Click [Finish]. The Web page files are saved in a folder named as your Web page in the location you specified in step 3.

At this time, you should have a folder named MY CAD DRAWINGS, which contains many files. Among these files, acwebpublish.htm is the main page that calls up all the other files to form the Web page. When you move these files to your Web server, they should stay together in the folder as they are now.

- When you copy the folder to your Web server, you may need to change the folder name to comply with the naming convention of the operating system of the server. For example, if you have a server using UNIX, you cannot have space between letters in folder or file names. Therefore, you may need to change MY CAD DRAWINGS to MYCADDRAWINGS or MY_CAD_DRAWINGS.

Testing the Web Page

In this step, you will open the Web page with a browser and practice working with the dwf image.

1 Quit AutoCAD without SAVE.

2 Start your Web browser (Internet Explorer).

3 Click File in the menu bar, and choose Open. The Open File dialog pops up.

4 Locate the acwebpublish.htm file in the MY CAD DRAWINGS folder and open it. Your Web page opens.

5 Click Floor Plan to view the plan in the image frame.

6 Right-click in the image frame. A menu pops up (Figure 13.15).

Floor Plan

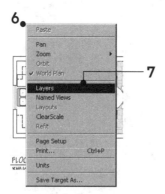

Figure 13.15
The pop-up menu.

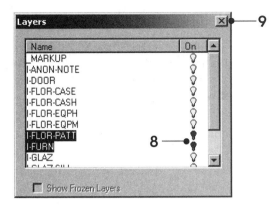

Figure 13.16
Turn off layers.

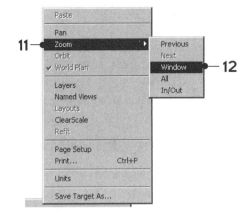

Figure 13.17
Use the Zoom-window tool.

- This menu provides a few useful functions to view the drawing image. We will try the Layer tool to change the display of the image, and the Zoom tools to look at a particular area of the drawing. You may want to try other tools yourself.

7 Click Layers… The Layers dialog box pops up (Figure 13.16).

8 Click the On/Off icon to turn off the I-FURN and I-FlOR-PATT layers. The layers turn off.

9 Click the Close button to close the Layers window.

10 Right-click to bring up the Tool menu. The tool menu pops up (Figure 13.17).

11 Move your cursor over Zoom. A submenu pops up.

12 Click Window on the submenu.

13 Click and pull out a window around the sink, and click again. A close-up view of the sink shows in the viewing area.

14 Press [Esc] to finish the ZOOM-window command.

15 Right-click to bring up the Tool menu.

16 Move your cursor over Zoom and select Previous from the submenu. The prevous view returns.

17 Experiment on your own.

18 Close the browser.

Summary

In this chapter, you learned the procedure of creating a Web page to post your drawings on the Internet. By using an inserted raster image in a drawing, you can present rendered images along with line drawings of your work on the Web. The following concepts, procedures, and commands were presented in this tutorial:

Knowledge/Concepts

- DWF file and Volo View Express
- html (htm) files and Web pages.

Procedure

- Use Publish to Web wizard to create a Web page to present AutoCAD drawings in the DWF format.

Command

 ● PUBLISHTOWEB

Appendix

Resetting the AutoCAD Program Window

This tutorial was compiled based on the standard (default) AutoCAD program window. If your program window looks different, the following instructions will set it back to the default settings.

1 Enter OPTIONS command. The Options dialog box pops up (Figure A.1).

2 Click the Profiles folder tab. The Profiles folder opens.

● Profiles store the program window settings, such as the configuration of the menus and toolbars. There may be one or more profile names in the list. One of them is the current one.

3 Click [Add to List...] to create a new profile. The Add Profile dialog box pops up (Figure A.2).

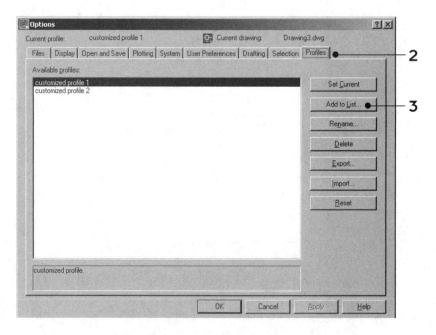

Figure A.1
The Options dialog box.

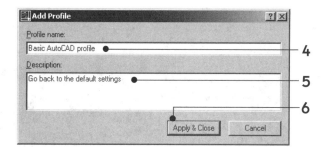

Figure A.2
TheAdd Profile
dialog box.

4 Enter a profile name, such as **Basic AutoCAD Profile.**

5 Enter a short description, such as **Go back to the default settings.**

6 Click **[Apply & Close].** The Preferences—Profiles dialog returns with the profile name added to the list (Figure A.3).

7 Click to highlight the new profile name on the list.

8 Click **[Reset]. An AutoCAD warning pops up.**

9 Click **[Yes].**

10 Click **[Set Current] to set your profile as the current window.** The program window changes in the background.

11 Click **[OK].** The program window is reset (Figure A.4).

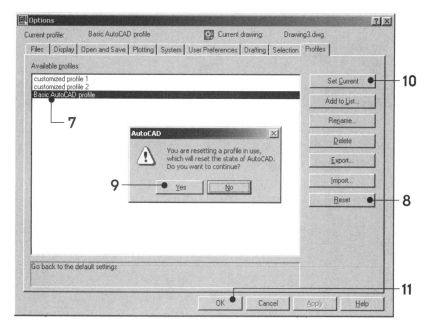

Figure A.3
The Profiles window.

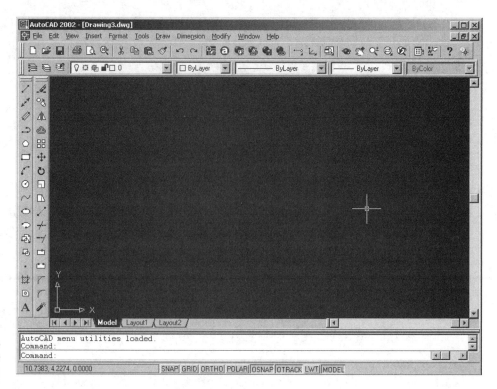

Figure A.4
The default AutoCAD
program window.

If someday you need to go back to the customized profiles, you can reset the profile to current using the OPTIONS command.

A p p e n d i x

AutoCAD Commands, Aliases, and Tool Icons

This list gives you a cross-reference of AutoCAD key-in commands, command aliases, and toolbar icons. This list contains only those commands that have an alias and are discussed in this tutorial. Since the alias can be customized, these aliases may not work with customized AutoCAD workstations. The same is true for toolbar groups.

Key-in Command	Aliases	Tool Icons	Toolbar Group
3DFACE	3F		Surface model
ARC	A		Draw
ARRAY	AR		Modify
BHATCH	H		Draw
BLOCK	B		Draw
BOUNDARY	BO		
BREAK	BR		Modify
CHANGE	CH		Properties
CIRCLE	C		Draw
COPY	CO, CP		Modify
DDATTDEF	ATT		
DDATTE	ATE		Modify II
DDEDIT	ED		Text

Key-in Command	Aliases	Tool Icons	Toolbar Group
DDIM	D		Dimension
DIMALIGNED	DAN		Dimension
DIMBASELINE	DBA		Dimension
DIMCENTER	DCE		Dimension
DIMCONTINUE	DCO		Dimension
DIMEDIT	DED		Dimension
DIMLINEAR	DLI		Dimension
DIMRADIUS	DRA		Dimension
DIST	DI		Inquiry
DTEXT	DT		
DVIEW	DV		
ERASE	E		Modify
EXPLODE	X		Modify
EXTEND	EX		Modify
EXTRUDE	EXT		Solid model
FILLET	F		Modify
HATCHEDIT	HE		Modify II
HIDE	HI		Render
IMAGE	IM		Reference

Key-in Command	Aliases	Tool Icons	Toolbar Group
INSERT	I		Draw
INTERFERE	INF		Solid model
LAYER	LA		Properties
LINE	L		Draw
LINETYPE	LT		
LIST	LI		Inquiry
LTSCALE	LTS		
LWEIGHT	LW		
MATCHPROP	MA		Standard
MIRROR	MI		Modify
MOVE	M		Modify
MVIEW	MV		
OFFSET	O		Modify
OSNAP	OS		Object snap
PAN	P		Standard
PLINE	PL		Draw
PUBLISHTOWEB	PTW		Standard
QLEADER	LE		Dimension
RECTANGLE	REC		Draw

Key-in Command	Aliases	Tool Icons	Toolbar Group
REGEN	RE		
RENDER	RR		Render
ROTATE	RO		Modify
SCALE	SC		Modify
SNAP	SN		
STRETCH	S		Modify
SUBTRACT	SU		Modify II
TOOLBAR	TO		
TRIM	TR		Modify
UNDO	U		Standard
UNITS	UN		
VIEW	V		Standard / view
XATTACH	XA		Reference
XREF	XR		Reference
ZOOM	Z		Standard

Index